The Eidolons

Louise Darwen

eidolon
ʌɪˈdəʊlɒn

Noun
LITERARY

1. an idealised person or thing.
2. a spectre or phantom.

Marilyn Monroe in *The Prince and the Showgirl*
Milton H. Greene, Public Domain.

The Eidolons

Louise Darwen

First Edition

Published 2023 by Shin Publications
England. Copyright © 2023

First edition, all rights reserved
This book, or parts thereof, may not be reproduced
in any form without permission.

ISBN: 978-1-9163365-7-5

http://alchemical-weddings.com/

Cover image credits: Portrait of Helena Blavatsky, Hermann Schmiechen (Public Domain); Head of King Arthur, Peter Paschten (public domain); Illustration from "The Lady of the Lake" by Sir Walter Scott, Bart. Illustrated by Howard Chandler Christy (Public Domain).

Dedicated to the
Dear (Un)Known Friends

Season of the Mysteries, 2023

The Fool of the Rider-Waite Tarot
Pamela Colman-Smith

Contents

1.	Acknowledgements	1
2.	The Occult Imprisonment of Madame Blavatsky	5
3.	Prologue	11
4.	The Brotherhood	14
5.	Jack and Maloney	18
6.	Lost Continents	28
7.	What a Flapdoodle	39
8.	The American	47
9.	The Chair	57
10.	Malaya Lubyanka Street	63
11.	Mysteries	74
12.	The Catacombs	80
13.	Dreamland	89
14.	Virgin Atlantic	93
15.	The Queen	101
16.	Cloud of Unknowing	110
17.	Bridge	115
18.	Stolichnaya	127
19.	Swords	137
20.	Order of the Seven Sacrifices	144
21.	Whistle Stop Tour	152
22.	The Tomb	164
23.	VITRIOL	170
24.	Persephone	182
25.	Aleph, Mem, Shin	193
26.	To my Friends: Andrei Bely	200
27.	The Castle	201
28.	The Musician	210
29.	Poker	216
30.	The Mem Key	225
31.	A Miracle	236

32.	Night School	243
33.	Dinner	255
34.	Sphere of Eros	260
35.	Spells of Attraction	270
36.	Recollections May Vary	280
37.	Percy	285
38.	The Pleiades	288
39.	Orphic Sacrifice	294
40.	The Crossroads	301
41.	Kalki Scala	306
42.	Epilogue	315
43.	Marxisits or Rosicrucians?	321
44.	Dramatis Personnae	325
45.	The Higher and Lower Minds From Pneumatology by V. Shmakov	338
47.	Endnotes	361

Acknowledgements

Thank you to all those around me for the continued inspiration, thought-provoking discussion, advice, fun and laughter. There are too many to name but if our paths have crossed, the chances are this includes you!

More particularly, thanks to Billy Bishop for being a wonderful sounding board in the early stages of this book's conception and for insisting the hero should be called Marc. Thank you as well for seeing the CERN connection and having the idea of a Mandela effect occurring somewhere, somehow.

Thank you as well to Fr VPIS, who inadvertently gave me the book's title. This was certainly necessary as my original working title was The Occult Imprisonment of Madame Blavatsky, which doesn't exactly roll off the tongue! Eidolon is such a good word that it has already been employed for many other book titles, but I can live with that as it fits the present purposes so well.

I am also grateful to the irrepressible Paul Weston for being a tireless champion of the Arthurian mythos and general font of knowledge when it comes to royalty. As well as being a successful author and historian in his own right, Paul also gives tours around Glastonbury Abbey. He very kindly allowed me to use material from his essay on Richard Whiting, Last Abbot of Glastonbury Abbey, in chapter 22, The Tomb. (See the endnotes for a link to this article online).

Thank you as well to dear Ramon – a much-loved individual in the realms of esotericism - for talking to me about the 'flame throwing' incident I refer to in the Epilogue and which gave me the impulse to write this book.

Big thanks to ArtTheurg – whose wonderful tarot card images feature in the English edition of Vladimir Shmakov's The Holy Book of Thoth - for his fascinating insights into the history of Russian esotericism given on his Mysterart Оккультуривание channel on Telegram.

For the inner workings of the occult order, EMESH Redivivus, Daniel Shubin's[ii] fascinating work, New Rosicrucians in Early Soviet Russia, is an invaluable resource, along with a couple of online publications, links to which are given in the endnotes.

Last but certainly not least, thank you to the Company of the Inner Abbey - for the well that never dries, the fire that is always lit, the breath of the Spirit and the Earth you help to sanctify. Thank you for being part of the Golden Chain.

Those to whom I dedicate books in the Shin Publications series are figures of great spiritual significance, not only to me personally but also to Heaven and Earth.

The Mebes Tarot Majors is dedicated to Our Lady of Guadalupe and St Francis of Assisi; his Tarot Minors to Our Lady of all Nations and St Bartholomew. Nina Roudnikova's beautiful book, The Solar Way, is devoted to Our Lady of Walsingham and St Seraphim of Sarov, in honour of England's re-dedication to Mary on March 29 2021 and the pilgrimage made in that year; The Magi & The Fool was accompanied by an upsurge of love for Our Lady of Fatima and Pope John Paul II, whilst the English translation of The Holy Book of Thoth by Vladimir Shmakov was dedicated to the divine feminine Sophia.

Which brings us to the present work and its dedication to 'Unknown Friends'. This unusual epithet will mean a lot to some people and nothing at all to others, depending on whether or not they're familiar with the legendary Christian Hermeticist who inspires such love in those who are drawn to his work.

VT, as he is often known, came to the world from Holy Russia and it is to this shining link in the Golden Chain – and others like him - that we pay tribute in The Eidolons. His beloved wife Maria, collaborator on his occult works – once herself a student of Mebes – also appears as herself. Likewise do G.O.M. and *his* wife Maria Nesterova, appear at the same table, alongside Vladimir Shmakov, Serge Marcotoune, Mikhael Chekhov and his star pupil, Marilyn Monroe, Vsevolod Belustin (the 'Moscow St Germain') and Nicholas Girs, another Mebes initiate who taught the Tarot Minors course to Martinist students in Germany and then Chile.

There were many other individuals who clamoured to be properly included but space did not always permit. Primary amongst these is Maria Dorogova, who despite several arrests and brief periods of incarceration, continued her occult work and mystical beliefs until her death in the early 1980s.

The Eidolons I present in this book are in a hypothetical grouping, but most of them were at least aware of each other, even if they did not meet up in person. The Occult Encyclopedia of Mebes, in particular, was consulted by pretty much every mage – or would-be mage – in Russia at that time. Not to mention the present time. Along with Martinist his forebearer, Czesław Czyński, G.O.M. was instrumental in the inception of the pivotal occult order, EMESH Redivivus. More of which later!

Nina Roudnikova occupies a pivotal position at the centre of the dramatised company. This is in tribute to the crucial role she played in her life as the rallying point and spiritual mentor for the Russian émigré community in the hard years that followed the Revolution. Not only was she the favourite pupil of Mebes and a leading member of the Prometheus Group for female initiates (headed up by Maria Nesterova), she was also the initiator of VT himself in Tallin, Estonia.

Nina served as a spy for a faction of the White Russian army in exile, whilst her publishing work and acknowledged position as a spiritual teacher and healer in her community, were reinforced by her friendships with Nikolai and Helena Roerich. She frequently corresponded with them and others via the respected magazine published by Alexander Aseev, Occultism and Yoga.

Roudnikova' premature death in her 50s came as a profound

shock to her friends and those she had mentored, who struggled to make sense of their loss from a karmic perspective. With the bulk of her life's work lost when a refugee daughter was forced to leave the heavy bag of papers at a station as the train departed, there is sadly little surviving information about a woman who was a doorway to the inner initiatory schools of the displaced Russian intelligentsia. She has passed to the realm of legend and mystery, coloured by the wonderful spiritual reality of The Solar Way and one or two other surviving pieces.

Whilst Mebes, Roudnikova and Shmakov inspired VT directly and had a deep (but often underplayed) influence on the development of his own occult work, I cannot help but recall his telling words about a certain 'R--', a gifted adept who had been reduced to writing 'ghost stories', for want of a suitable student to whom he could pass his magical legacy.

Whilst I don't pretend to high adept-hood, I can't help seeing a few parallels with the present work, as in many respects The Eidolons is merely a ghost story of the kind that Mr Tomberg might utterly disdain! As the same esteemed gentleman was in possession of an excellent sense of humour, I can only hope he would overlook my indulgence and accept this tribute in the affectionate spirit in which it is given.

The Occult Imprisonment of Madame Blavatsky

This book went through several strange turns since its conception in late summer 2022, when I was caught up in one of the minor flame-throwing incidents that is so characteristic of occult groups and is why VT himself warns plaintively against joining them.

The heated discussion, which occurred on Facebook – something our Dear (Un)Known friend would surely have abhorred and denounced as the work of the anti-Christ – centred on an obscure piece of occult lore which has always fascinated me: The occult imprisonment of Madame Blavatsky (HPB).

A prominent member of this group – a long-time devotee of Joséphin Péladan - took strong exception to the claim that said imprisonment of the Madame actually occurred. Though she fell short of calling me a fool (not that I'd have taken this as an insult), her imperious denouncements piqued me into a robust defence of the (in)famous Madame and the mysterious events in question. Such a defence I would probably not have contemplated in earlier years.

Several members of this particular group express a disdain for HPB and all that she spawned, which I myself – as an earnest and zealous Christian Hermeticist - shared for many years. For any serious student of the Primordial Mysteries and Perennial Philosophy – especially if they are Christian - the sprawling New Age Theosophy of HPB can be infuriating and even alarming if you're easily spooked: If you want to get lost down any rabbit holes, this is one of most well-worn routes.

The controversies surrounding HPB are well documented and need no repeating, but her unique and irrepressible character

– the immense influence she exerted and still exerts - looms large over the esoteric environment. Whilst it is undoubtedly true that HPB and the school she founded had a seismic impact on the social, political and spiritual framework of not just their own generation but those which followed, some have viewed their seemingly uncontrollable egregore as being formed almost exclusively of 'NABS' (New Age BS). Others hear talk of 'Lucifer' and the 'Lucis Trust', or consider the influence of Theosophy upon the German Thule Society, and their Christian blood runs cold.

As indeed did mine, until I made my third trip to India in the Spring of 2014 and took the opportunity to visit Adyar from our base in Chennai. The faded splendour of the place, with its solemn and sad but still rarefied atmosphere, overturned my hackneyed aversion to HPB – and Theosophy by extension – over the course of an afternoon spent wandering the house and gardens. Striving, as ever, for fairness, I asked myself if I had not been a little too harsh in my judgement of the remarkable lady, who was such a divisive figure in both life and death. At the very least it must be admitted that her influence on the world of occultism – in fact, the world in general - was and still is enormous.

Here it is worth noting VT's own thoughts as they are expressed in Arcanum V of Meditations on the Tarot, The Pope: "With regard to the statements of Éliphas Lévi and Joséphin Péladan that we have quoted, they add their conviction that it is the Universal or Catholic Church which represents for humanity the decad or fullness of manifested unity. For them, the will united and bound to the essence of the Church is expressed by the good pentagram, understood in the sense of Saint-Martin, and the will that is purely and simply personal is expressed by the evil pentagram. This is why Madame Blavatsky accused Éliphas Lévi of Jesuit politics and why Joséphin Péladan's old occultist-friends regretted his lapse into Roman sectarianism.

"But now, it is not a question of taking sides in the 'war of the roses', nor of accusing or regretting. Here it is a matter of the problem of personal arbitrary magic (the quinternary separated from the decad) and personal sacred magic (the quinternary united and bound to the decad)".

I've highlighted this remark as it usefully illustrates the background to the Bridge and Poker chapters, where HPB can be found playing cards in the astral 'White Room' with a trio of French mages. Whether or not these characters might really have downed their swords and engaged in some healthy banter, who knows! I like to think so.

Further on, in Letter VIII, Justice, VT explains: "Christian Hermeticists are unanimous concerning the pre-eminence of the mission and the person of Jesus Christ in the spiritual history of mankind. For them, Jesus Christ is to other spiritual masters (Krishna, Buddha, Moses, Orpheus, etc) as the sun is to the other visible planets in the heavens. In this they distinguish themselves from modern Theosophists of the school of Blavatsky and from oriental occultists and esotericists, eg, Yoga, Vedanta, Sufi, Madzaznan, Gurdjieff's school etc. They are Christian, therefore, in the sense that they recognise the uniqueness of the divine incarnation who is Jesus Christ."

In Letter X, The Wheel of Fortune, he references Blavatsky again, this time within the context of the Fall, where he compares the Biblical account of the six days creation and ancient Indian lore about kalpas, manvantaras and yugas "with the exposition (following the Stanzas of Dzyan) of cosmogony and anthropogony according to the Indo-Tibetan tradition, given by H.P. Blavatsky in the three volumes of her Secret Doctrine." Also up for consideration is "the grandiose tableau of the spiritual evolution of the world through seven so-called "plantetary" phases that Rudolf Steiner has bequeathed to the dumbfounded intellectuality of our century", as well as the "cosmogonies and eschatologies" to be found in the arcanology of Hermes Trismegistus and Plato, the Zohar and "diverse gnostic schools".

Further into the same letter our friend sadly observes how several prominent occult authors of the nineteenth and twentieth centuries "have striven to restore the cult of the serpent, this time in intellectual form. Thus "H.P. Blavatsky did much in her Secret Doctrine to honour the serpent as the philosophical idea of ancient wisdom. She interpreted it as the principle of universal energy, *fohat*, which has a unique and indispensable place between the universal intellect, *mahat*, and universal matter, *prakriti*. She evoked the ancient legends and traditions of the teachers of childlike humanity, who were creators of civilisation - the "sons of the serpent" - the benefactors of mankind at the dawn of its history."

We are then reminded that for Éliphas Lévi and Stanislas Guaita the same serpent was the "great magical agent" and "principle of realisation, that which in practice translates the will into events."

It is also observed that the very sign of the Theosophical Society is the age-old Ouroboros - the serpent biting its tail - within whose circle is a hexagram (also known as the Seal of Solomon) as well as an Egyptian Tau.

Whilst admitting the reality of this ancient magical agent, VT is ever mindful of the Christian centre and goes onto remind us that "there is not only another agent and another magic" but also "another consciousness and experience than that due to the brain." It was not the serpent that John the Baptist saw descend upon the Master of sacred magic the greatest thaumaturgist of history, but rather a dove."

VT asks why this dove of the Gospel - of the Holy Spirit - was rejected by the otherwise titanic intellects and dedicated spiritual seekers to whom he elsewhere pays tribute. Why do so many occultists prefer to serve the serpent instead of the dove, the mind instead of the heart, the Luciferian rather than the Christ principle? "Why did the Theosophical Society, which values truth above all belief, not choose the dove of the Holy Spirit as its standard? Why did Stanislas de Guaita not write a book entitled The Dove of the Gospel? Why did

Éliphas Lévi not turn to the new great magical agent, the dove, which is called to replace the ancient magical agent, the serpent? Why did H.P. Blavatsky refuse to see that there are two principles of cosmic energy, that of the fohat or the energy of the serpent, and that of the Holy Spirit, or energy of salvation?

In the second part of Meditations on the Tarot, Letter XVII, The Star, he invites us to recall that the great ongoing work of synthesis has its own history. "It was born after a long series of continuous endeavours from century to century", of individuals who include (in his estimation and in this order): Heraclitus, St Augustine, Martinez de Pasqually, Fabre d'Olivet, H.P. Blavatsky (for her opposition to Darwinian materialistic evolution and "breath-taking vision of the spiritual evolution of the universe) and Rudolf Steiner, leading up to the beautiful synthesis achieved by Teilhard de Chardin and his genius conception of an "omega point". Not bad for a girl who used to ride wild horses on the Steppes!

Having softened towards Madame Blavatsky – the original heroine of this book - through objective experience, I became intrigued not so much by her writings as her incredible life story, which – as with all such Mages, Masters and Magicians – is a history lesson in its own right, with bonus psychology, sociology and theology classes thrown in for good measure. The course of my research (many moons ago now) led me to the Transcendental Universe written by enigmatic anthroposophist, CG Harrison, which is our primary source for happening in question: The occult imprisonment of Madame Blavatsky.

I have provided an extract from this excellent work as the Prologue, for it outlines the basis of the position that HPB was subjected to a form of psychic/astral imprisonment at the hands of antagonistic American adepts, who were opposed in these efforts by European counterparts who baulked at what they perceived as an abuse of magical power.

The present volume is not intended to either prove or

disprove this notion, but is rather a creative interpretation of a legend I find particularly compelling. In retelling the various tales of Madame Blavatsky and the Russian Rosicrucians I'm aiming for the yoke to be easy and the burden light.

We see more hints of why a light-hearted and imaginative approach may be appropriate in a study of HPB, as it reveals an important aspect of her natural character, as described by her sister, Vera Zhelikhovsky:

Helena used to dream aloud, and tell us of her visions, evidently clear, vivid, and as palpable as life to her…It was her delight to gather around herself a party of us younger children, at twilight, and after taking us into the large dark museum, to hold us there, spellbound, with her weird stories. Then she narrated to us the most inconceivable tales about herself, the most unheard of adventures of which she was the heroine; every night, as she explained. Each of the stuffed animals had taken her in turn into its confidence, had divulged to her the history of its life in previous incarnations or existences.[iii]

This excerpt sheds light on the title of the present volume, which points to phantoms and spectres, astral vision and psychic quests, egregores and esoteric 'Chains'. Those who students such as myself have sought in the subtle realms as we attempt to understand the roles they played in the great initiatory chain which reaches through time like prayer without ceasing.

Cameo appearances from such illustrious individuals as Serge Marcotoune and Vsevolod Belustin gave me the opportunity to share a few golden nuggets of their original teaching. In 'The House on Malaya Lubyanka Street' chapter I also offer a glimpse behind the scenes of the order, EMESH Redivivus, which occupies a unique place in history of Russian occultism and – in my view – secret world history. For more information about this group I refer you to my (free) Youtube[iv] podcast of 2nd August 2021 - The Dark Order which Targeted Valentin Tomberg.

Prologue

From The Transcendental Universe by C.G. Harrison

A person who was known to exist, but who had not been discovered, suddenly appeared in Paris, presented herself at an occult lodge, and demanded admission into the brotherhood on terms which could not be entertained for a moment. She then disappeared, and the next thing that was heard was that a certain Madame Blavatsky[v] had been expelled from an American brotherhood for an offence against the constitution of the United States[vi] and had gone to British India in order to carry out a certain threat which it would seem there was a fair prospect of her putting into execution.

It is only within the last few months (1893) that I learned the details of this Homeric struggle in which poor Madame Blavatsky played the part of Patroclus in the armour of Achilles. Like Patroclus, she spread consternation at first, but was soon (metaphorically) slain, or rather, taken prisoner. Then it was that the real battle began, and for several years raged around her unhappy personality…I gathered the following information:

That the phenomena of the séance room are not due to the spirits of the dead, but of the living; that modern spiritualism is an experiment on modern civilization decided on, about fifty years, by a federation of occult brotherhoods for the purpose of testing its vitality and ascertaining whether it is capable of receiving new truths without danger.

That there are what may be called a "Liberal" and a "Conservative" party amongst occultists, and that the rank and file are strongly Conservative, though about two-thirds of the leaders are more or less inclined to Liberalism; and that owing to the preponderance of Conservative opinion,

"spiritualism" is about to receive a severe blow which will have the effect of throwing discredit on "phenomena" generally.
That the "aspect of the heavens" at the time of the birth of Madame Blavatsky frightened the Conservatives and resulted in a kind of "coalition ministry", which gave place to al Liberal one in the year 1841.
That a "Brother of the Left" revealed this fact to Madame Blavatsky in Egypt about 20 years ago[vii], that she returned to Europe immediately, and imposed certain terms as a condition of reception into an occult brotherhood in Paris, which were indignantly refused; that she was subsequently received in America and expelled very shortly afterwards.
That in consequence of a threat from Madame Blavatsky that she would soon make the American brotherhood "shut up shop", a conference of American and European occultists was held at Vienna and a particular course of action decided upon.
That during the time Madame Blavatsky imagined herself to be in Tibet, she was, in reality, in Kathmandu in the state known to occultists as "in prison".
That certain Hindu occultists who, for patriotic reasons, having sided with her against the American brotherhood, had nearly succeeded in procuring her release from "prison" by their own efforts, consented to a compromise whereby she was to be set free on condition of their non-interference with anything that had already been accomplished.
That Koot Hoomi is a real person, but is neither a Tibetan nor a "Mahatma". "He is", said Mr. X – "a treacherous scoundrel I the pay of the Russian government, who, for a time, succeeded in deceiving Madame Blavatsky, but whose true character and personality she at length discovered". Her chagrin at being hoodwinked caused her a serious illness. But as the "Mahatmas" were the foundation stone of the Theosophical Society she was obliged to keep up the deception. She contrived, however, to let "Koot Hoomi" gradually disappear as the author of "phenomena" and

substituted for him a mythical "Mahatma M." who never appeared in his "astral body".

That incredible as it may seem, she allowed herself to be again deceived after her return to England; this time by a renegade Jewish man who had been expelled from a continental brotherhood for the practice of evil arts. It was decided not to warn her against this individual, because he was keeping her alive. In her wretched state of health, the withdrawal of the stimulus of his control would have been fatal. The man waited until she had completed the second volume of the "Secret Doctrine" and then threw her over. She succumbed to her next attack and died in 1891, unsuspicious (as far as it is known) to the last, and serenely unconscious that she had been all her life a tool in the hands of designing persons, very few of whom were her intellectual equals, and who made disgraceful use of her extraordinary mental activity and unique gifts.

The Brotherhood

As God creates, so man can create. Given a certain intensity of will, and the shapes created by the mind become subjective. Hallucinations, they are called, although to their creator they are real as any visible object is to anyone else. Given a more intense and intelligent concentration of this will, and the form becomes concrete, visible, objective; the man has learned the secret of secrets; he is a magician[viii] -

Helena Petrovna Blavatsky, Isis Unveiled

Helena Petrovna Blavatsky, c1868, {{PD-US}}

The circle of magicians steeled itself for confrontation as they approached their target in cautious increments, holding back to regroup as they passed through the magical gateway to New York City. They had instinctively huddled close together. Not given to moments of self-doubt – and certainly not with respect to their magical prowess and birthright – they were, to a man, uneasy nonetheless.

Two of their brothers had point-blank refused to participate and one of those had condemned the others outright and quit the circle in disgust, absconding to a rival order in undignified but understandable haste. This was not the only reason for their cautious and sombre mood, however, for their target was an extraordinarily dangerous individual. Indeed, this was why the decision to take their risky present action had been taken in the first place. It had been a highly controversial decision to risk so much, to break the magical law.

Calmly made but insistent, a telepathic reminder from their leader stiffened the resolve of those hovering in the grey lower astral state:

She is most dangerous. Must be stopped. Remember your oaths.

On this much they had all agreed and their chain[ix] visibly strengthened. Their physical bodies remained still as corpses in the upper room of their lodge in Virginia Beach, where they were being assiduously watched over by their mystical sister, Nora Maynard-Levin. A psychic seer of some renown, Nora had had quite enough of the insults and challenges that were continually levelled at her by their target and fully supported what she saw as the courageous mission of her brethren.

A total of eleven were participating in the complex and volatile ritual. It was a less than ideal number but would have to do as nobody else could be persuaded.

Certainly not those lily-livered old boys across the water in London or Paris, though the leader with silent annoyance. *And as for the Italians…* it appeared they were actually *on her side*, which made the present action all the more urgent. Many of those unhelpful weaklings had been trying to reach his ritual circle in a last-ditch attempt to halt their progress – make him see reason, as they put it - but the Hidden Superior had pushed the irritating fellows from view with a powerful astral shield.

They were perilously close by this point - almost at her New York residence, the Lamasery – and he indicated for his brothers to pause a moment while they summoned the fulness of their astral resources and got any last-minute doubts of their chests.

Their fellows in tradition across the Atlantic were on all of their minds and it was deeply regrettable that the brotherhood had been so divided over this. It was symptomatic of how infuriatingly divisive the Madame had proven to be since the beginning of her public life. Even her private life. The squares of her horoscope pointed not just to her alarming personal power but also to a life riven by conflict.

If only the London lodge could have been persuaded. Perhaps the Fabians had got to them; wolves in sheep's clothing indeed... The Superior was unable to prevent the thought reaching his fellowship and nine of the eleven immediately concurred whilst the other two remained impassive. He sensed their brooding emotions. One of them, an Indian brother, loathed her with a passion so intense that she was actually afraid of him. This hatred alone would guarantee them at least some success; the difficulty might come later in the form of a magical rebound, but they would cross that bridge when they came to it.

It is regrettable we couldn't get them on side, gentleman, but not terminal. We CAN bind her. Now, is everyone ready?

From her place of power in an apartment close to Central Park, Nora's eyes snapped open. Just as she telepathed her assent to the Master her breath had caught in her throat and a feeling of dread came over her. The Spirit standing sentry behind his hypnotised body had raised a hand to its ghostly face, as if to cover it from view. A quick glance around the room told her that all the guardian spirits had done likewise and one or two of them were even melting away.

Her instinct was to warn him that the mission should be aborted but the gunmetal shade of his astral body, which formed a jagged blade, effectively silenced her. Indicating that there was no other path but forward with the plan, he raised a hand before the circle and issued his order:
Surround the Lamasery and proceed as we decided.
Lest anyone should falter in their resolve he had a little good news to steel them with: Henry was downstairs and she was in bed, for once alone and unaccompanied by one of her many friends or acolytes. A stroke of luck indeed.

And remember that your bodies are quite safe, Nora is keeping watch and she will not fail us, no matter how bad things get.

The eleven felt more assured and seven of their number began to look forward to the dolorous blow they were about to inflict upon Madame Blavatsky.

Jack and Maloney

My godmother, who saw the fairy-ladies, was held as a good woman, not a diviner or a witch

Margaret Alice Murray, The Witch-Cult in Western Europe

Margaret Alice Murray photographed 18 June 1928

And so it begins.

Jack's eyelashes trembled over her closed eyelids and the Sanskrit word for 'no', an almost imperceptible moan, escaped her lips, which were turned downwards into a deepening frown. A battle line had just been drawn on the boundary of the magical shield she had set about the property. As those pale eyes rolled back beneath their short flickering lashes and a flush began to rise over her white cheeks and brow - still smooth despite her advancing years and state of physical decline – a lone pigeon decided to take its chances on the window ledge. From this excellent vantage point it cast a marble eye towards the untidily bundled up woman who was hovering an inch above the bed.

After several moments of sickening magical tension a peculiar sort of inbreath stilled the atmosphere. The figure on the bed looked for all the world like a ghostly life-sized doll of black satin and silver lace, porcelain and gold. Ornate heirloom rings stacked on plump white fingers were glittering like secret incantations in the half light. The bird was still as a statue, its gaze fixated on a single ruby that winked from her wedding finger that was resting on the crimson silk divan. Alarmed and alarming, a pair of icy-blue eyes snapped open and bored like gimlets into the ceiling as their owner fell back onto the bed with a messy rustle of fabric and compressed air.

The nerve of it, by Shiva! BLAST THOSE COWARDLY RUFFIANS!

Flustered by the dramatic change in energy from unbearable potential to electrified drama the pigeon flapped its wings against the leaded glass and cooed anxiously. The large head on the pillow rolled to the side which faced the window. "For heaven's sake, Henry, go to sleep!" She muttered an incantation in a guttural voice and the pigeon tucked its head into its breast obediently. "Good boy." She grunted in approval, but the satisfaction was short lived.

My God, I am AFLAME... DAMN THEM ALL! Oh, I must

think now...where the hell is...."MALONEY!" She roared into the bowels of the three-storey house, which seemed to shake on its foundations at the sound reverberating through its antique bones.
The law has been broken! How can they think they will prevail! Where on earth was..."MALO!"
A small brass bell was rung with such violent force that the chain inside broke and its mallet flew out at formidable speed, ricocheted off the mahogany bed post and crashed into the oval dressing table mirror, which instantly shattered and thereby provoked a horrified gasp in the one left holding the bell's useless neck. Seven years down the pan in one hit! Jack suppressed a horrified sob and only with a superhuman effort was she able to hold back the hot, bitter tears which finally threatened to dampen those plump, powdered cheeks. In a flash they were replaced with impotent rage.
"DAMN YOU ALL!!" she roared into the abyss of the house, which cowered into its frame, but not before hurling a flurry of alarmed raps against the oak bedroom door, which rattled noisily as if a train had just thundered past. With emotions that shifted with their customary baffling speed, her eyes suddenly narrowed and the unfallen tears shrivelled in their sockets. Her inner eye fixed a baleful – really quite terrifying - glare upon her invisible enemy.
Run along now you despicable cowards; this won't be the end of it! BE OFF WITH YOU!
All but one (including the Master) melted away quickly, a few of them rocketing back to their somnambulant bodies in sudden panic. She steeled herself; with a quite superhuman effort attempting to control her own fear as her mortal enemy took a measured step forward. He had masked his face in a sort of makeup that was clearly intending to make him look more menacing.
Like a Vampire. She felt herself falter a little and her body trembled slightly as her mind raced to find an ally. With a stab of near terror she quickly discovered that every door in

London was closed and Paris might as well not exist. Her real friends were blissfully ignorant to her plight, lacking the magical strength to even perceive what was happening. He was moving slowly closer, tightening a long black cloth between his hands. In mounting desperation she reached for the motherland.

If only Mr '___' were not dead and Vladimir had been born! But wait, yes, maybe there is someone who could help, if only I can reach him…

Sensing that she was about to make a breakthrough, her enemy made his move with devastating speed, darting behind her astral form and in one fell swoop wrapping the black cloth tightly around her eyes, binding it with a magical knot of terrible dark power while she shrieked in terror. He smiled grimly at the sight of her misery, stepping backwards to slowly savour the sight as her desire body flailed before him.

She gasped a curse in her native tongue, which his waiting body perceived as poison dripping into his left ear, rousing him instantly and causing him to raise his hand to touch it. The others were already awake and stood watching him with eyes like saucers. Nora knelt before him, concern etched onto her keenly intelligent face. "Are you all right Hurrichund – can you remember what she said?"

She had tried to steady her voice but he could hear the anxiety and see it in the face of his brothers. He waved her away in irritation. "Of course not; the witch said it in Russian!"

They glanced at each other as the Master stepped forward. "It was a heroic deed, Chintamon, you have my word that the order will do everything it can." He paused. "Did you tie it very tightly?"

"Of course I bloody did, you don't think I was playing games out there, do you!"

The Master stepped back and bowed his head, triumphal satisfaction at the outcome of the ritual easily outweighing any irritation he might have felt at the inappropriate conduct of his apprentice. "No of course not, Chintamon, you did

superbly. We shall rally in an hour's time when we've had a chance to get ourselves in order, then see what we can do about this. In the meantime you must let Nora help you, it's vital we try to recall some of the wording she used."
Elsewhere in New York – by now enveloped in the darkness of night – somebody else was attempting to get herself in order. Her eyes were wide open, staring at the rose on the ceiling, unable to escape the sense of despair that she knew would probably not quite leave her again. Not in this lifetime. Her sight had changed. That devil Chintamon had bound her with a blindfold so dark that it was as if a thick fog was all around her; a barrier between her astral vision and the upper spiritual world she had always been able to access with ease. Her astral body itself – part of it, at least – had been set upon a chair by the one she would not name, who had come to her aid as soon as he'd heard her plea, but not in time to prevent her adversary from doing his worst deed.
Resigning herself to the situation for the time being she agreed to allow her astral body to remain waiting on the chair and agreed to meet later with the Master, at the more magically auspicious time of 1.30 am GMT. She would set a few physical wheels in motion in the meantime.
Back in the real world, her innate cunning came irrevocably to the fore, gunning for her survival with customary zeal.
I shall bide my time, let them think they really have me....Ach! so what if they DO have me; such a travesty will never be allowed to stand and the monster is going to have a devil of a time overcoming that curse! After all the world keeps turning and karma will have them sooner or later; my chain is sure to avenge me.
She attempted to shift her bulk on the high, well-padded mattress. *If only it were easier for ME to turn!*
A snort of laughter burst through her lips, saving them from an aghast grimace which had begun to take hold. The situation was dire but her sense of humour was virtually indestructible, her fire still volcanic in its intensity.

They are fools if they think I will be unable to bear this, I've cheated death more than once and I shall cheat this binding come hell or high water!
Where in God's name was Mal? At that moment a portly bearded fellow burst through the door and stopped dead in shock at the terrible sight of broken glass and a clearly distressed Jack on the bed. Had she had another of her funny turns?
"Maloney, thank God!"
"JACK! What on Earth...he hesitated, startled anew at the troubled expression in her usually implacable gaze. He sank to his knees with some difficulty and clutched her right hand, which was dangling over the side of the bed. "What on Earth has happened?"
"The fools have really done it now Mal."
Confusion crossed his face. "I don't understand, who...."
"For God's sake, Mal, do I have to spell it out! They've done the ritual and that devil Chintamon has forced on me a blind!"
"Chintamon! But I thought he was with *us*?" Her companion visibly paled beneath the massive beard.
She frowned unhappily. "I've had my suspicions about him for a while but didn't expect such a volte face, I didn't realise the Jesuits had got to him so seriously. We shall need to confront him in person, you know, I fear there is far more to all this than meets the eye and this is bad enough. We must leave for India as soon as we possibly can....perhaps there will be a hidden blessing to all this, after all," she murmured thoughtfully.
Maloney's mind raced in a flash over his many commitments in the United States. To leave in a hurry for India would really put him on the spot, not least of all with his wife. Removing a handkerchief from his waistcoat, he dabbed at his forehead, which was bright red from his exertion up the stairs and was now beaded with sweat. "My God," he began feebly, "it's worse than I imagined. I thought we were safe here, although London might have been better, you *were*

assured that the lodge there refused to have anything to do..." She waved a hand around impatiently, rudely signalling that he should both stop talking and direct his attention to more subtle realms. "The devils have blindfolded my astral body, which is currently sat on a chair that the Master has protected with a magical shield. The good news is the shield is impenetrable by that lot, the bad news is I can't go anywhere. Unable to assault my astral body further, they shall henceforth attempt to break my mental centre. We must prepare ourselves for a long siege, Mal, as this won't end in my lifetime. I am to reconvene with the Master at the magical hour to discuss counter measures; you and I are to think very carefully now about the future of the society. It's a terrible business, Mal. From this point on there will be no rest for me; the Unpopular Philosopher is reaping the whirlwind!"

A wry chuckle was sent his way but Maloney - whose real name was Henry, but Maloney suited them both just fine – creaked and puffed to his feet, far from reassured. In fact, he was indignant and alarmed in equal measure, trying to get his brain around the seismic shift in his life that were about to take place. "How dare they, by God! I'd dearly love to hear the Master's thoughts on all this." His voice took on a more professional tone as something definite occurred to him. "It is against the law."

He drew himself up to his full height and took a generous bunch of tobacco from the preserved head of a Siberian fox that was on the bedside table. He quickly rolled two small cigarettes, lit them at the same time and passed one to the Madame, who seized it gratefully and drew on it hard through pursed lips, nodding slowly.

"*Yes*....yes it *is* against the law. I didn't think they'd dare, but I'm weaker than I was, Mal, and they caught me unawares." She inwardly kicked herself for letting her guard down even for a minute. "I do not think I can fully overcome the blindfolding, even with help from..." She pointed upward with the forefinger of her left hand, looking exactly like an ancient sage through that simple gesture, and Maloney nodded. "But I do think we can inflict a comparable blow against their order, which over time will effect the brotherhood more and more profoundly." She chuckled wryly. "And at least I managed to give Chintamon a real earful, he'll be suffering now, to be sure, that awful woman is going to have her work cut out! We need to think very hard about how to deal with him and the others from now on; you know the Jesuits will never give up I'm totally destroyed and the Society with me. Part of me wants to carry on as normal to show the outside world haven't got to me…"

Maloney gave her a searching look, not daring to question the nature of the earful she'd given to her adversary, who he happened to know she was afraid of. This in itself he found strange, as she was an unusually courageous woman who'd faced individuals and situations which Maloney personally considered to be far more dangerous than that weaselly-looking Indian fellow. She'd fought and almost died in Garibaldi's volunteer army that was ranged against the Papists at Mentana and all-but conquered the Steppes, for heaven's sake, yet this Hurrichund character had her spooked like a skittish pony before a fluttering cape. Why she had wanted to give him money was beyond Mal, but Jack often did things that were beyond his comprehension. "How many of them did it take?" He picked up an almost overflowing ashtray from the chaotic dressing table and put it between them on the divan.

She looked him in the eye and he was relieved to see a glint of the customary cold blue steel. "Nine tried to stick it out. There were 11 to start with if you include the woman, but one of them panicked and fled the moment I noticed the little rat...He couldn't help himself, it would have been rather amusing if it weren't so terrible. The rest of them turned tail and left *him* alone with me shortly after. If their chain had not been broken I'd be done for now, I can tell you. Whatever the case though, Mal, to a man they shall live to regret it, every single one of those traitors. One way or another I shall be avenged". She felt a reassuring flash of her usual confidence. Maloney nodded in agreement as his own resolve began to shore up. "Their magic shall rebound of course…" He fell silent, watching her intently, searching for a sign of power draining away, vitality seeping out or a mind unhinging, but she looked exactly the same as she had done earlier that day, before this abomination. She was doing a heroic job of covering up the injury he intuitively knew to be real.

Jack crooked a pudgy forefinger around her bottom lip and cupped her chin, looking into the space between worlds that was still as real to her as the dozing pigeon on the window ledge. She was genuinely puzzled. How could they not see that they had succumbed to a grave transgression and thereby courted disaster; how could they have been so rash; what did they think would happen next? She still had some cards to play, though she was astute enough to realise that a very long game was ahead of her. Ahead of all of them.

Maloney was thinking along similar lines. He patted her hand. "Those fools will live to regret this."

She eyed him in a flash. "If not in this life then surely the next! But in the meantime, Mal, they shall do all they can to wear me down, to cast me further down into this prison. I fully expect a second attack to come very soon. They will have to reinforce their magic and appoint a jailer if I'm to be kept down. It wouldn't surprise me if that Maynard witch is being prepared for a very serious challenge, you know how she hates me…"

His eyes widened at that and then he sighed. "I'm so sorry Elena, you do not deserve this treatment, especially not from those creatures who should know better."

At the sound of her real name tears glistened freely in those limpid eyes. "Oh Henry, you are a true friend to me, I shan't ever forget it you know…"

"As you are to me, the truest and the best." He clasped her hand again. "Tell me what I can do?"

"You shall bring me pen and paper, Mal, for I am to summon my allies on Earth as well as those of the ether. If they are to inflict on me this gravest of injustices then I shall bring forth their worst nightmare, even if it should kill me. Their Empires shall fall. The Ganges shall burst open across all they hold sacred and the NAGAs shall speak. The Gods of India and Tibet shall be ranged against them. We shall see what will become of those who dare commit such acts against HPB!"

Lost Continents

Is it possible for great people and historical movements to escape from life?

P.D. Ouspensky

Peter D. Ouspensky, before 1953, {{PD-US}}

Two pairs of eyes

Were fixed on the front door of Lost Continents as the sign on the door was turned to 'Open' by a ghostly white hand emerging from a green silk sleeve. The first pair belonged to an equally ghostly figure who was standing in the entrance of Café de Paris, incongruously but impeccably dressed in an expensive top hat and tails, his back ramrod straight and his moustache oiled.

It was not, of course, la belle Paris itself – the croissants and macarons, whilst good, were not quite *that* delicious – but the coffee was excellent and the ambience suitably cool, an implied shrug of the shoulder and insouciant expression served with every cup.

Perched upon a leather-seated stool, elbows wedged onto the wide oak bar in front of the window, the owner of the second pair of eyes peered over the top of his newspaper and studied the bookshop opposite. It was, of course, 11:03 am, for she opened at precisely that time every single day, often to a waiting book worm or two, keen for their next fix. On this particular morning, soft and warm in London's autumn sunshine, the street outside was oddly quiet.

"Can I get you anything else?" He started a little at the voice in his right ear, roused from ponderous thoughts by the pretty but bored-looking waitress who raised a pointed eyebrow at the empty cup he'd been nursing for the past hour and a half.

He glanced around the small room by way of response. Save for a pair of students – bushy-tailed first-year exam-takers from the University of London a few minutes' walk away – he was the only person in there. Not exactly short on tables were they? The waitress shrugged imperceptibly and, taking the cup with her, glided back to the counter where she began to rearrange pastries stacked inside Perspex-lidded trays.

He turned back to look at the shop and was startled to notice the door closing shut and a flutter of mild disturbance behind its turquoise-painted façade.

He cursed under his breath. There he was yet again - sitting for the entire morning - and no sooner did he turn his back for two seconds when a mystery man (or woman, but it was usually a man) shows up! He gestured for another cup of coffee, earning himself a raised eyebrow and curt nod in return. Experience taught him that people who entered Lost Continents tended not to come out for an inordinately long time, with some of them sitting in there for hours reading some fabled tome or other and hoovering up the complimentary biscuits.

He wondered when the American would come. He'd been told to expect him within the fortnight and thanks to the wonders of modern technology had several high-resolution photographs from which to match a likeness. In the meantime, however, it was more important to find out who, exactly, might be paying a visit to Granny. As visitors could show up at any hour of the day or night he was forced to keep the long, dull vigil until his colleague arrived to relieve him in the early afternoon.

Outside in the fresh air Mr Moses took a glittering golden fob-watch from a waistcoat pocket and raised it to his eyes, squinting a little in the September sun, which had just emerged from the rooftop horizon of Museum Street. The hands of the watch pointed, as ever, to 11:11, the moment of his death on 5th September 1892.

He put it back in his pocket and raised his hat at a passing Hansom cab, swiftly pulled along by a pair of smart black horses. He received a raised hat in return from a member of his Lodge who was sitting inside with his eldest son. About to have a sherry, no doubt. Perhaps Moses should join him?

He gazed into the depths of Lost Continents, trying to assess out how long Mrs Pixley was likely to remain holed up with Mrs Roudnikova in the upper room. Surmising it was likely to be quite a long while he turned on his heel and walked in the direction of New Oxford street, where he would hail a cab of his own and then partake of some much-needed sherry with

George and the Earl of Zetland.

From her vantage point about a metre inside the shop – exactly the point where she could see them without anybody inside (or outside) Café de Paris seeing her - Ana Morgan watched Stainton Moses walk away with his customary long strides. It was the same little routine she watched every day and whilst her great-grandmother invariably told her to ignore him – "he's just trying to prove a point, my darling, but he's got the wrong end of the stick" - Ana always found him rather unsettling. If he wanted something – the right end of the stick, for example - why didn't he just come in?

"Don't be worrying yourself with ghosts, darling, there's nothing much he can do now even if he did find the nous to approach you directly."

The regular sight of Mr Moses, which she could never quite get used to, once again distracted her from the more sinister character who was sipping hot black coffee in Café de Paris. She walked to the back of the shop and opened the door to the stairs just in time to see an elegant camel-coloured coat disappear around the bend. "I'll bring you some tea Mrs Pixley" she called politely as she set foot on the stairs behind her. "And some of that nice shortbread."

"Thank you my dear" returned the clipped but muffled tones of her great-grandmother's friend as the door to the upper room closed behind her.

Ana gave a little smile to herself. It was lovely that granny's friends were still in such good shape and could pay regular visits. The two of them made old age seem like a wonderful thing. Ana had a particular soft spot for the genteel Mrs Pixley, whose wonderful stories from a life well lived were almost as enthralling as her great-grandmother's jaw-dropping yarns about escaping from the Bolsheviks. Her insights into the history of Silbury Hill were especially interesting and Ana resolved to pump her for more information if she got the chance later. Maybe she would make a stop at Silbury when she headed out West to visit her father later that month.

Once the narrow stairs were negotiated, the duplex flat above the shop was surprisingly spacious, extending not only across Lost Continents but also the top floor of the shop next door, which specialised in a curious bric-a-brac of lead toy soldiers and animals, military memorabilia and ancient-looking ephemera. The great-grandfather of the little old Italian man who owned this shop had fought alongside Garibaldi in the Italian war of Independence. He also had a tale or two that he didn't mind telling Ana, who often shared a cup of cocoa with him on cold winter evenings when the sun sank down before their shop signs turned to 'closed'.

The upstairs kitchen was a quaint old-fashioned jumble with hand-made painted cupboards, bunches of dried herbs hanging from various hooks and an inordinate amount of pottery. Some of this was rather good, ranging in style from delicate gilded tea-sets to the sorts of contemporary pieces that were prominently displayed in craft galleries.

Ana lit a ring on the gas hob and set down the copper kettle which her great-grand mother insisted upon, refusing to allow any electricity to be used in the house unless it was totally unavoidable. For granny and Mrs Pixley it was always fine black Ceylon tea brewed in an heirloom silver teapot and served with slivers of unwaxed lemon and an exotic, honey-like substance called Chrysopoeia acquired from somewhere on the continent. Ana suspected the fine-looking elixir, which she had never even tasted, was inordinately expensive, thereby accounting for her great grandmother's secretive behaviour regarding its supply, which never ran out.

She was just arranging generous chunks of her freshly baked shortbread onto the prettiest of plates when a loudish tinkling sound from downstairs – evidently the front door opening - had Ana wiping her hands on a tea-towel and heading back down to the shop. It was a rare and especially courageous thief who might venture into the arcane bazaar of Lost Continents but she didn't like to keep anyone waiting alone in

there. They might get scared and just leave, for one thing.
Breezing into the front of the shop with a suitable greeting forming on her tongue, Ana paused in surprise when she got past the stack of shelves. Not only was the shop completely empty (quite unusual, really, as there was usually someone sat on the armchair reading by now), but it was obvious that nobody had come in at all since Mrs Pixley's fleeting entrance. The atmosphere was still as the statue of Queen Victoria at Blackfriars.

Ana was just about to turn around and go back up the stairs when something on the front desk caught her eye. A thin sheet of paper folded in two - clearly a note of sorts for the initials 'A.M.S.' was written on it in bold indigo letters – was placed where it would easily be found, right in the middle of the desktop. Another one of those letters!

Half curious, half sceptical, Ana unfolded the paper and began to decipher the text, which had to be from Granny again as it was written in the Old Russian alphabet using fountain pen. Maybe even a quill. Ana swore this elaborate ritual was to ensure she never forgot her mother's tongue – and it was, in fact, rather a sweet habit, entertaining at times and sometimes revelatory – but it was a bit early in the day for this new trick of Granny's. Ana's brow furrowed in concentration and her eyes narrowed as the contents of the note became apparent.

....spirits of the dead cannot return to earth – save for rare and exceptional cases...nor do they communicate except by entirely subjective means.

That was debatable, thought Ana. Apparently so, for in the following sentence Granny contradicted herself completely, which in itself was strange because she was lucid to a quite astonishing degree and never disagreed with herself at all.

...it is because I believe in these disembodied spirits (at least,

Ana thought that's what it said, the word next to 'spirits' was rather indistinct) *that I revolt against such phenomena with all my being. You really need to sharpen up, my girl, for you'll end up opening the door to a swarm of 'spooks' – for better or worse, good or evil – and if it's the latter, they might enslave you for life! Then you really WILL be in a flapdoodle!*

M

PS – have you moved my tobacco?

What a Flapdoodle

We have this roving disposition of mind, it goes off at a tangent...

Olive Pixley, The Armour of Light, Part II

Olive Pixley, origin of photograph unknown

What was a *flapdoodle?*

Ana shook her head with a snort of laughter and tucked the note into the back pocket of her jeans. She'd never heard her great-grandmother utter such an archaic thing. *Tobacco!* Granny had, by her own admission, given up smoking and drinking decades ago.

Pushing back a stray lock of hair, which had escaped the thick blonde rope that swung across her back, she went back up the stairs, moving briskly as she heard the old-fashioned kettle start to whistle.

She pushed up the long silk sleeve of her favourite green shirt before pouring hot water into the teapot, giving the aromatic leaves a stir and loading the heavy silver tray with crockery and biscuits. Keeping a close eye on the two stacked cups as the top one rolled precariously and the bottom one slid on its saucer, Ana took small steps out of the kitchen and stood outside her great-grandmother's door. Experience had already confirmed it would be locked from the inside. "I've brought the tea Mrs Pixley!"

"Coming my dear!" The guest held open the door with a tiny bird-like hand which bore a simple gold band on the ring finger, her bright eyes fixed on Ana. She politely stood aside whilst the tray was divested of its treasures – white linen napkins, shiny silver teaspoons, cups and porcelain plates – and the tea was dutifully poured.

"Two slices of lemon and a teaspoon of honey isn't it, Mrs Pixley?"

"That's right, my dear, but you don't have to do all that. Just set the pot down and I'll see to the rest."

Ana straightened up as her great-grandmother looked on approvingly from her usual chair, an enigmatic smile on a face that had once been very beautiful and remained radiant into extreme old age. It was not a comfortable, well-stuffed lounger, as you might expect, but a formal sitting room chair which had carved wooden arms adorned with gilded scrolls.

Her hands were resting serenely on the rounds of these scrolls, multiple sapphires and other precious stones twinkling in the narrow chink of light that was permitted to fall upon them from the slightly parted curtains at the back of the room.

She was sitting very upright on the red padded seat, her back just grazing the elaborate caduceus pattern that was embroidered on the back with heavy golden thread, its top appearing like wings behind her squared narrow shoulders. The whole thing rested on slender wooden legs carved into spirals atop ornate golden feet in the shape of lion's paws. The chair, which really resembled some sort of throne, was very over the top and Ana never stopped wondering exactly where it had come from. Her great-grandmother had made vague comments about the summer palace of the last Tsar and escaping with the army, but that didn't fully explain how she'd come to acquire the amazing piece of furniture.

The elderly lady was impeccably attired in a high-necked lace-covered cream dress of very high quality but totally inappropriate for just sitting around the house. As always, she looked like some kind of High Priestess but minus the veil and head dress, which were nonetheless implied by her overall countenance.

"Won't you take some tea, my darling?" Mrs Roudnikova's voice was clear as crystal – albeit with a pronounced Russian accent - and it produced a coy smile in her great granddaughter.

"I'd love to, but the shop..."

Mrs Pixley pointedly locked the door and sat back down on a chair opposite her friend. "Have a cup of tea, dear."

Before Ana could protest further, amber liquid was poured into flower-adorned porcelain. This was another strange thing, as Ana could have sworn she'd only brought in two cups. "Ah, well, if you insist!" she gave a pleased little laugh and knelt down before the two ladies. "Shall I get the Golden Fleece [their nickname for the elixir]?"

"That's alright darling, I have it here…"
There was a meaningful pause in which Ana's great-grandmother ignored the unspoken question and coiled a generous scoop of the precious golden liquid around a tiny silver spoon. She stirred it into her own cup and then handed it to Mrs Pixley.
Wondering what the honey actually tasted like and if she'd' ever get to try it, Ana held out the plate of shortbread.
"Would you like some? It's freshly baked from last night."
"No thank you, dear, tea is just perfect. Exactly what I needed after that journey."
"Did it take you very long to get here?"
"No more than usual."
There was a lull in the chit chat. Ana devoured a huge piece of shortbread, chewing thoughtfully whilst honey-tea was sipped over gilded China on either side. She had a strange sense of déjà vu as the same old questions arose in her mind, minor mysteries that never unravelled but only moved in circles of infinity around the vortex of the upper room.
Staring at a drawing of Arthur Dee, which she had only just noticed in the jumble of old portraits crowding the walls. It was next to one of Lewis Carroll's original drawings of Alice, Ana couldn't help feeling curious. "Where *do* you come in from Mrs Pixley, I can never quite remember, it's terribly *rude* of me to keep forgetting!"
Her great-grandmother interrupted. "You should eat less sugar, my darling, it's terribly *bad* for you".
Nothing to say to that, she was right, as usual, although Ana did pointedly glance at a half-full bottle of Stolichnaya that was on the sideboard. Her grandmother gave a tinkling laugh. "You know perfectly well that it's just for show; we can't disappoint people, can we!"
"The day when you disappoint is unlikely to come in this lifetime, Granny… longer may it last!" This was naughty of Ana and butterflies danced in the pit of her stomach to prove it. Her Great-Grandmother's age was the biggest taboo in the

family by a very long stretch and if anyone so much as thought of it they got a wag of her right forefinger, as indeed happened to Ana at that precise moment.

All three women laughed and took a third sip of their tea. Mrs Pixley gave Ana a look. "Tell me, my dear, how are *you* and *how* is that lovely young man of yours?"

Ana looked startled. "I'm very well, thank you" she replied cautiously, wondering what lovely young man she could possibly mean. "I'm glad that dreadful heat has finally broken, aren't you?"

"Oh yes, it was perfectly dreadful, I thought it might never rain again, it even stunted the potatoes!"

Ana nodded slowly and did another circle, still wondering who she could have meant. "Dreadful, yes." There was another pregnant pause whilst she blew on her tea and looked askance at the house guest. Curiosity finally got the better of her. "Which young man do you mean, Mrs Pixley?" Ana took a sidelong glance at her great-grandmother, who remained silent as a sphinx, evidently prepared to give nothing away about this mysterious heart throb.

"Oh, you know...." Mrs Pixley waved her hand vaguely.

"I don't." Ana shook her head, nostrils flaring as she got a heady waft of the frankincense that her great-grandmother liked to burn

"You know..." Mrs Pixley reiterated, waving the hand around her head this time. "The one with lovely dark hair."

At that moment a black Persian cat minced slowly onto Ana's lap and dug its claws into her thighs, purring loudly. Their guest gave a pleased little laugh. "I'm sure you'll remember, soon, my dear!"

Ana arched an inquiring eyebrow at her great-grandmother, only to be rewarded with a total change of subject.

"What did the letter say, Ana-Maria?"

"Which letter?"

"The one you just received, of course, what else?"

"Oh Granny!"

"Yes darling?"

"You already know what it says, seeing as you wrote it. All that talk about spooks and enslavement, whatever did you mean!"

A sharp glace darted between the two older women which did not escape the younger one sat between them. Her great-grandmother held out a bejewelled hand; her tone suddenly imperious. "Show it to me now, Ana-Maria-Sophia."

Alarmed by the unexpected use of all three of her Christian names in a row, Ana reached obediently into her skirt pocket and handed over the folded-up note, watching as her great-grandmother studied it by the light of several candles lined up across the mantlepiece. After a moment or two she passed it over the table to her guest. "See what you make of this, Olive."

Ana was about to protest that there was no way Mrs Pixley would be able to understand what was written, when a flutter of the open paper as it passed in front of her face revealed that the note was somehow now in English. She caught her breath in surprise. "Oh!"

"Hush darling, let Mrs Pixley concentrate."

Mrs Pixley studied the contents of the letter and then held it close to her body, her eyes closed. It seemed like an eternity passed before she finally opened them again and Ana could let out her breath. "You're right, Nina. I do believe it's from her!"

"Just as I thought! I suspected during Easter that she was making an approach but this is a definite sign." Her smile was archaic and inscrutable.

"It's about time," murmured her guest. "Have you received many of these?"

"Quite a few…They've been appearing for a few months but I thought you were sending them to me to help me with my languages."

She was about to say more but her great-grandmother interrupted a little sharply. "Do you still have them?"

"Yes, I've been using them as bookmarks..."
"Bring them to me this afternoon."
Ana was surprised but acquiesced. "I will do."
Her great-grandmother considered her for a second. Very good, Ana-Maria, now drink up your tea, a delivery is about to arrive and you'll need to sign for it."
Ana gave her a blank look. "Oh, but I didn't order anything, unless it's more of those candles they keep sending us from..."
"It'll be here any minute, darling, you go now."
Mrs Pixley clasped Ana's hand as she rose to her feet. "Thank you so much for the tea, my dear, it's so lovely to see you. Do take care of yourself; we worry about you so!"
"It's lovely to see you as well, Mrs Pixley". Ana said quietly, stooping over to kiss her cheek before turning back to her great-grandmother. "Let know if you need anything else, Granny, just ring the bell".
Her great-grandmother smiled warmly and put a cool hand to Ana's cheek. "You're a good girl, Ana-Maria. Try not to worry. We will *always* look out for you. *Always*." Mrs Pixley nodded in return and both elderly ladies took a resolute sip of their tea by way of closure.
Ana felt herself blanche. Their odd behaviour was finally making her nervous. "OK, thank you..." she muttered uncertainly, pulling shut the door behind her. A key could be heard turning in the lock as she trudged back down the stairs, the wind in her sails having sunk a little.
Her great-grandmother was given to extravagant turns of phrase at times –even more inclined towards the cultivation of mystery at *all* times – but this latest turn was bizarre even by her standards. Nevertheless, a definite warning from someone like Nina Roudnikova could hardly be ignored. Ana felt that a part of her innermost self had grown increasingly wary of something and she physically shivered when she realised it had been growing for quite some time.
The phone rang loudly, making her jump. It was a great old

heavy thing that looked like it belonged in a museum but they preferred it to slick modern machines. "Lost Continents, how can I help you?"

A deep voice boomed down at her from on high. "Hello Ana-Sophia, it's me!"

Another surprise: "Daddy!"

"Are you alright, duchess, has anything happened?"

A flush rose high on Ana's cheeks. "Like what? Honestly, you're all acting so strangely at the minute. Stranger than usual, I mean."

"Don't worry sweetheart, I just miss you that's all, I think you should come to see us soon."

"How soon?"

"How about tomorrow?"

"But you know I always come down for the Equinox anyway, what's the rush?"

Her father ignored the direct question and asked to be put through to Ana's great grandmother.

"She's got Mrs Pixley with her," Ana replied, feeling rather mutinous. "Maybe they're getting a cloak and dagger ready for something."

"Yes maybe," her father replied in all seriousness, apparently not noticing the sarcasm. "As soon as Mrs Pixley leaves ask Granny to give me a call, there's something I need to discuss with her." He interrupted Ana just as she started to protest at yet another cliff-hanger from her exasperating family. "And do give Olive my regards, it'd be marvellous if she had time to pay us a visit here sometime, we have so much to discuss."

Ana put down the phone with a clatter, her inner peace well and truly disturbed. It was intolerable how they were all behaving!

A pair of large, middle-aged Wiccans bumbled into the shop with a flurry of door-bells, rustling robes and more clatters, but she hardly even muttered a hello, despite the welcome blast of fresh air they brought in with them. They beamed at her like Cheshire cats. "Hello Ana!"

She took a deep breath. "Hello! hi, how are you…"
They both stuck their thumbs up and paused in front of Gerald Gardner on the third bookshelf from the left, avid expressions plastered onto their faces while they rummaged through the selection he nudged towards them.

The door swung open again and a very tall man dressed top-to-toe in black, except for a red scarf wrapped round his hat, stalked inside. He doffed the hat and headed straight for ceremonial magic cabinet, looking serious. It was a welcome return to normality and Ana sat down behind the desk to take up a book she was wrestling with.

The Holy Book of Thoth
Eleventh Arcanum, Metempsychosis

Lo and behold, there was another note folded up inside, which Ana read with new eyes. If it wasn't from her great-grandmother, then who on Earth had sent it?

Dearest AMS

It is difficult, sometimes, to know what to call the 'Brothers', even when one knows their real names…

Yours affectionately

e

PS – turn ahead to page 262.

Only the true adept has the quite great art of rearranging the whole mechanism of his or her consciousness under the influence of his will alone, whenever the need arises. By rearranging his consciousness to completely coincide with the consciousness of another person, he thereby gets the opportunity to experience the same sensations, get the same perceptions, get the same experience as this person.

....If a person cannot fully associate with a given idea, it passes away without leaving any trace in his soul, like a ray of the moon on an icy surface; but if, on the contrary, he rearranges his consciousness so that it completely embraces the idea, it, like strong acid on metal, will leave once and for all the imprint of its contour, after which a person has the opportunity to study it in detail, to deepen analysis and learn its connections and relationship with the whole mass of other ideas....

....Transubstantiation into the composition of a person, as opposed to identification, which takes place instantly, takes place over a more or less long period of time, sometimes extending for many, many years and sometimes does not have time to complete before the death of a person....with the death of a person, with the destruction of the brain, everything that is not transubstantiated into his inner essence is lost forever; this is why the ancient Hindus denied reality behind purely intellectual knowledge, behind the 'knowledge of the eye'; only the inner, fully felt knowledge, which is strictly analysed in all its parts, true wisdom, 'knowledge of the heart', was considered the true and inherent wealth of man."

A white van screeched to a halt outside the shop, breaking her concentration. The driver yanked up the handbrake, leapt out of the driver's seat and extracted a heavy-looking parcel from the back of the van before shoving open the door of the shop.
"Delivery for Mr Marconi" he announced.
Ana shrugged, feeling mutinous. "Nobody here by that name, have you tried next door?"
The driver – who happened to have dark wavy hair - looked at the parcel label again. "Care of Ana..." he raised an eyebrow at her. "*Anastasia* Maria Sophia Morgan?" He gave her a cheeky wink. "And there was I thinking you'd disappeared!"
She flushed. "Just leave it there, thank you."
He put an electronic device in front of her and tapped the screen. Ana tut under her breath. She hated these ridiculous

contraptions, what on Earth was wrong with pen and paper? She sighed as he left the shop and drummed her fingers on top of the package. It was tightly wrapped in thick, brown paper and string which covered a solid box at least two feet long and 12 inches wide. It was heavy. The name on the hand-written label was totally unfamiliar. *Marcus Marconi.* Sounded Italian. Visions of dark wavy hair crossed her mind again. Could Mrs Pixley have meant this guy? surely she hadn't meant the driver! *Probably meant the cat.*

At that minute the door at the back of the shop opened and Mrs Pixley emerged from the stairs, ignoring the pair of Wiccans and lone thelemite who were deeply absorbed in their respective sections and didn't even look up as she passed. She stopped in front of the counter and nodded. "I see that it's arrived..."

"Yes", Ana replied. "For a Mr Marconi apparently... is this the man...."

Mrs Pixley raised a discreet hand. "No, no, my dear, someone quite different, but you'll be seeing both of them very soon."

Ana felt a little thrill at those words and Mrs Pixley smiled at her kindly. "Lovely young man, my dear; very kind."

Ana smiled. "Well, I could do with an extra pair of hands round here, that's for sure!"

"But of course, dear, he'll be a marvellous help, but first we have to deal with Mr Marconi. I do hope he'll be reasonable. You never know with that type. He's an *American*, you know," she added, as if that explained everything."

"What do you mean, Mrs Pixley? I'm so confused now. I didn't make much of the letters. I assumed they were from Granny but now I'm not so sure. And now this mysterious box and strange men – as if things weren't strange enough around here." They both looked up and fell silent as the thelemite approached with a large, expensive book and a blunt ornamental dagger topped with a stylised dragon head.

"I'll be going now, dear, you're very busy. Give my love to your Father. Tell him I'll be along to see him after the

Equinox; I must be at the barrows first and Silbury Hill needs some attention."

"Oh yes, that reminds me. I wanted to ask you…"

"Not just now dear, I'll talk to you about that when all this business is cleared up." She looked over her shoulder as she exited the shop and there was something in her expression that made Ana shiver again. "Tell your Father I shall come sooner if needed".

"Bye Mrs Pixley, lovely to see you…" Ana tailed off as she took care of the customer - who happened to be rather a good one – and resolved to put the peculiar morning behind her until further notice.

After wrapping up the parcel and sending the thelemite on his way she took the mysterious package into the storeroom and put it under a heavy black cloak that sometimes got wheeled out for exhibitions. Until Mr Marconi showed his face – *if* he showed his face – she would forget all about it and carry on as usual; that was quite enough wyrd for one day and it was only just gone noon!

• • •

The American

For wisdom, renounce; for glory, persevere. These two verbs suffice to conquer time and colossal human stupidity

Joséphin Péladan, How to Become a Mage

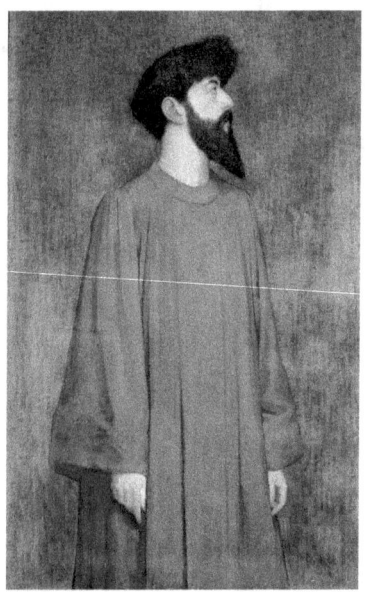

Portrait de Joséphin Péladan, Alexandre Séon, c1892, {{PD-US}}

Endless lines of code

Which had no apparent meaning. Marc sighed inwardly. The screen in front of him was a sea of minute white figures on a black electronic canvas. He pushed his black-rimmed square spectacles back on his nose from where they'd slipped down from the bridge, a result of him furtively looking down to read the book sandwiched into his ring-binder:

The Arthurian Formula, Dion Fortune, Margaret Lumley Brown and Gareth Knight, page 123:

Arthur was meant to be the Priest-King of these Islands and thus to carry on the tradition of Atlantis. In the Lost Continent the chief ruler was chosen before birth which was carefully planned by esoteric means. After birth, special training both as warrior and priest-magician were given to the future ruler. Hence the legends of Arthur's prowess, for actually he was set to perform esoteric tests and, to put it briefly, he achieved as a warrior but failed as a priest. Hence also, all the legends wove round Excalibur. "Take me up" was written on one side of the magic weapon and "Cast me away" on the other. Arthur indeed could take up the Sword but only cast it away by proxy until the time at length should come of his return.

The hair prickled on the back of his neck and Marc flipped shut the ring binder before the team leader, Nick, reached his desk.
"Hey Marc, how's your progress with the demo? We need completion on test phase one before they decide whether or not to take this further?" His voice was tetchy. There was no real need for him to repeat what everyone in the department had their backsides tattooed with two weeks ago, but he just

couldn't help himself.

It was, to be fair, a genuinely huge commission and by far the most important thing his firm had ever worked on, but for some reason Marc couldn't get excited about it. Truth be told he didn't think Nicholas was up to the team leader job and it was difficult to get enthused with such an idiot in charge..

Keeping his eyes locked firmly onto the sea of cryptic white text he leaned into the screen and allowed his mouth to fall open a little, as if in intense concentration. His voice was soft and thoughtful. "It's going pretty good....yeah, it'll take me a couple weeks but I'm getting there."

Nicholas was making a superhuman effort to stay calm. Much though it pained him to admit it, he needed Marc. In fact, he had been specially requested by his counterpart at CERN, but Nicholas wasn't about to tell him that. It was so frustrating trying to manage belligerents. "OK, well, let me know as soon as you're ready to move forward. Just bear in mind that we have to make significant progress on this before I go back out there on the 19th".

"Sure". Marc felt more like a tormented artist than a crucial cog in the wheel of a high-tech firm. There was NO WAY Nick should be heading up a project like this, he thought again. Just because he was anal about deadlines didn't mean he was qualified to manage someone of Marc's calibre.

As soon as the reflection in his screen informed him that the team leader was safely out of range, Marc flipped open the book again but his concentration was broken. He decided to do a bit more actual work before heading out for lunch.

Mandela Module. Here we go.

***

12.34

Nobody could deny it was a respectable time for lunch, even if the guys around him were hard at work and the atmosphere was tense, borderline frantic.

Marc glanced out of the window. It was a lovely sunny day out there. Fact was, no matter how busy things were, a proper lunch break was his human right. Maybe he'd take his coffee and sandwiches down to the beachfront promenade. Virginia Beach was especially nice in early September when the bulk of tourists had disappeared but the sun was still going strong. *Yeah, time for a stroll.*

He pushed back his chair, ignoring the scowls and incredulous glances from his colleagues, who appeared to be welded to their desks for 12 hours straight every day. He wasn't even sure they took bathroom breaks but nor did he care. The usual flat white from Julie's was calling him, as were the sandwiches his wife had prepared that morning.

Marc cast his mind back to breakfast with his family as he left the contemporary low rise building and headed towards his favourite coffee shop. It had been mildly chaotic as usual but nothing remarkable had happened. Also as usual.

Marc was slightly depressed. He hated work. Even the CERN project – which should have been exciting if the brief was anything to go by – was just a bunch more hard graft and lines of code. He was more likely to find a parallel universe in the troubadour legends than Nick the Prick's glory boat.

In his state of ennui, Marc definitely *wanted* something unusual to take place. He longed for it, in fact, with an intensity which bordered on desperation. He sighed despondently but a glimmer of his more usual optimism broke through as the sunshine warmed his face. At least it was a nice day. He wished he could spend the entire afternoon strolling by the beach and day-dreaming about Arthur and Guinevere, or even England generally.

Marc and been adopted at birth and knew nothing about his natural parents, but his lovely adoptive mother hailed from Britain. She made much of their heritage and had taken the young child to London once. Too young to remember much about it, at the top of Marc's bucket list was a return trip to his motherland. He even had half a mind to emigrate there some day and was building up to a reconnaissance mission.

He pushed open Julie's front door, which tinkled sweetly and greeted him with a delightful aroma of coffee and fresh pastry. He breathed in appreciatively. Their coffee really was the best in town. "Hey Ambrose!" he raised a hand to the barista and flashed a smile.

"Hey brother, how goes it - flat white?"

"You got it!" Marc got together some change. Life was dull but it wasn't bad and the coffee, at least, was good.

On his way out of the cafe and heading in the direction of central Virginia Beach, Marc failed to notice a man who was leaning against the corner of the block, two shops down from Julie's. There was nothing special about his beige slacks and short-sleeved shirt, nor about the newspaper he was holding in front of his face as Marc walked by. Just something in the man's general demeanour spoke to hidden agendas and shaded secrets.

Not that Marc was any the wiser. Passing at a loping pace, his mind deep in thoughts of Merlin and Morgan le Fey, the IT professional didn't spare a glance at the older grey-haired fellow who was about to stalk him to the beach.

He was barely five metres past when the spy took out his mobile phone and without removing his eyes from the target pressed the first number of his speed dial. He didn't bother to lower his voice. "Target on track and headed your way."

Blissfully ignorant to the life changing events that were being set in motion, Marc took a slurp of coffee and peeled off right towards the well-kept boardwalk, where he would begin the hunt for an empty bench. It was lunchtime but he could usually find somewhere to perch, his brooding presence and peculiar aura tending to move other people on sooner rather than later. Passing one of a few alternative bookshops which he regularly frequented, Marc didn't notice a poster in the window, although it did garner interest from the man who was trailing him.

Discover The Sleeping Prophet!

Fall Gathering of the Edgar Cayce appreciation society

Saturday September 3rd
7.30 – 9.30pm

Join society leader, Douglas Carr & psychic medium, Emmaline Clearview, on a journey to Atlantis with the Sleeping Prophet.

Tickets: $7.00 ($3.50 concessions)

After taking a photograph of the poster with his phone the man strolled in the direction of the boardwalk, where he could already see his associate waiting by a brightly-coloured ice-cream kiosk. A few elderly residents trundled up and down on ornamental buggies whilst one or two skater girls glided along, easily overtaking the slow-moving vehicles, glossy hair flowing behind them like mermaid tresses.

Marc had stopped in front of a bench that was currently occupied by a lone teenager smoking a cigarette. The stalker smiled to himself as Marc perched down on the opposite side of the bench, prompting the teenager to quickly suck up the last of his smoke and exit stage left.

Marc was not an unpleasant or sinister person, but there was something strangely powerful in his aura which made a lot of people nervous. As you would expect from the son of...

The man watched intently as his associate approached the bench and occupied the space left beside Marc. How would he take the truth bomb?

"Do you mind if I sit here?"

Marc looked up in surprise, mildly irritated at the intrusion

into his thoughts about the Arthurian formula but conceding that he didn't own the bench and it was still a free country.
"Sure." Marc studied his half-eaten sandwich, hoping the new arrival wouldn't attempt to strike up a conversation.
"So how's work?"
Marc felt his hackles rise. Couldn't a man get some peace to eat his lunch and focus on daydreams?
The man's lips stretched into a half smile but ignored the unspoken comment. "You work in the new building over on ---- Avenue, I'm opposite in Lockheed..."
"Oh..." Marc was confused but something indefinable compelled him to engage further. "Is there anything I can help you with?"
"I'm glad you asked. As a matter of fact there is."
"Oh!". Marc pushed his glasses back up his nose and folded the wrapper over his sandwich.
"You see, we're working on something really big right now and I heard you're the top guy at AstroLink when it comes to the..." The man lowered his voice and leaned towards Marc conspiratorially, gaining his full attention in the process. In the intrigue of the moment Marc entirely missed the man who approached from behind, deposited a brown leather briefcase on the floor beside him and then strode off quickly without looking back.
"Uh, I didn't quite catch that, I'm guessing you mean the new CERN thing but that's really confidential and we only just started?" Marc gulped as he realised he'd already said way more than he should have done, but it was almost like the man had hypnotised him. He was also desperate to know what he was the top guy for according to Lockheed, but his new-found friend had another surprise.
"Is that your briefcase."
Marc looked down and started in surprise. "No it's not, I'm sure it wasn't there before either!"
"Maybe someone left it, you should check."
Marc peered at the case uncertainly. "I'm not sure about that,

maybe it's got some kind of loaded device in it!" He let out a nervous laugh and fidgeted with his sandwich, suddenly keen to get up off the bench.

"Here, let me". The man stood up and took a pace to where the briefcase was resting on the floor beside Marc's feet, picked it up and examined the surface. "There are initials carved into the top: M.A.V.I.M.

At the sound of his initials, which hardly anyone knew, read out loud by a stranger, Marc physically jumped. "No way, let me see that!"

The man's smile was ironic. "I'm sure it's yours."

Something in his tone of voice made Marc peer at him over the top of his glasses. There was clearly more to this enigmatic Lockheed fellow than met the eye. Maybe he had put the briefcase there without him noticing? He looked back down at the obviously antique case, on top of which were embossed his initials in startlingly large gold letters. He ran his finger over them and whistled softly. "Well would you look at that, what a coincidence!".

"There are no coincidences, Marc".

Marc looked up at him sharply, surprised for the third time in as many minutes. Had he even mentioned his name to this guy? "What do you mean, how do you know…"

"Why don't you open the case?"

Marc hesitated for a moment and looked back down. "OK, well, I guess it couldn't hurt to check it out, at least we can find out who the owner is…" he flipped open the unlocked catches, opened the lid of the case and blinked. For a long moment he simply stared at the contents, which at first glance consisted of a chunky bundle of hand-written, old-looking papers held together with red silk ribbon, a ceremonial silver dagger with his initials engraved on the hilt, a large and ornate ring which had a very unusual stone in the centre and a few antique photographs of people who appeared to wearing formal Victorian dress.

He looked uncertainly at his companion. "I'm not sure about

this, err, what was your name again?"

The man gave him a strange smile which did not quite meet his eyes. "You can call me Frater Saturnus."

Marc knew his mouth had fallen slightly open but felt unable to close it right away.

"Do you know who your real father is, Marc....or your real great grandfather?"

Marc felt his jaw slacken further and his eyes widen. His heart had begun to pound and his hands were suddenly clammy. He shook his head. "Not really...my aunt told me a few things but it always seemed to be a closed conversation."

Saturnus grasped Marc's left shoulder with a strong hand. "The documents in that case are going to answer a lot of the questions you've had about your life. I want you to take it away and read the contents thoroughly. It is better if you don't say anything to your family about this right now; wait until you've digested it all first." He gave Marc a stern glance to make sure he understood, receiving a nod in return. Reaching over to close the case, he added. "On your way back to work take a look in the window of Mysteries. There's an event you should attend this Saturday. That gives you two full days to familiarise yourself with the contents of the case. "You may bring the ring with you, but don't wear it. Don't try to find us, we'll find you. Is that clear?"

Marc felt himself nod. Now that something was finally happening to him he felt an exhilarating mixture of wild excitement and plummeting dread."

Saturnus nodded curtly. "Good. Speak to no-one. NO-ONE, Marc, it's very important." As he headed off along the boardwalk Marc raised a hand by way of farewell, still speechless. Like a man who really was hypnotised he arose from the bench, case in hand, and walked directly towards Mysteries bookshop with a solitary thought floating in his head:

AM I HERE?

The Chair

An enchanter I shall be today - and failure transmute to success.

Nicholas Roerich, The Key from the Gates

Nicholas Roerich, The Modern Review, 1937, {{PD-US}}

Thou askedst

Who wanted to defraud Thee? ... Is it astonishing![x]

Jack nodded miserably at the lamentation of her Master and he crouched closer to the chair upon which he'd placed her. They were in a region known to occultists as Kathmandu, at one side of a great, wide plateau, before which was an incredible-looking but faraway vista of the sub-continent.
"How do you like the view?" He asked, hoping to ease the blow of her capture with an excellent platform from which to view that which she *could* still see. Whilst the abyssal blindfold made it impossible for her to access the heights of spiritual vision in the way that she had done previously – and her physical body was suffering in sympathy - her physical sight was clear as day and the middle astral realm more real to her than ever.
From that moment on, however, her physical mobility would start to decline in a serious way. Only after her death would she regain a degree of movement, but even then just downwards or sideways, not straight up. Not for as long as the blindfold was still fastened about her mind.
Her piercing blue eyes roamed across the immense plane, which stretched out endlessly in every direction, the colours of the land made pale and misty by the ether of the mountain peaks. "It is a sight for sore eyes, she murmured. "The soul of India. I'm fully resolved to set up here for real. A cold climate will be no good for me.'"
"It's a good view," the Master agreed. "I shall give you something more to look at."
She turned to watch as he moved a few metres behind her to the mouth of a cave in the mountainside, unusually round and blacker than pitch inside; black as the blind around her eyes. To her curious surprise, he stopped at the very edge of the entrance to the cave – not even allowing a toe to creep over the threshold – and let out a sudden cry.

Wholly unexpectedly, a group of slender, black-bearded men, identically dressed in red and white loin cloths and turbans, rushed out of the cave and sat down on the plateau in orderly lines, bowing before the dawn horizon. There were 40 of them in total, she observed, wondering who on Earth they might be. Some class of monk, priest or adept, of course, but of which cult?

"It's a good spot, this", said the Master with a smile, and you can come her anytime you please. There's more; watch again." She followed him with his eyes as he stepped back over to the cave and paused once more at the threshold. "Look out," he said, turning back towards her. "I think this might be a big one."

Taking this as an urgent warning, Madame Blavatsky hastily wheeled her chair in the opposite direction, just as he bellowed inside the cave. Before the echo had died the smooth 'O' of its mouth burst open into a jagged roar, right across the width of the plateau, as a river of souls poured out in a great chaotic torrent.

As she watched in amazement, a huge golden statue of what appeared to be Brahman, taller than two men and sitting in the Lotus position, one hand raised in teaching, floated outside. It was hovering a short distance from the ground by some unknown mechanism, apparently independent of the crowd. *How on Earth is it moving*, she wondered, as it floated straight towards her, also observing that herds of cows and other animals were trotting out with the horde.

That wasn't all. Also manifesting were two more aspects of the Indian deity. The second emerged in a dynamic standing position a few metres in front of her chair. The apparently sexless being, which resembled Sanat Kumara, radiated calmness and control, but also expressed an energy so strong it was almost fierce. Smaller in stature than the Brahman figure, with long black hair and a strange blueish tint to its bare limbs, its unutterably exotic, long-lashed eyes were impenetrable shining pools of the deepest Prussian blue.

Before she could get lost in those mesmerising eyes, knowing and yet innocent, ancient yet childlike, bold yet shy, a third figure burst into view between them with a breath-taking whirlwind of force.

She held her nerve as the incredible entity with multiple whirling arms, blue-black in colour, zoomed straight towards her at breakneck speed and with a silent shriek. Willing herself to remain calm, Madame Blavatsky felt as if a clear, strong breeze passed through her astral body and back out again to the beyond. *"WHOOO!"* she exclaimed, unable to help herself. That *was* something! She watched in fascination as the soul of the river just kept on coming.

"It's somewhat like the Mouth of the Ganges," he told her eventually, on this plane, at least. There is much you will learn here about the Secret Doctrine. As long as you account for the astral reflection. Now we shall go to the main reception room so you can become familiar with the environment before you return to face life on Earth".

"How much longer?" she asked.

"A while yet"

The next thing she knew they were facing each other in a very different and even stranger no-man's land, where everything was white.

"The situation on Earth will soon become very serious", he told her. "The Pax Britannica will hold for one more generation and then – when you have passed over - all hell will start to break loose".

She pondered this a long while. "War?" *Armageddon.*

He nodded. "All four horses are to be unleashed. There will be great wars on Earth and spiritual battles in the Heavens. Bloodshed, disease and death. Wickedness in high and low places. The enemy will attempt to control the astral space and mental space by subverting a plan set up by those who wanted to serve the light, albeit misguidedly at times". *As with you. As with me.* Jack was passively seated with the blindfold blacker than the abyss wrapped tightly around her astral eyes.

Her submissive countenance was diametrically opposite to that of the persona she cultivated in the earth dimension, which was domineering, brash, chaotic, infuriating and often rude, although she did have a natural ability to charm.
The telepathic communications from her revered Master were carefully absorbed with every fibre of her being. His present astral form closely resembled his earthly body and was of indeterminate age. Judging from his features, which were framed with thick, straight black hair, he might equally have been a native of Russian Siberia, Mongolia, Tibet, Peru, Greenland, Nepal, Shambhala or Atlantis.
Rather than appearing in the heavy ceremonial gear he could often be found wearing on Earth, he was simply dressed in a dark woollen poncho with matching wool trousers, fur boots and a round fur hat. Somewhat unusually, as he only brought them with him when emergency situations suggested he should do so, he also had with him two mountain-dog puppies. He knew she preferred cats but still hoped the friendly dogs would offer some comfort to Mrs Blavatsky, who remained silent, her mouth turned down at the corners. She knew she was in a terribly bad position. Her thoughts were black.
The magnetism of that man is sickening; his lying is beastly; his slander of Hübbe Schleiden, his intrigues unaccountable but on the ground that he is either a maniac – utterly irresponsible for the most part, or allowed to be possessed by his own dugpa Spirit
[xi]"I expected the Jesuits to get involved," she added, more conversationally, "but I was sent into a spin by the Amilius brothers; their involvement threw me for a crucial moment and enabled them to capture me unawares".
The Master was similarly disappointed. "The brotherhood in America has been infiltrated by a cell of Belial initiates. They managed to stay hidden by manipulating the crystals."
Jack felt even more gloomy at that. The forces of Atlantis in their entirety – dark *and* light – were working against her,

which was ironic, as she was nothing if not committed to spiritual unity amongst all people.

"There are definitely three," infiltrators," the Master continued, "four with Chintamon as the new recruit, whatever his other stated allegiances are. Two of them came via Opus Dei and the third turned when his land deal failed..."

There was a query in his tone and HPB was forced to admit that she had acted to stymie an immensely valuable land contract. She'd known at the time that she was sowing the wind and would reap the whirlwind. She felt a pang of regret but a touch of defiance remained. "I might have overstepped but you know how they tried to defraud me. My entire legacy could have been lost had I not turned the tables".

"What's done is done, but you have a good heart and history may still be kind to you if you can make peace with the White Guard in future. They will think deeply and forgive everything in their synthesising impulse. You will also have opportunities to make amends with some of your most ardent critics from other quarters and settle karmic scores.

He gestured around the white expanse. "All who pass through this room must somehow come through, by or past you. Your vision above this point might have been cut off, but your access to the earthly, astral and mental realms will henceforth be strengthened. Not only will you inspire a school of high adepts in Russia – the leaders of which are already incarnate - the Theosophical Society will come to exert enormous influence on Earthly culture and politics. Far beyond your wildest dreams, Elena, for their magic shall rebound more badly than they can even imagine".

He paused. Now for the bad news. "All of this will take time. Certainly more than a century; maybe as long as 200 years. The rest of your life on Earth will be passed in this prison in Kathmandu. The zone of Maya is what you shall see in place of your former high vision and your ability to reach the higher astral has been greatly curtailed. Your chariot is now a chair and this immobility will have a malign effect on your physical body".

Jack's head bowed as her worst fear was confirmed. Her physical decline had been apparent for some time and with searing foresight she was painfully aware of how bad things could get. She could clearly see herself being pushed around in a coffin-like contraption by solemn-looking acolytes and felt perilously close to howling with grief.

Her Master's calming presence saved her from this loss of composure. "We shall focus on our vital work in this sphere, Elena, secure in the knowledge that not only will the time of Theosophy come, but the Mages of your homeland shall write the blueprint for earthly power".

She perked up a bit at this. "I am ready to work on the next book. Something to help with the unlocking of doors".

"Completing the Secret Doctrine will be very difficult. It may be impossible to do it correctly. In your weakened state you will rely on others to complete it for you. The most unscrupulous characters will attach themselves to you and attempt to drain you of all psychic and spiritual vitality. They will use you most grievously and you must bear it all for the good of the mission, For the sake of humanity."

The House on Malaya Lubyanka Street

When you really concentrate, you will get a sense of expansion. You will feel that you are larger person than you are physically, as if you become a person two or three sizes bigger than your ordinary physical self, and that you are flowing with all your being toward the object of your concentration.

Michael Chekhov

Mikhail Chekhov, pictured in
The Russian Theatre by Sayler,
Published by Brentano's, NY, 1922

What an evil night.

Madame Blavatsky peered with a glum expression into the basement of number 7 in house 16 on Malaya Lubyanka Street[xii]. A dark, malignant shadow hung over the holy, white-walled mother city of times past, its golden-domed churches either razed to the ground or desecrated by devils. In the 37 years since her physical death the same grim realisation had plagued her on many a night. Saving a decade or so when the Tsar had announced the Edict of Toleration of Religion[xiii] and opened the astral doors of Russia to the work of occult schools, things down below had gone from bad to worse. *Poor man*, she thought, shaking her head. The die had already been cast with the attempted assassination and subsequent death of his saintly father, Alexander II.

Perhaps the greatest evil had begun on that fateful day, she brooded. *Never did I witness such a sincere, unanimous grief. Never did I think that a ragged crowd, 50,000 men strong, composed mostly of our working factory heads, peasants, and beggars, vicious and half-starved as the Moscow populace now are, could stand for two long hours, suffocating each other around the many Kremlin churches and weep, as I have seen them weep today. . . . It seemed as if their hearts were breaking. . . . It was a terrible strain upon one's nerves*[xiv].

She shuddered to think of what had unfolded since that time. The slaughter of the Imperial family – most of them, at least – had come in the midst of a horror so great she had never believed it possible. *A sinister fate seemed to have pursued the Romanovs, she wondered, of whom not one had met a natural death, since Peter the Great*[xv].

Dark clouds looming on the horizon – fulminating in the distance and clearly visible from her vantage point in Kathmandu – told her that hell was bubbling over.

In the basement of number 7, the zealous Mr Vadim Karlovich Chekhovski[xvi] – a physicist of some renown who worked in the Moscow branch of the Leningrad Brain

Institute – was adjusting a dial on the psychic machine. It stood at one corner of an enormous table which spanned the length of the room. The earnest young man had found, to his chagrin, that Madame Blavatsky was still blocking its receptors and once again he attempted to reason with her.

"I *know* that it is dangerous, Elena Petrovna, but surely you can't expect us to sit here and *do nothing*. Just look at what those devils are up to. The Emperor is long dead and poor Master Butator is locked up in Solevski in the worst of all worlds; no end to their depravity is in sight!"

He was right, of course, but Madame Blavatsky was nonetheless determined to do everything in her power to divert him from his suicidal course of action.

Time was running out. As their exchange became more heated, sparks began to fly from the machine and sweat started to pour down Vadim Karlovich's face. This would be so much easier if she would only get onside with his plan, but since the debacle with Lenin and the Roerichs she'd refused to intervene directly with the Soviet hierarchy.

"The more you interfere, the worse it gets", she repeated for the hundredth time, her patience running thin. "They've found a way to feed off your energies and they will keep turning things around. These are no ordinary human beings, Vadim Karlovich, They're *vampires*. You've seen what the American branch did to me all those years ago. A firing squad will be the least of your worries if the Reds discover what you're up to. *When* they discover it. What makes you so sure you can escape the fate of the Petrograd circle?"

"Because members of our circle have higher positions – we're better organised - and we have the blessing of the Unknown Philosopher. I'll remind you that when he left Russia he began to set the wheels in motion from a base in central Europe. And Nina Pavlovna is doing magnificent work. She's already infiltrated the upper levels!

Madame Blavatsky inhaled deeply on her cigarette. "They're far more powerful than you realise, Vadim Karlovich. They will take the work of EMESH and twist it to suit their goals. Why do you think Vladimir Ilyich is embalmed in a Ziggurat, with a 33rd degree conferred upon him? They are subverting your efforts to work black magic". She paused before delivering her parting shot. "You're letting your personal desire get the better of you...or should I say Evgeny Karlovich's desire?"

This stung the younger Chekhovski more than he cared to admit, for his father – who also inhabited the spacious apartment - had said the same thing to him over breakfast that very morning.

"It's easy for you to say," he implored. "We have to live through this reign of terror; all you have to do is watch and criticise our efforts. If you would free up the machine I'll try to reconnect with Nikola Tesla and obtain the blueprints for a weapon that will destroy them. Even Rasputin would be useful *if only the line was free* to call him!"

"The lights on the machine were flashing red but Vadim Karlovich could not prevent his feelings getting the better of him. "Admit it, Elena Petrovna: You're afraid of them!"

No sooner did the thought escape his brain when he regretted it. It was a sore point which he and the others had skirted around for years, because he was right. She *was* afraid of them.

As if in response to the tremors of his ego, the machine shuddered violently for a moment and then shut down completely, as if it were dead. He sighed in frustration and pulled off the head piece, yanking at the tangle of wires until they were lying in a mess on the table before him.

He poured a glass of Stolichnaya and gulped it down, followed by another. The liquid burned his throat and numbed his brain with reassuring speed. *God, what a night*, he thought again. The disastrous conversation with Elena Petrovna, the latest in a long line of disputes, had left him shaken.

Despite his contrary arguments, he took very seriously her warning. Ice dripped into his bones as he felt the web of the spider being drawn around him. He lit a cigarette and looked around the darkly cavernous space with his clinical scientist's eyes and philosopher's soul. He wondered what an OGUP[xvii] report might look like if they happened to discover such an unrivalled cache of illegal documents and equipment:

Imagine a table running the entire length of the basement; and you know how huge those basements are, General Secretary. On the table were occult books – works of black magic and sorcery - documents of an illegal secret organisation. But it wasn't just theoretical, General Secretary, oh no! These are cunning scientists of the first order, employed by our State Brain Institute, no less! There were many pieces of equipment, chemical reagents, strange glass bottles and stones, animal bones, resin and exotic herbs.

Yes, General Secretary, almost like the lair of that damned scoundrel Rasputin. Worse in fact! What really came to mind when I saw the cursed secret laboratory of Vadim Karlovich and his henchmen, was the first black magician to taint our land: Arthur Dee himself, subverter of the Tsar and spy to that Queen of the wicked Empire, Elizabeth I of England.

"A pile of hair was found at one end of the table and nearby in the corner was a device they call a "psychic machine. Vadim Karlovich swore it wasn't working but at that moment it began winking with lights. He refused to say who the hair belonged to, but we made later enquiries and, well…"

At this point, Vadim Karlovich thought, the man would go pale and hastily change the subject.

"Also confiscated were various electronic instruments – including a very large device that they use for teleportation - illegal printing equipment and weapons that included an ancient sword. A sword! As you know, General Secretary, the father, Karl Nikiforovich, is a *Roman Catholic* of noble birth." Vadim Karlovich imagined the eyebrows being collectively raised at this. Someone might swear under their breath or even spit into a fire.

"In the clandestine laboratory, General Secretary, magical experiments were staged – ranging from investigations into hypnosis and telepathy to "killing at a distance" with the help of wax figures. All under the registered guise of finding a cure for eczema and haemophilia. We did find the formulas for such medicines amongst their many papers, he added as an afterthought.

"And how does Vadim Karlovich explain all of this, you might well ask. He gives the appearance of being a respectable man and is so naïve as to believe himself innocent. He says he was driven by the desire to combine the mystical experience of Orthodox ascetics with the data of contemporary science. He wishes, so to speak, to master grace on a scientific basis.

"The result of all this, General Secretary, is that entirely by chance - for we were really visiting this house to arrest the father, the People's Commissariat of Railways, Karl Nikiforovich Chekhovski - we happened upon the headquarter of the Russian Rosicrucians: The order EMESH Redivivus[xviii]!

"The purpose of this order was, with the help of scientific experiments conducted in the laboratory, to master the forces of nature and to find a mechanism for changing the human psyche. The maximum programme included the construction of a magical Temple and a city of initiates who would possess inexhaustible magical resources up to immortality. Wholly by accident we found ourselves amidst the self-styled ancestors and reincarnated souls of the Atlantean race, which perished when their abuse of magic created a vortex in nature which destroyed their realm.

"We know all this because a large archive of manuscripts which completely exposed the existence of the occult order was also found in the building. I cannot help but notice, General, that this very same building is just 350metres away from our own head office. It is an outrage!"[xix]

And what of this psychic machine, the General Secretary

would naturally ask, with eyes like black stones extracted from the bowels of hell. You say that a piece of hair was found close to this...psychic machine. Do you know who the hair belonged to, comrade?

At this dreaded question the OGPU secretary would steady himself on the back of a chair and (looking straight ahead, his voice beginning to waver), would reply, almost in a whisper. "It was yours, General Secretary...the hair belonged to you".

What came next, Vadim Karlovich hardly dared contemplate, for the hair did indeed belong to Joseph Vissarionovich Stalin, sequestered from the General Secretary's own barber. Through this odious black clump the EMESH inner circle was attempting to control the tyrant's psyche. Worse than this (if that were possible), they were trying to exert this control by influencing the OGPU employees, who were stationed nearby. Practically across the road.

As he considered the likely contents of a prosecution that could be brought against him – against every member of EMESH, whose records were kept in that very same basement - Vadim Karlovich realised it was almost time for the next general meeting and began to arrange the papers and light candles.

Whilst he was going about this pleasantly dull chore he reflected back upon the group discussions of the past few weeks. Every member of the inner circle had sworn himself without reserve to their goal of regenerating the egregore of Atlantis and creating a magical seat of world government at their heart. Once this seat of control was established they would be ideally placed to bring peace and happiness to the entire Earth and its peoples.

The men considered themselves to be Rosicrucians and, as Vadim Karlovich's founding partner, the diplomat Evgeny Karlovich Teger, had said, they: "Sought to surpass all existing occult organisations, including Masonic ones.... to realise [magical] theory in practice by attaining power that enables implementation...to establish initiation to magic on a worldwide scale.

Their name *"EMESH - אמש - Redivivus"* - signified the reborn unity of the three planes of being through the three Hebrew mother letters of: Aleph (Mental plane), Mem (Astral plane) and Shin (Physical plane). Their core literature, which included a few huge illustrated volumes, was stacked up on the table. It included their foundational text, the Encyclopaedia of Occultism by G.O.M, who had also assigned the group its name; Karl Brandler-Pracht's Occultism and assorted works by Swami Vivekenanda and Sar Dinoil[xx].

The group had evolved out of the Order of World Secrets and there were now four levels. The first was for those individuals who knew nothing about the existence of the organisation and consisted of a few exceptional students at elite Moscow and Petrograd[xxi] institutions. Fewer in Petrograd since the infamous case of the Leningrad freemasons, which had resulted in the arrest of G.O. Mebes and his wife, Maria[xxii]. Second was the level for those who, whilst following the course and perhaps attending one or two informal meetings, had begun to suspect the existence of a hidden occult order with a magical agenda. Numbered amongst them were friends, colleagues and older students of the leading members, Evgeny Karlovich and Vadim Karlovich himself.

As Evgeny Karlovich was an important diplomat, he had also done much to extend their network beyond the borders of the Soviet Union, into Afghanistan and Western China. These efforts were greatly assisted by the work of the White Russian Sisters led by Nina Pavlovna Roudnikova, who served as the Shin element for their White Guard and loyal Russian citizens in the Eastern European diaspora.

The third level of EMESH Redivivus admitted those who had been told about the magical inner circle and had begun to understand its aims – some of its aims, at least – but without knowing its name, organisational structure or identity of the leaders and officers.

Finally came the innermost inner core of the group, ranged around Teger as commander, Chekovski as procurator and a man named Preobrazhenski as assistant. Those in the inner circle, which also included Chekovski's wife, knew the name and aims of the organisation and were granted the right to use its materials and facilities. All had pledged to devote themselves to EMESH, to the exclusion of other occult groups and their materials.

The incognito magicians at the veiled heart of this Order must, according to Teger: "be higher than the spiritual and secular authorities" in the entire world," committed to the Russian Rosicrucian dream of re-creating the culture of Atlantis, which would enable them to influence all planes of existence and to thereby govern the world by magical means.

Vadim Karlovich wondered how the Chekist regime would react to the disclosure of the stated aims of EMESH, as set out in the manifesto he'd just filed away beneath a treatment for haemophilia in an ordinary-looking filing cupboard. This nine-point manifesto ran broadly as follows in dramatic calligraphic script that was repeated in 12 languages: Six ancient, the others modern:

1. The scientific study of meta-psychical phenomena, especially works on telepathy and clairvoyance.
2. Arcanology and preliminary occult training.
3. Magical praxis.
4. Formation of the conceptual centre EMESH Redivivus and its astral egregore, which was the confirmed level achieved by the group at the current time: 18th February 1928.
5. A development of EMESH into a suitable base for serious occult work and magical praxis over a number of years.
6. The greater expansion of EMESH, which could

only follow the attainment of certain results, chief amongst which was the establishment of a world centre for occult magic. This might be physically head-quartered either in the USSR or abroad. Here certain preferred countries were listed, including Brazil.
7. A global occult centre and magical headquarters which has full control of the astral plane.

As he considered this seventh point Vadim Karlovich trembled from head to toe, as if a phantom had crossed his grave. Already the rival egregores had reached monstrous proportions. The untold sacrifice of so many noble and innocent souls – human and animals together– during the Great War had unleashed astral forces of previously unimagined power. These had left their root nations in a parlous state, but the great Western powers were largely in denial about the extent of the precipice they were falling over. They had not come to terms with their loss and nor would they until even worse came.

The same titanic forces had facilitated the growth of EMESH to an electrifying degree and Vadim Karlovich knew, deep down, that the group egregore had become extremely volatile with the huge and rapid influx of power. Huge enough, perhaps, to propel the group through stages 7 and even 8 if the base could be consolidated in time.

8. A global occult centre and magical headquarters which has full control of the mental plane. This had to be done, Vadim Karlovich thought desperately, or the reds would seize the initiative and gain an upper hand. Already their propaganda was proving highly effective and spreading like wildfire.

9. A global occult centre and magical headquarters which has full control of the Divine plane[xxiii].

His partner, Evgeny Karlovich, arrived early ahead of the general meeting. It was agreed they would attempt to psychically influence their captors by whatever means they had at their disposal and - most crucially – that the identity of the Moscow St Germain must be kept hidden at all costs[xxiv].

As the rest of their members began to arrive – one-by-one stating the password from the other side of the door, the psychic machine had sprung back to life, its red lights blinking the alarm signal. This time it was accompanied by a note, which Vadim Karlovich snatched up at once. It bore only two scrawled words, written in capitals with a grim finality:

THEY'RE COMING[xxv].

Mysteries

This will go on until A.D. 2025. During the years intervening between now and then very great changes will be seen taking place, and at the great General Assembly of the Hierarchy—held as usual every century—in 2025 the date in all probability will be set for the first stage of the externalisation of the Hierarchy. The present cycle (from now until that date) is called technically "The Stage of the Forerunner"–

The Externalisation of the Hierarchy, Alice Bailey

Ellene Alice Bailey, c1893

Mysteries' window

Glowed with a warm light as Marc arrived there at 19.28 hours on Saturday 3rd September 2022. He paused outside it for a moment, searching the faces of those who were already crowded inside. Failing to spot Frater Saturnus or anyone else who stood out from the regular throng of oddballs, he pushed open the door with a great tinkling of bells. A large woman wearing a lot of clothes bore down on him with a clipboard.
"Are you here for Sleeping Prophets or just having a look?"
"Yes I am, I should be on the list: Marc Marconi"
"Aha…yes, here we go, M." She ran a pen down the clipboard and crossed out his name. "Welcome Mr Marconi, we're just about to begin. Do help yourself to a glass of wine, it's included in the ticket price." She gestured to the back of the shop and smiled pleasantly.
"I will, thank you." The bookshop was familiar territory for Marc and he'd been to events there in the past. The last of these had been an interesting talk given by someone called John Eastern about the myths and legends of Glastonbury and the surrounding area. He learned this was known as the Glastonbury Zodiac, named after the work of someone called Kathleen Maltwood. Marc had enjoyed John's acerbic wit but hadn't been totally convinced by the Zodiac idea and suspected that only a very thorough reconnaissance mission to Glastonbury would convince him on that point. He was therefore unlikely to be convinced in this lifetime as he couldn't see himself getting to South-West England at any point in the future. Maybe London one day but even that was doubtful as his wife hated flying.
Safely installed close to the drinks table, passably good glass of red in hand, he scanned the crowd again whilst the advertised hosts of the meeting introduced themselves. As the talk got properly underway, he became increasingly absorbed in what they were saying. Edgar Cayce was one of Virginia Beach's most famous stars and whilst Marc was well-versed

in the lore surrounding this legendary clairvoyant, the expert speakers were honing-in on a subject of special interest to occultists: Atlantis.
A young woman who was also standing guard over the wine and nibbles leaned towards him. "That stuff they're saying about the Amilius and Belial groups seems to have lasted to this day", she whispered.
Marc gave her a sidelong glance. She had glossy brunette hair with bright blue highlights and even in a room full of dandyish characters was notably well dressed. "Yes, it's interesting, the forces of darkness and light…"

In the beginning, the Atlanteans were a spiritual people ruled by a peaceful group Cayce termed the Law of One. But gradually, the Belial influence began to manifest. An ongoing spiritual and material battle was waged between these two groups. The Sons of Belial worshipped self-aggrandisement, sought power over others, and practiced human sacrifice. Cayce stated that they had no standard of morality, no sense of right and wrong. In contrast, the Children of the Law of One worshipped one God, sought spiritual and physical attunement with the Creator and espoused the idea of treating others as oneself in their day-to-day lives….according to Cayce, there was a more etheric or spiritual component in the Belial Group's conflicts, which led to ill-defined destructive forces entering the earth. These destructive forces were, in part, responsible for the series of catastrophic events that befell Atlantis.
Cayce's story of how the destructive forces were unleashed is entwined with the mysterious crystal. The story begins with the 'White Stone', a stone "in the form of a six-sided figure", which was also referred to as the "Tuaoi stone." Initially, this stone was used for communication with the divine, in a way that appears similar to how Native American shaman utilise crystals. A priestess of the Law of One would gather together a group and concentrate on the stone, eventually entering an altered state of consciousness. From the stone would come a form of speech interpreted by the priestess. The speech came

from what Cayce referred to as the "saint realm", which imparted "understanding and knowledge" to the group. As the Sons of Belial came to realise the unlimited power inherent in the stone, they began using it for selfish purposes... By 28,000 B.C....the Tuaoi Stone, once a conduit to God, had now become a "terrible crystal" or a "firestone" - an energy source that could be easily utilised as a powerful weapon. [xxvi]

"I'm fascinated by the Tuaoi stone," the woman whispered at him from behind her hand. "I heard that it was some kind of copper ore, a form of Lapis."
"First time I've given it this much thought," Marc replied, wondering what the unusual crystal embedded in his new ring was made of.
"Yeah, Cayce and a friend took off for some mines to see if they could find any of the stuff; it was covered on the Dark Journalist show a few months back."
"Sounds cool, I should check it out".
"It's the best show on Youtube in my opinion but - full disclosure - I help moderate the group chat during podcasts, so I *would* think that!"
"No kidding!" Marc was impressed. "So you're some kind of Wingsgirl who controls the ideas room?"
She laughed at that. "You must be psychic, Mr, err?"
"Marc. Marc Marconi".
"You must be psychic Mr Marc Marconi, our chat hangout is known as the Idea's Room!"
He chuckled as well. "I'd call it a good guess! My wife says I'm psychic but personally I think she's the one who can read minds. She can read mine, anyway!"
The woman smiled. "I'm Olivia." She held out a petite hand, which Marc shook politely, glad to be meeting a cooler person than he usually got to hang out with. By the time it came to the end of the presentation he had filled his glass for the third time and was in a pretty good mood. The talk had been better than expected and he'd almost forgotten why he'd

come to Mysteries in the first place.

"So what is it that you do?"

The question brought him back down to earth and he was suddenly conscious of not having achieved the object of his evening, which was to reconvene with Frater Saturnus. "Nothing as cool as you, I'm afraid. I'm your regular IT man."

"Nothing wrong with IT. DJ used to edit a tech magazine; he's a bit of a geek at times, loves his gadgets!"

"I wish I were editing a tech magazine! To tell the truth I'm pretty bored of my job right now, I can't seem to build up any enthusiasm. It might be time for a career change."

"You have to follow your dreams!" She clinked glasses with him and they both drank to that. "So which firm do you work for, is it Mystics, Data Services, AstroLink…"

He stopped her before she could reel off the names of more tech companies. "Yeah, AstroLink." He was surprised to sense her ears prick up.

"Aha! Rumour has it that you guys are pitching for a big CERN project, that's got to be exciting?"

She gave him a piercing look and he was suddenly conscious that he was in fact speaking to the press and the press somehow knew about the secret project he was working on." He blushed. "Gee, Wingsgirl, you're calling *me* psychic, how the hell did you hear about that?"

"So it *is* true!"

Oh jeez. Marc felt a burning need to extract himself from the pickle jar he'd somehow fallen into. "You must excuse me, there's someone I was supposed to meet here and I still haven't found him."

She looked a bit contrite. "I'm sorry, I shouldn't have pried, that's my journo instincts getting the better of me. Forget I said anything." She held out a square business card, which was black with a bold white X across it. "If you ever feel like blowing a whistle, you know who to call. We're keeping a close eye on CERN as we believe that it ties in with what's happening out there in the hot zone." She touched his arm and lowered her voice. "And I can assure you that we NEVER reveal our sources".

Marc pushed his glasses up and blinked at her. "That's really kind, thanks Olivia. It was nice to meet you. I'll be sure to check out your show!"

"Friday nights at 9.00", we'd love to see you in the Idea's Room. She gave him a conspiratorial wink and melted into the crowd, where she was soon surrounded by people who seemed to think she was a minor celebrity. He looked after her for a moment, wondering if her strange insider knowledge about AstroLink was a matter for concern. A voice very close to his left ear made him jump.

"Glad you could make it".

Marc swivelled round. "Mr Saturnus!"

The Catacombs

..all at once the light burst forth from all parts, the priest cried, Rejoice, O sacred initiated...

Manly P. Hall, The Secret Teachings of all Ages

Manly P. Hall, late 1920s

Come with me

Saturnus inclined with his head towards the back of the room. There was a door which must have led to the basement as the stairs to the upper storey – home to Reiki, horoscope and tarot card reading - were on the other side of the shop.
Marc's heart gave a little leap. He'd not yet managed to penetrate that inner sanctum of the Virginia Beach occult community. Society there was awash with rumours about that basement, where magical rituals were meant to have been held with surprising regularity over the decades. Maybe more than a century if you counted the infamous activities of the prior owning of the building.
He was aware of Olivia watching intently as he followed Saturnus to the basement door, where the lady who'd earlier held the clipboard was now waiting for them. She gave him a knowing smile as she produced a key from her voluminous skirts, unlocked the door and then closed it shut without following them into the basement.
A single bulb that was dangling from the ceiling cast a dull orange glow which only just adequately lit the way down the narrow wooden stairs. Keeping a close eye on the steps so he didn't lose his footing, Marc toyed with the ring in the left-hand pocket of his jacket. He wondered again what it was made of and resolved to ask Frater Saturnus.
In the breast pocket was a letter retrieved from the briefcase, which he must have read twenty times or more since it had come into his possession two days ago. The ceremonial dagger he had prudently decided to leave at home, although he'd seriously toyed with the idea of bringing it. That it might have been needed in some form of ritual was opposed by the chance of being arrested for carrying a dangerous weapon. The knife, therefore, was at home where it could do no harm.
"How long have you known Miss Hepburn?"
The question took Marc by surprise. "Who?"
"The woman you were speaking with."

"You mean Olivia?"
"Yes".
"I don't really; we just met…"
"I advise you to take care when dealing with the press; she might be genuine but the press aren't necessarily on your side". There was a meaningful pause. "On *our* side."
Marc was silent. The remark pigeon-holed him on the other side to whatever the first side was but he had no idea what either side really stood for.
The bottom of the stairs opened up into a small boxy room which, Marc was thrilled to note, had a pentacle drawn inside a circle on the concrete floor and what appeared to be a rather beautiful ebony altar cupboard up against the Eastern wall. The stubs of variously coloured candles were ranged on top of it but the rest of the contents were securely locked inside. Marc would dearly have loved to take a peep.
The walls were crowded with all kinds of framed portraits and group shots. Some of them were very old looking and many of them were signed. It was an eclectic mix of characters, which reflected the curatorial instincts of the bookshop's owner, Nora Boleskine. Aleister Crowley, Jack Parsons and L.Ron Hubbard were all up there, although Marc only noticed Crowley's distinctive challenging glare. Edgar Cayce had pride of place on the Western wall, surrounded by prominent members of the Association for Research and Enlightenment. Madame Blavatsky was of course present – opposite Cayce and above the alter – along with Jiddu Krishnamurthi and several other famous theosophists. They were flanked by Rudolf Steiner and an army of anthros.
Deadly handsome with his liquid dark eyes, a young Gurdjieff gazed into the astral world from his high place on the North wall. A wonderful image of Nicholas Roerich holding the peace banner amidst a crowd of international ambassadors was proudly displayed on the South. Dion Fortune, Gerald Gardiner and a few more English occultists could be spotted in one corner, though they were somewhat

concealed from view behind a very large candelabra on a plinth that was placed on the floor in front of them.

In another corner were ranged many formal looking portraits that most people would not recognise, however well versed they were in occult lore. These included an almost forgotten chain of Unknown Russian philosophers, who'd become targeted individuals as soon as the Bolsheviks revolted.

Marc had to take all this in very swiftly, as Frater Saturnus pulled aside a black velvet curtain on the North Wall (directly below Gurdjieff), revealing an intriguing looking door. Marc's heart skipped a beat as he realised that his years of beating around the edges of occultism were about to take him to a centre.

He was suddenly filled with longing. Desire to know more about his long-lost father and the contents of the briefcase; curiosity about the true identity of Frater Saturnus and the group or order behind him; concerns about the veiled warning from Olivia – who he instinctively felt was a good egg – and the grey but magnetic aura of Saturnus. He had to admit that he felt rather uneasy. Finally being privy to a genuine Mystery was one thing, but what if he'd found himself on the wrong side of the good vs evil binary?

Saturnus unlocked the door and held it open for Marc before stepping inside after him and locking it behind them. They were in a very dark, cold corridor and with eyes that and had not adjusted to the near-total gloom, Marc was unable to see anything at all. Despite this, Frater Saturnus made him jump again by tying a blindfold around his eyes and tying it tightly at the back of his head. He then manoeuvre in front of Marc in the narrow space. "Hold onto the back of my jacket, I'll lead you through".

It seemed he had no option but to obey. His heart really racing by this point, Marc clung like a child to the tailcoat of his elder, wondering what the hell he was getting himself into and how long it was all going to last. Where on Earth were they going and would he ever get out of this hole?

Having initially expected a short walk to another room, his unease grew exponentially as the journey through darkness progressed along a route of strange angles which never seemed to end. For most of it he was aware of being in a tunnel of sorts, the unyielding stone walls making their close presence felt by the chill on his skin, but at other times he was conscious of passing through more open spaces; other rooms, he supposed.

On more than one occasion he was unhappy to sense there were nameless others watching him, whilst fluctuating light conditions – just about perceptible from behind the blindfold – added to his sense of dislocation. After what seemed to be forever he was commanded by Frater Saturnus to stand still. Marc felt very alone and vulnerable, standing in his personal darkness whilst his guide whispered at length to some indefinable other.

The hairs on his neck stood on end and for no particular reason the project he was supposed to be hard at work on for AstroLink came to mind. He was suddenly overwhelmed with fears about the state of his employment, conscious that he was treading a fine line between relative prosperity and an empty can, jeopardizing the entire stability of his family in the process. What on Earth had he been thinking! The CERN project was genuinely exciting – the kind of thing that comes along once in a lifetime for employed IT professionals – yet instead of embracing it wholeheartedly and showing Nick and the rest what he could do, Marc had kept his head firmly up his own ass, fixated on the quest for Excalibur!

The inner vision of this legendary sword of British mythology triggered a mental picture of the ceremonial dagger that was nestled inside the leather case bearing his initials. The case was safely tucked inside a cupboard in his home office, also known as his man cave, which his wife and children knew better than to poke around in.

Despite the coolness of the atmosphere he began to feel extremely hot and even broke a sweat. Everything about his life that was bothering him, or he had neglected, taken for granted or abused, reared its head simultaneously. The unfixed light on the back porch; the minor disagreement with the other church elders which he'd allowed to turn into a cold war; his slothful attitude to work; his pride, in fact. The wedding anniversary he'd forgotten three years ago because he'd been too busy making wine; neglecting to take his kids to Disney World because it wasn't the Louvre; *I DRANK TOO MUCH WINE UPSTAIRS!* He panicked, his thoughts running amok. *I need to loose ten pounds; I need to do more housework; oh my God, I'm a terrible person!*

After this harrowing bout of self-flagellation, which reached the intensity of eternity, someone removed his blindfold. Marc squinted at his surroundings. He was in a surprisingly large room with no windows – still underground as far as he could tell – that was octagonal in shape and lit by an array of flickering candles which cast dancing shadows on the walls.

Standing around him in a deathly silent circle were twelve cloaked and masked individuals of indeterminate age or sex. One of them, he assumed, was Frater Saturnus. He turned slowly in a circle, looking at each one of them in turn, at a total loss for words. He felt like a rabbit caught in headlights and the thought of hitting this gathering with a bunch of pre-prepared questions now seemed ludicrous. The sound of a staff being forcibly struck against the wooden floor behind him made him jump out of his skin. This was followed by a thundering voice and a sword pointing straight at him from the front, which froze him to the spot in terror.

"MARCUS AMILIUS VLADIMIR IAHMEL MARCONI?"

Marc was dumbstruck. So *that* was what the A and the I stood for! It hadn't even been detailed in the letter, which was one of many reasons he'd brought it with him.

"MARCUS AMILIUS VLADIMIR IAHMEL MARCONI?"

"**YES**". He shouted back out of nervousness. "I'm here!"

'We have received the charges against you. How do you plead?"

Oh my God I'm going to die.
"HOW DO YOU PLEAD?"
How do I plead, how do I plead, how do I plead!
"HOW DO YOU PLEAD?"
A lump had formed in his throat and he felt dangerously close to crying. He knew his voice would sound small and pathetic but if he was going to die he may as well do it with a clear conscience. "Guilty. I'm **GUILTY!**" he screamed, close to tears.
It was the right answer. Much to the relief of his adrenalin-heightened senses there was a subtle change in the atmosphere of the room, from horrifyingly inquisitorial to somehow conciliatory. He even thought he detected a murmur of satisfaction.
"We accept your plea. Will you accept our judgement?"
Marc hesitated as the tension ramped up again. Did he have a choice? As it tended to do in moments of crisis, the iron like core of his being quietly asserted itself. There's always a choice; I'm a sovereign human being. I don't have to take any shit from any of these guys but..
"WILL YOU ACCEPT OUR JUDGEMENT?"
If he was one of them, as Frater Saturnus had suggested, reason should dictate that the judgement would not be to his detriment. Fancy name notwithstanding, as a middle aged IT professional Marc was hardly the ideal sacrificial lamb. Or so he surmised. He reached again for the ring in his pocket and took a deep breath. "Yes, I accept it."
There was a long enough pause for him to regret saying guilty and think about the nearest exit when another voice rang out from the opposite side of the room.
"The neophyte has spoken well. The son of our founding superior merits a merciful judgement." Saturnus.
"Will you vouch for him?"
"I will."
"Do you accept him as your disciple"
"I do."

"Do you accept that any errors he commits shall henceforth be yours?"
"I do."
Marcus Amilius Vladimir Iahmel Marconi, do you have the seal of Amilius?"
Marc slipped the ring onto his finger and held out his hand. "I do."
"Do you have the dagger of Iahmel?"
Damn it, wrong decision! "Yes I do… but it's at home."
There was a just audible sigh of irritation. "Very well. It is not ideal but we can use a substitute for now. Now you must kneel and recite your oath to the brotherhood founded by your father."
Part of Marc felt like saying, '*to hell with that*', but the greater part of him felt hypnotically compelled to obey the command. It was all moving pretty fast but going with the flow seemed so much easier than getting out of it and after all, what did he have to lose? If the letters and their words tonight were anything to go by he was pretty important already. Furthermore, if it was anything like the masons this could be a really good career move! He knelt without a word and held up his hand.
Frater Saturnus moved behind him and placed a hand on his shoulder, whilst the first speaker mirrored his gesture and held up his hand. "Repeat after me: I, Marcus Amilius Vladimir Iahmel Marconi, do solemnly swear."
"I, Marcus Amilius Vladimir Iahmel Marconi, do solemnly swear."
"That henceforth my life shall be for the Brotherhood of Amilius.…"
"According to the laws laid down by our Father, Victor Iahmel Amilius and the Dauphin priests of Atlantis."
Marc faltered. He had to think about that one for moment, which became increasingly pregnant as the seconds ticked by. He thought back to one or two nuggets he'd heard from Dann and Emmaline earlier that evening, especially the part where

the Amilius group was highlighted as the good one, in opposition to the dark forces of Belial. "Could you repeat that please?"

Ultimately, yes, he would agree to that as well and to all the other clauses that were sent his way. He would drink something alcoholic from a ceremonial goblet; he would be daubed with anointing oil, dressed with a matching cloak to all the others and apparently knighted with a ceremonial sword. it was more than Marc had dreamed could even happen to him and his dislocated expectation had the curious effect of making his mind a blank slate. For the duration of the ceremony, at least.

After it had ended, he was blindfolded once again and taken back the way he had come through the tunnel, out of the secret door, into the basement room of Mysteries and up into the shop again. By that time it was totally deserted and almost dark, except for the voluminous lady who was quietly reading a book by the light of a lamp on the front desk. Marc breathed a sigh of relief when he saw her. Finally he was coming full circle on this crazy evening.

She smiled at them and he thought that she also looked tired. Frater Saturnus spoke to her. "Thank you for your patience, Mrs Boleskine. Do you have the documents for Mr Marconi?"

"Of course, Brother Saturnus, it's right here." She handed an envelope to Marc. "Open it when you get home," Saturnus commanded, but don't delay too long, we need you on that flight on Thursday."

The remark hit its target like a bolt from the blue, but Marc didn't have time to protest as Saturnus and Mrs Boleskine ushered him from the building with a combination of goodbyes, farewells and good lucks. God knows he would need it.

Dreamland

The key to the Apocalypse is to practise it...for as the Apocalypse is a revelation put into writing, it is necessary, in order to understand it, to establish in oneself a state of consciousness which is suited to receive revelations.

Meditations on the Tarot, Letter IV, The Emperor

The Emerpor Arcanum, Vasily Nikolayevich Masjutin

The peculiar tea party,

Letters from the ether and mysterious parcels still in her mind, Ana stared at the ceiling of her small but pretty bedroom, a colourful bazaar of floating fabrics and flower fairies. Though she had tried to have a normal rest-of-day following a rather trying morning, now she was finally in bed she felt tense and uneasy.

She would have loved to put the apparent eccentricities of her great-grandmother down to old age but Mrs Roudnikova was Markedly more lucid than any other person she knew. There was no possibility of writing the letters off as being the concoctions of a gently-going senile senior citizen. Besides, there was Mrs Pixley – also in possession of one of life's great mental centres – who was clearly in full agreement with her friend and they both seemed to know who the *actual* scribe was. So why hadn't they just told her?

Then there were the warnings from both ladies AND her father, who'd phoned right on cue in that infallible manner of his. His startling power of pre-cognition was something she admired the most about him and usually found highly comforting, but on this occasion he had scared her. It was blatantly obvious that all three of them – four if you counted the invisible scribe - were trying to warn her about something. So again, why didn't they just tell her! She didn't even want to think about the mysterious Mr Marconi and his unwelcome parcel. An American!

In situations like this, the only thing she could think of doing was turning to her dreams to help clarify things. It had been at least a week since she'd had a dream of any worth and it was high time for another. *Something prophetic, if you don't mind*, she thought stubbornly. Or any kind of clue whatsoever.

***

Why is everyone so sad?

The most enormous crowd, silent and solemn, stretched out as far as the eye could see. Flags were fluttering at half mast and people everywhere were weeping. It was definitely somewhere in London. In fact, it was like she was seeing all of London - all of England; the entire UK - through one lens. The longer she stared at panoramic scene, the farther it seemed to extend, until it appeared to signify the whole of the *world*. Some event of great import had clearly taken place.

She suddenly had a bird's eye view of The Mall, the long broad avenue which ran from Admiralty Arch to the Victoria Memorial outside Buckingham Palace. The city had fallen silent and the lips of the watchers who lined the street were sealed. The heads of young and old alike were bowed. And yet it was confusing because some sort of parade seemed to be happening in the road itself. Surely parades were positive occasions? Soldiers and sailors in full military regalia were marching in a line which stretched for more than a mile. There was music. Ahh! Beautiful and heart-rending. Bagpipes! In London; *why bagpipes*? But wait, the music had changed and now it was completely different. A single loud drum, solid as a heartbeat. Then a rat-tat-tat that accompanied the marching shoes of soldiers who swayed from side to side like a gently undulating wave. *The heartbeat of a nation.*

Beethoven.

Imperatrix.

императрица умерла

Ana was awoken by the sensation of tears running down her cheeks. She felt unbearably sad but did not know why. Her family were all safe and well, she could feel that much. So what had happened? What was *going* to happen? She was pulled back to the land of hypnosis in the next minute.
There was a pause of sorts whilst she entered a void in

consciousness and then opened her astral eyes onto a zone she'd never seen before. It was like a no-man's land - a grey zone - like a tunnel with nothing in it, not black or white but all grey like heavy clouds. Something abyssal like the sphere of Da'ath.
Standing ahead of her, maybe five metres away, was a huge and ancient horse. It was a red horse. It had a white stripe on its nose and white socks with great big feathers like a shire horse, but with very long legs, skinnier than a typical shire horse. Something told her what it was. It was an *ancient Russian War Horse and very special*, because it was *able to withstand extremely cold temperatures of up to -50 degrees*. Strange that the temperature was so specific.
Ana was unafraid of this huge creature and slowly walked towards it as the horse did likewise, heading in her direction with short, measured steps until it was standing right above her, as if she were a child. It must have been huge. It reached down its nose to nuzzle her face in the usual manner of old and friendly horses. It was gentle but not beautiful, with a Roman nose. It seemed incredibly ancient. She stroked its nose in pleasure and keenly felt how lucky she was to be seeing this animal, without any kind of thought or idea about the black shrouded figure who was sitting astride it with his sword upturned.
The horse and rider passed her by and paused another five metres or so behind her. Ana turned her head to look back at it and the horse did the same. Once again she noted the colour: Red hide, white feet and an extremely long mane and tail, which it swooshed slowly from side to side. It was an ancient Russian war horse.

An atom and also an archetype of some great horse

Virgin Atlantic

If it were possible,
Having flown centuries,
Flying over the graves,
In the body to rise in another

Nikolai Belotsvetov

Nikolai Belotsvetov

The flight took off

And Marc settled back in his seat with a quiet sigh of relief as the Boston lights fade from view and the nose of the plane pointed to London. It already felt like quite a long journey, involving an overnight stay in Richmond, an internal flight to Boston and the inevitable airport crowds and queues which his wife loathed so much.
He felt a twinge of sorrow as his beloved came strongly to mind. Apart from the fact he missed her a lot already, their parting had not been a happy one. Justifiably aghast at her husband's sudden decampment to London – which had come even more out of the blue for her than it had for him – she'd spent the last couple of days accusing him of having a midlife crisis and acting like a jerk. Their twins were refusing to even speak to him.
It was hard to disagree with her point of view under the circumstances. Not only must his present actions with their inadequate explanation appear totally outrageous for a married father of two, but Marc really *had* been acting like a jerk for the past 9 months. Bored of work and ever-more inclined to hide in his man cave, but not quite willing to buy a motorbike and re-enact a Bruce Springsteen song, he had floundered in a state of ennui for most of that year.
Niggling problems with his house, petty arguments with the church community and a few family health scares had taken their toll and he was close to burnout. What he really needed was a holiday, so the business class ticket to London and a credit card for expenses he was handed in an envelope three days ago had been impossible to resist.
Marc had never flown business class before and he couldn't help relishing the comfort, even as he lamented over the furious arguments his wife had levelled at him. Knowing he deserved it gave him a self-indulgent sense of peace, of inevitability, which conspired with an equal understanding of his desperate need for a break to make him feel secretly

pleased. Denial sure felt fine as he ascended to 36,000 feet, surrounded by tasty snacks and affluent fellow travellers. Better to be hung for a sheep than a lamb, he thought calmly, accepting a glass of champagne and flicking through the inflight entertainment options.

In the back of his head were complex concerns regarding the fulfilment of his appointed mission – the flight didn't *really* come for free, he realised - but he wasn't in the mood for addressing those just yet. Nor would he think too much about the oaths he'd recently taken or the mind-blowing facts about his father. It wasn't at all clear that these things had even sunk in yet. The odds were strong that they had not.

Am I here? Marc thought for the hundredth time that September as he took another swig from his glass. Whether he was or not, he would enjoy the charming hospitality that Virgin Atlantic had to offer and worry about the rest when he arrived in London.

Although he had managed to doze for a few fragmented hours on the plane, he was exhausted by the time he got to London, which was in the throes of an autumn chill. The early elation and state of denial he'd experienced during take-off had sunk just as easily during the descent and he now felt lonely, cold and vulnerable, desiring only to settle into his hotel and speak with Alice and the kids. He would have preferred to be at home with them getting ready for dinner, but it wasn't to be. He very much hoped her anger had softened and that she was missing him as much as he was missing her. This would have been so much more fun if she'd been with him, but there'd only been one ticket in the envelope.

It took a lot longer than expected to clear customs at Heathrow airport, which was surprisingly chaotic, he thought. Having not been abroad for over eight years he was a bit out of practice and felt very much like a fish out of water as he patiently stood in the slow moving 'all other passports' line. When he was finally through he shunned the Heathrow Express train to Paddington in favour of a black cab straight to the hotel, even though it would cost an arm and a leg as they said in England. Expenses paid had major benefits, that was for sure, but Marc was done with crowds for one day, regardless of who was covering the fare.

Despite it being well past 10.00pm local time it took longer than expected to reach the hotel. The city, it seemed, never slept. He was informed during check-in that the well-appointed place in Bloomsbury was in easy reach of shops, bars and restaurants in nearby Soho, Mayfair and Covent Garden. It was also within easy walking distance of the British Museum and an occult bookshop called Lost Continents in the same vicinity. *So far, so good.*

It was quite an expensive hotel, he noted, gratified by the opulent interior and beautiful restaurant cum cocktail bar. Whilst he greatly appreciated the unaccustomed luxury, it also made him somewhat uneasy. The sense that he might have been somewhere in the ballpark of a condemned man eating a last meal of lobster and champagne crossed his mind, especially when you put it all together with the fancy flight and bizarre chain of events he'd gone through at Mysteries.

Sitting down on the bed and dialling home on his mobile, the insanity of his recent actions began to dawn on him properly for the first time. He had the weird sensation of awakening from a hypnotist's show where he'd been the main attraction, mesmerised into doing anything the Master told him and scrutinised by the faceless crowd. Well, it was a bit late to worry about all that now, wasn't it. He'd already taken the carrot. Heaven only knew what the stick might be.

It was pretty late in London by the time he called but round about family dinner time at home. Alice picked up on the third ring and his heart leapt to hear her voice. "Hi sweetie, how are you?" Much to his relief, her tone had finally softened and he knew she was also feeling the pain of their separation. "How are the kids?"

"Still a bit upset but they're OK. Just finishing up dinner. You want to talk to them?"

"Not just yet, I want to talk to you first."
Despite having been warned against it and undertaking oaths to that effect, Marc was tired of keeping the world's biggest secret from his wife and desperate to hear her advice and reassurance. He poured out his heart without restraint, hearing her mounting astonishment in the non-judgmental silence with which she received his confession.
It was a long confession and by the time he got to the end they were of one mind again, both as amazed as each other. Sharing the burden of the past days' events had broken their spell and he could see them for the first time with the same objective eyes that Alice was looking through. How had he let things go so far was the incredulous question on both of their lips. Soul searching answers connected with his long-lost father and unfulfilled potential aside, they agreed there was more to it than a mere moment of madness, although such a moment had surely struck him hard. Neither of them really understood what the urgent purpose for the London trip might possibly be; the documents he'd been given were strong on instructions but hazy on explanation.
"I really think the Saturn guy might have hypnotised me, Alice; I seemed to fall under his spell from the moment he spoke to me that day at the beach. I can't believe I just went along with all this. What do you think I should do?"
There was a mindful pause whilst the eminently wise and wonderful woman he had married thought things through as rationally as circumstances allowed. "Well..." she began slowly, "you're committed now, right?"
"Sure, but nothing's really happened that can't be undone. If I had to pay them back for the plane ticket and hotel it'll hurt, but we can do it.."
"What about all those oaths and promises you made?"
"Nothing can override my promise to you."
"I know. But all the same, honey, you've got this far, it seems a bit of a cop-out to quit now. You should at least go to this Lost Continents place and find out what the score is and do a

bit of sight-seeing in London while you're there. You've always wanted to go so why not just see this as a golden opportunity. A gift from the proverbial gods, if not necessarily 'God'?"
For the millionth time in the past two decades Marcus Marconi congratulated himself on his choice of wife. Just as the sound of her voice had brought calm to his troubled heart, so did her advice dispel the doubts from his mind and inject some much-needed courage into it at the same time. All at once he felt truly at peace. It was so much more real than the false peace he'd felt on Virgin Atlantic, flying like an Eagle on somebody else's wings.

***

The grounding effect of his reconciliation with Alice, coupled with a good night's sleep and excellent breakfast, gave Marc the wholly misguided impression that Thursday September 8 would be a more regular day than the others had been of late.
He was in an inordinately good mood as he read the morning papers and enjoyed a 'full English' as they called it. As an Anglophile American he was fascinated to see how news was covered on London's side of the pond and glad for a break from the full force of the political nightmare he judged to be permanently installed on his usual side of the Atlantic.
Brits, of course, felt as if their own political nightmare was just as bad and it was interesting to read about the factional in-fights that he usually only saw through the distorted lens of American press. The country had a new Prime Minister called Liz Truss who, he was informed, had recently met the Queen at Balmoral. That was so cute! He loved the fact their leaders had to meet a Queen. It made him feel like he was in the middle of a Medieval fantasy just by being in Britain.
Marc didn't quite understand how or why the last Prime Minister, Boris Johnson, had been made to leave office and the newspapers gave him no sensible clue. He found it

hilarious that with all that was going on in the world the Brits would ditch a Prime Minister over something they variously called Partygate or Cakegate. Surely that couldn't be it?!
He actually laughed out loud but then recalled seeing recent pictures of the Queen with Paddington Bear at her Platinum Jubilee. Perhaps, after all, 'Cakegate' was something to do with the supremely eccentric way in which Britain functioned.

As was the case Stateside, the war in Ukraine dominated headlines of the broadsheets. There were rumours that Russia's cornered President might actually do the unthinkable and unleash nuclear bombs on the world. *Satan II is the last thing we need right now,* he thought, shaking his head.

The energy crisis was also getting much worse. The Nord Stream pipeline was apparently at risk, Marc noticed in an explosive article by Seymour Hersh, thinking that he wouldn't be a bit surprised if it got blown up American forces, as the President was already threatening[xxvii].

There was nothing in the paper about Hunter Biden's laptop, WHO Pandemic Treaty or the Wuhan Military Games, but there were a lot of pictures of the Duke and Duchess of Sussex. He sighed and turned the page. He didn't understand the ins and outs of royal titles, the status of royal babies or similar puzzles which seemed to drive the British to distraction but were an impenetrable mystery to everyone else on Earth.

By the time he'd had a couple of cups of the great coffee – almost to the standard of Julie's – Marc was full of beans and ready to take London by storm. He was curious about Lost Continents and thought he understood what had to be done, but was also looking forward to a spot of sight-seeing, as Alice had encouraged. Not Buckingham Palace or the Tower of London, though, as he wanted a clear day for all that.

He checked his watch. It was 9:45, which meant he had plenty of time to finish up breakfast and go upstairs to read through his notes again before walking to Lost Continents.

Sitting on the bed with notes in hand, he reconfirmed that the shop opened daily at just past 11.00 but was also warned against arriving too early as the shop was under surveillance. The reasons why were a bit too vague for Marc's liking and he resolved to choose a moment when the shop looked busy and he could enter more discreetly. If it were anything like Mysteries there would be a lunchtime rush of people whiling away their free hour, which meant he had some time to kill.

He looked again at the map of the area he'd been given by a helpful concierge. The short walk to Museum Street would take him right past the British Museum. This was the ideal place to pass some time and work his way up to what he hoped would be a denouement of sorts at Lost Continents. It also meant he could take a look at the Elgin Marbles, the Rosetta Stone and John Dee's scrying glass en route.

Hugely looking forward to all of this, Marc exited the hotel with a spring in his step and a pack on his back, rather like a divine Fool about to walk over the edge of an abyss, oblivious to the fox that was snapping at his feet.

The Queen

"In these uprooted times there is a great need for constancy, for those who can rise about the clamour, the din and the sheer pace of our lives, and helps us rediscover those truths which are immutable and eternal. A need for those who can speak of that eternal wisdom, which is called the perennial philosophy".

HRH King Charles III

Queen Elizabeth II on her Coronation Day, 2 June 1953

The silver tray

Was loaded with porcelain and biscuits as Ana stood outside her great-grandmother's door and called to be let in. It was already 10.00 am but Mrs Roudnikova had always preferred to break her fast later in the morning. As usual, the door was silently unlocked and pushed ajar but her Great-Grandmother somehow managed to get back to her throne before Ana had even put a nose over the threshold.
"Good morning darling!"
"Morning Granny!" Ana began cheerfully, but then stopped in her tracks and gave a little scream. She only just managed to avoid letting the tray crash disastrously to the floor. For the first time since her own mother had died – 16 years ago, when Ana was just eight years old – Mrs Roudnikova was dressed from head to toe in black. The effect was truly dramatic. Setting down the now at-risk tray, Ana sat down on the nearest chair. "Please tell me it's not daddy!"
"Hush now Ana-Maria, it's not your father, everything is fine. Well, sort of fine. I didn't mean to scare you. Now come, pour the tea."
The two women sat drinking their tea in silence until a greater sense of harmony had returned and Mrs Roudnikova was ready to explain herself. As soon as that moment came Ana noticed a portrait of Queen Elizabeth II placed prominently on the altar cabinet against the East wall of the room. She put a hand to her mouth. "Oh no, is it the Queen!"
"I'm afraid so. The Queen is on her deathbed and only has hours to live. Everything is about to change. You must prepare yourself." She held up a hand to prevent her great-granddaughter from asking pointless questions. "The American will soon arrive. Unless you feel that something is badly amiss, you may bring him to me when he asks".
"But what about the Queen, shouldn't we tell someone?"
"No you mustn't say anything. There will be an announcement later today. Change into more suitable clothes

and say the Mass for Mary; candles must be lit in the shrine."
Ana looked down at her green dress. "I'll change now before the shop opens."
"One more thing, Ana-Maria. As you know, we are always being watched. It is better if you don't draw too much attention to the American. Let us try to ensure our movements go unnoticed, at least until Tristan arrives.
"Why is Tristan coming?" Ana asked, puzzled. Tristan was a long-time student of her Father's and whilst she'd known him all her life, he never came up to London and they only ever met in Glastonbury.
"He's going to drive you to the West Country."
Ana felt a pang of fear again. "Why won't you tell me what all this is about and who you think is watching us?" To her great discomfiture, the (much) older lady avoided her eye, which was most unusual. "You will find out soon enough. I am not permitted to interfere in your karma, I can only try to keep you out of harm's way."
That was more than Mrs Roudnikova had ever said on the subject and the admission truly alarmed her great-granddaughter. "Shouldn't we call the police?"
"And tell them what, Ana-Maria, that there are ghosts in the streets and nameless people who like to sit in Café de Paris and look into the shop window for hours a day? There is little we can do except try to give them the run around and marshal our forces"
As soon as Ana had left the room Mrs Roudnikova took out a large set of tarot cards from a secret drawer inside the table. Over a century old, they were hand-painted in a distinctive art deco style and there was no other deck quite like it in the world. Reverting to her native tongue, which was the Russian equivalent of old-fashioned Queen's English, she whispered under her breath to the members of her chain, who were never far from mind:
Maria! Maria! And dear Grigori Ottonovich! Esteemed Vladimir Alekseevich, my friend, Serge; Vsevolod

Vyacheslavovich; beloved Valentin; fellow traveller, Nabusar.... A Russian cannot be happy alone, he or she needs the participation of others[xxviii]".

One by one or two by two they materialised around the table and held the space in reverence. *Happiness on Earth begins only when a person, having forgotten himself, goes on to live for others.*[xxix]

All were reminded of a rule of their order and reason for their gathering again at that moment. As it is written, *people who have gathered in the name of an idea and its implementation develop a common plan, rebuild their psyche accordingly, and their association becomes an organisation with a mental face and a mental collective body. It is good to place the sun in the centre of its planetary composition and coordinate the other planets around their natural centre*[xxx].

A moment of deep reverence passed between them, as heads were bowed in devoted remembrance of their shared fraternal ideals. After a time, Butator spoke up in solemn tones. *"The highest good a person can obtain in this world is unity with his fellow men*[xxxi] and women. I thank you for bringing us together at this time, Nina Pavlovna. We have prepared for over a hundred years and the veils are parting at long last".

Mikhael raised his voice next. "I received a letter from our brother Leonid". He looked around the table as he reached into his breast pocket and took out a folded paper. "I think you will agree that it strikes to the very heart of our mission":

"The foundations of human deeds are so complex and diverse, in particular the art of politics, like black magic, so dark and subtle...

There was a ripple of assent around the table and Mikhael looked up with raised eyebrows, nodding grimly as he continued. "

Today there is no electricity in Berlin, tomorrow there is no coal in London, but it will not be long yet, and who knows? Maybe all the roads will stop, steamboats will stop at their harbours, and bony Famine will reign over Europe, sweeping away the living remnants of the right and the guilty. So Fate will avenge the violation of oaths, which the Agreement swore before the God of Humanity

"Like a telegraph operator on a sinking steamer, that through the night and darkness send out calls: "come to the rescue! We are dying! Save our souls!

"So I, moved by the love of human goodness, throw into the dark space my plea for the dying people. My friend, I will not tell you how painful and scary it is for us in our present Russia. Mountains of verbal lies have piled up in the world - and under this pile of powerless and sluggish it seems a true word, rejected by a thousand ugly lives. How can I open my mouth for prayer when the drunken Satan himself is serving the throne?

"Every single Englishman, to you I turn: save our souls! It's you, on yours. Understand that this is not a revolution, what is happening in Russia has already begun in Germany and from there onwards! This is Chaos and Darkness caused by the war of their black underground, and the same war, which was created for the destruction of the world.

"Hundreds of millions of money have been thrown into the purchase of printing, thousands of machines are being manufactured, lies are being washed away, thousands of liars are screaming, screaming, murdering water, inhabiting the world with monstrous phantoms and masks, among which a living human face is lost, The very air is bribed and lies: these fake radio that diabolical circles entangle every editorial office, these nocturnal passions that intrusively knock on the door, climb into the ears, muddy the mind. But I also know something else: as there are people among bipeds, so there are people-journalists, you, to whom it has long been given the name of the knights of the Holy Spirit, who writes not with ink, but with nerves and blood, and to them I appeal ... to everyone individually!

"Help me![xxxii]"

The heart-rending testimony was followed by a shocked silence, whilst Mikhael folded the letter, placed it back in his pocket, and made a prayer of his hands.

"Oh my God." Vladimir got to his feet. "It is more than a century since the first horror. The planets of the Aquarian Age have aligned as we forecast. The mirror of Atlantis is reflecting our eidolons and we stand at the breaking dawn of new horror. Our brothers are being sacrificed to murder our brothers, the vicious wheel keeps turning and our Chain is still missing a vital link. Will she help us resolve it as Christ intended?"

His voice broke with emotion and Serge raised a calming hand. "Vladimir Alekseevich, I know you received a letter from her long ago, but there have been no communications other than that. She will not admit any of us to her presence. It's been the same since Vadim Karlovich got arrested. She loved him very much, you know. It was a great blow to see the young ones sacrificed."

Serge looked around at them all. "But time has passed and although she is still held within the ring-pass-not, her binding is loose enough for her to go free if she so desires. But how much does she desire it? The binary is not yet resolved and she perceives a certain advantage in her present position, which is something her Master secured from the outset".

Vladimir got to his feet again. "You are right Serge! Elena Petrovna may be deprived of her highest faculty but she has forged alliances in the most unexpected spheres. She has made peace with many former opponents, even those in Paris. Those who once shunned her entirely now sit with her at cards. They have come to understand that they have a more unified cause than once they surmised. They see that at some stage there must be unity between path walkers, as the field widens up ahead of the gateway. As you know, brothers and sisters, all of us are waiting at the same final gates".

His face fell. "All the same, I admit that it irks me how the French are granted visiting rights whilst us – her countrymen and women – are kept waiting. René is her visitor as we speak. Can you believe it, after all he said in Paris? I'm told they get along tolerably well now!"

There was an ironic chuckle at that, but then the tone became serious again. "Perhaps she feels that members of her folk soul did not rush quickly enough to her defence", Maria murmured regretfully."

"Or perhaps she felt bad when the Babalon Working went ahead because she wasn't able to combat Hubbard's black magic?" Chekhov mused. "She shouldn't blame herself, though, it all went awry when Aleister lost control of Jack and The Witchcraft was founded. The Scarlet Woman performed a rite to birth the Wormwood Star during the Summer Solstice of 1953, but she was very confused, as you know" he added, pulling a face. "My atmosphere, presence and radiation techniques were also subverted", he added, looking round the table. "The war engines[xxxiii] arrived."

"All hell has broken loose," Vladimir agreed. "We have been forced to witness the most terrible of egregores birthed and grown to an almost unimaginable scale. As we step further into the fourth industrial revolution the very concept of humanity is under threat. The enemy is using the qualities of Kali Yuga to its advantage. She has to help us contain the behemoth."

"Most certainly this is true", agreed Chekhov. "People are worshipping false idols. The doctrine of binaries has been wholly misconstrued and subverted by the sorcerers. Many of the church faithful are moving into the catacombs as Valentin predicted. The time has come for us to act."

Serge took up the baton. "Somehow, they comprehend that the start of dualism marks the beginning of our life and our thought. Just as two parallel lines meet to infinity -- which mathematically is right but remains concretely incomprehensible to us - even the dualism of our thought finds its point of fusion in the world of the absolute. But for some of those called to bring it down to the sex centre is traumatic to witness.

"Let us recall a third of the Great Arcanum, the binary Eternity and death; positive and negative attributes (+ and -) of the mystery unified in the Oneness of the Androgynous Lord. This fusion of more and less in the absolute world represents for the initiatory teaching, the mystical wedding of the two poles of the Androgynous.

"The Inconceivable Father - the Absolute - and the mystical marriage of the Androgynous will always remain first fruits of our dualistic thinking. These first fruits give the supreme point where is found the inherent contradictions, by virtue of its very essence, to the dualistic thought. When the Initiate passes from the sphere of the first fruits to the conceptions of our relative existence and our world from the Fall, he draws a line called by Tradition: Threshold of knowledge, curtain of the Sanctuary, veil of Isis.[xxxiv]

He finished his impromptu speech with a gentlemanly bow and sat back down as if oblivious to the fact that the atmosphere had become electrifying. The Master of the Group – mystery name of Butator - seized the moment of potential. "We must do everything our power to resolve things. Nina Pavlovna, would you cut the cards?"

They watched as Mrs Roudnikova shuffled her priceless Tarot cards and spoke a prayer over them in Russian, Hebrew and French. The rest of the gathering bowed their heads in concentration as she cut them and began to deal. Butator was dealt The Magician and his wife, Maria, The Empress. Valentin was dealt The Hermit and his wife the Guardian Angel. Serge was given The Sun and Vsevolod The Star. Vladimir took up the mantle of The Fool and Nabusar The Pope. Nina herself was High Priestess. All the cards had been signed by the artist on the reverse. Shmakov turned his over and smiled to see the name of his good friend Masyutin.

The Star smiled as well and finally spoke. "Why don't we deal for her as well, Nina Pavlovna. If the indications are good, we might proceed further?" He looked at Vladimir, who inclined his head in assent, and then around the table to see if all were in agreement. "Take two, Nina Pavlovna", urged Nabusar, one each from the Majors and the Minors."

It was a good suggestion and they all watched intently as Mrs Roudnikova closed her eyes in deep concentration.

The card which was drawn from the Major Arcana was The Emperor, which produced a delighted clap from both Marias. It was an excellent start, the best they might have hoped for. The guests began to join hands, forming a united arc in front of Mrs Roudnikova as she shuffled again. This time a card leaped out and set itself beside The Emperor, which had been placed in the centre of the table. She united her hands with Shmakov and Nabusar, who were seated at her left and right, respectively. "That settles it", said the latter in satisfaction. "The Queen of Wands has spoken".

Cloud of Unknowing

Beneath the broad tides of human history there flow the stealthy undercurrents of the secret societies, which frequently determine in the depth the changes that take place upon the surface.

Arthur Edward Waite

Arthur Edward Waite in London, January 13, 1921

Nearby in the British Museum,

Marc stood in front of an elegant glass cabinet of exceptionally rare curiosities, his jaw slack with wonder. His long-held ambition to view the collection of John Dee's magical instrument had not resulted in disappointment now he'd finally fulfilled it. He had been well primed by an astounding tour of the gigantic ancient statues of Egypt, Syria and Greece that were on display elsewhere in the museum and felt well primed for a visit to the world's most prestigious occult bookshop.
He checked his watch and was alarmed to see that it was almost 2.00pm, meaning he'd missed his preferred lunchtime slot entirely. The fact of being late for his one job served as an effective wake-up call and he at once made for the exit of the Enlightenment Gallery, strode across the magnificent Great Hall past the shops and out of the front door onto Great Russell Street. He breathed a little more easily as soon as got outside. At least Lost Continents was only five minutes away, which he knew because he'd already found the street where it was located earlier that morning.
Rushing across the outer courtyard of the Museum and crossing over the road which ran along the South side and which was quite busy by now, he ignored the souvenir shops that were opposite and took a left turn onto Museum Street. Still concerned about being late and moving at speed, he almost rushed straight past his target and stopped in his tracks when he noticed some crates of books on the pavement and a statue of Anubis in the window of a Turquoise blue fascia.
After a leisurely morning spent mooching around amongst the originals in full-on tourist mode, now he had reached his destination Marc felt entirely unprepared and started to panic. Why had he not spent his time more usefully; psyching himself up for the task, for example, mentally preparing himself? As soon as he asked himself this question he remembered that the shop was under surveillance and caught

his breath in horror. Not daring to look left or right, let alone enter Lost Continents, he followed the path of least resistance and dived into the shop next door.

The watcher sitting opposite in the window of Café de Paris gazed after him for a moment, wondering if he needed to investigate further. The man's behaviour had been peculiar but 90% of the people who entered Lost Continents or the place next door had something strange about them. As he'd had the hood of his anorak pulled far over his head it had not been possible to ascertain whether he was, in fact, The American. The American who he'd been told in a phone call late last night would be arriving that day. Half-inclined to call back to base, he decided against it for now. Until someone entered Lost Continents they were somebody else's problem.

From his vantage point inside the badly lit shop that was crammed with military-themed curios, lead miniatures, old prints, postcards, magazines, leaflets and other ephemera, Marc stared at the man who was trying to stare at him. It was very obvious that he'd attracted attention. Shit was getting real. His pounding heart told the story his eyes were relaying. Entering Lost Continents by the front door was clearly out of the question.

Wondering what on Earth he was going to do he turned further into the shop and locked eyes with a small, elderly man whose olive complexion suggested a Mediterranean origin. So kindly was the gaze that he was instantly put at ease and felt an urgent need to confide. "Can I help you, Sir, or are you just having a look around?" came the smiled greeting, in an accent which confirmed he was Italian.

"I sure hope so!" Marc replied with feeling, prepared to cast himself at the mercy of this reassuring, fatherly figure. The man behind the counter removed his reading glasses and placed both hands on the glass top. Beneath his palms were rows of old medals from centuries of wars. "Fire away!"

"I really need to get to the shop next door but I'm being watched and I don't want to attract any more attention t."

It was rather an astonishing confession for someone who'd been sworn to discretion, but Marc trusted his instincts more than the pages of notes presumably written from the safety of Virginia Beach. The man nodded slowly. Yes, you're right. The ladies next door are targets and I've been concerned for a while that they could be in danger." He gave Marc a searching look. "Perhaps you are too?"

"I don't know. Maybe. It feels like it!"

"If you want I can give Anastasia a call and see what she suggests?"

Marc was relieved beyond measure. "Oh my gosh, that's so kind of you." He placed his hands together in prayer. "Please".

"No problem, Mr...?"

"Marconi. Marcus."

That won him a raised eyebrow. "You don't look like an Italian," he pointed out as he reached for the phone beside the shop till.

"I've heard that one before!" Marc agreed, ruffling his mousey hair and pulling up the sleeve of a white forearm. Marconi was the name of his adoptive father and Marc suspected he was northern European by blood and didn't have a drop of Italian in him. His rounded cheekbones and blue-grey eyes with thick brows indicated that he might have had blood from further north and east than he, himself, suspected.

The shopkeeper spoke into the telephone receiver. "Is that you, Ana? Hello, yes, it's Giuseppe Gasco....yes, yes, I'm very well thank you. My dear, I have an American visitor here for you but he's concerned about you know who."

There was a pause during which Mr Gasco nodded slowly to himself before speaking up again. "Yes, that's right. He says he's called Mr Marconi". He looked directly at Marc again, his expression more serious now. Marc nodded back, also feeling struck by the gravity of the situation, albeit shrouded by the Cloud of Unknowing he was flailing around in.

When Mr Gasco got off the phone again he gestured for Marc

to come behind the counter, where he opened a door to the back of the shop. "It seems you are expected, Mr Marconi. Miss Morgan has asked me to show you into Lost Continents via the basement. There is a door between our worlds where you can enter safely."

Marc thanked his host once again as they walked past another room that was piled high with mounds of cardboard boxes and antique stock. "Don't mention it!" said Mr Gasco. "I like a little adventure." At the back of the shop, opposite a cramped kitchen and toilet, was another door. Taking a key from his front pocket, he quickly unlocked it and flipped a round metal light switch on the side of the wall. "Come, Mr Marconi," he urged, walking down the stairs with an agility which belied his advancing years."

Marc followed him silently, remembering the other basement under a bookshop he'd entered recently and starting to feel as if he were in a dream again. A line from a poem – he couldn't remember who by - came into his mind: *You are not wrong, who deem - That my days have been a dream;*

The room at the bottom of the stairs was dark but Mr Gasco did not bother to turn on the light this time, instead warning Marc to mind his step as he led him through the dank little basement to the northern side of the building. "I won't be a moment, I need to find the opening," he said quietly, apparently pressing both hands to the wall, although Marc couldn't see enough to figure out what he was really doing.

After a moment or two he heard a click. "Aha!" said his host in satisfaction. "There it is!" He turned to shake hands with Marc. "Here is where I must leave you."

"Yes of course," said Marc. "Thank you so much for your help, I can't tell you how grateful I am."

"Hush, hush, don't mention it! Now mind how you go. There's a light somewhere on the left if you get lost and the stairs up to the shop are through that room and to the right."

"I'm sure I can manage, thank you Mr Gasco, maybe I'll see you sometime again."

Bridge

The knowledge possessed by Western Occultists of the Esoteric Philosophy, and their range of perceptions and thought of the Eastern Occultism, is very superficial.

Helena Petrovna Blavatsky, Philaletheians

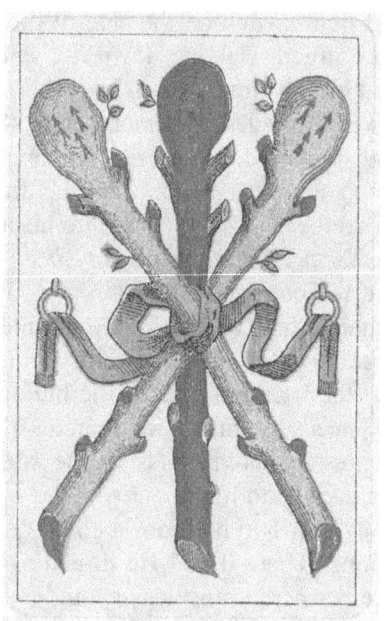

Three of Clubs, Aluette Deck, B. P. Grimaud

You deal this time, Joséphin,

We may as well make it the best of 33!"
A note of amusement rippled around the bridge table as an important-looking fellow with a thick black beard and enormous head of hair began to shuffle the playing cards with deft hands. His Bridge partner - an equally impressive, refined-looking man with a long nose – had soulful eyes the colour of rich, dark chocolate. The four of them fell into deep concentration while they organised their hands.

By far the best of them at card games - and despite the blindfold, which only prevented her seeing into higher realms and rendered the present one clear as day - Madame Blavatsky had hers swiftly under control. Cards fanned out before her, drumming her free hand lightly on the table, she looked askance at her companions, wondering how best to get a rise out of one of them. One particular subject was begging to be brought up, she decided.

"It's fascinating, don't you think, to see how one's acolytes reflect one on Earth. The mirror they hold up isn't quite what one would expect or wish for?" she said idly, as if she were simply making chit-chat.

"QUI! Yes, Mon Dieu" exploded her partner, another bearded fellow who was sat opposite Madame Blavatsky in an amazing robe. "I see mine wearing those outfits, waving pentagrams - praying to Baphomet! - and I can't 'elp thinking, what 'ave I done!"

"Yes! Yours are the funniest, Alphonse, which is ironic, really, as they're deadly serious for the most part. In fact, I think only *mine* have any sense of humour at all, the rest of you are breeding intellectual snobs on a grand scale."

"As indeed they *must* 'ave a sense of humour, given what you serve them!" the chocolate-eyed man could not resist interjecting, with a drop of acid from his tongue. The velvety softness of his eyes remained undiminished.

"Touché René, touché!" she hooted, pleased to have piqued

his interest. An unparalleled master of the art of annoying traditionalists, her tone became more conciliatory for a tactical moment. "Most of mine are completely crackers but very well-meaning, René, they really *do* want to save the world, bless them". There was a pause while she considered her own statement. "For the most part, at least", she conceded. There was another pause and then: "The masses, that is. The ones at the top of the triangle are a menace to society," she added with feeling.

"It is doubtless true," the chocolate-eyed man began keenly, "that the masses have always been led in one way or another, and it could be said that their part in history consists primarily in allowing themselves to be led, since they represent a predominantly passive element, a materia in the Aristotelian sense of the word; but in order to lead them today it is sufficient to possess oneself of purely material means, taking the word matter this time in its ordinary sense, and this clearly shows to what depths the present age has sunk; and at the same time these same masses are made to believe that they are not being led, but that they are acting spontaneously and governing themselves, and the fact that they believe this to be true gives an idea of the extent of their unintelligence."

"Precisely, René, which is why I have to entertain the blighters, it's to help them engage their brains: Bread and circuses, etc!" Madame agreed with a delighted grin.

René's partner, the man to Mrs Blavatsky's left, made an opening bid of one heart and, after following suit, they carried on in silence for a while, considering the relative (un)intelligence of their respective disciples.

Before long, Madame Blavatsky could not help herself but start up again. "I must say, Joséphin, that whilst you *do* have some talented offspring, some of your acolytes are much too self-important, by half. It's as if they've actually absorbed your ego. I mean, it's all very well insisting upon tradition, but the degree of pomposity and self-regard is quite extraordinary, especially considering the somewhat thelemite nature of some of your teachings. They really have no just cause to be holier than thou (or moi, as it happens) in their outlook."

The man to her left gave a good-natured smile, which disguised his almost violent need to overrule her point. "You are right of course, Madame, but they have good taste, you know and this brings a little arrogance; they understand that we must have a solid tradition or else we'll end up in an unholy mess! And it's not *thelema*", he hissed the word in disgust, "it's nature!"

There was a pleased chuckle from his partner. "Quite right, Joséphin, our people are taught to be clear about the truth and not to be blind-sided by the curse of modernity". And with that, he scooped up the trick on the table and stacked the four cards neatly in front of him.

Madame flared her nostrils and put down the three of Spades. "I see! Well let's not forget – and I do believe you have already insisted upon this yourself - *more than once*, René – that the tradition originates from the East, where it continues to be upheld?"

Seeing what was coming, her partner gave a delighted chuckle as he set down the King of Hearts, winning himself a trick in the process.

"And what of it?" said the man on her right with more than a hint of imperiousness.

The King of Hearts spelled it out. "Elena here is the only one of us who is actually *from* the east and spent much of her life living amongst the *actual* Hindus. She *might* argue that *you* only discovered the Eastern ways second hand..." he paused for effect before delivering the dolorous blow. "via colonialists".

If it *was* a killer blow, the chocolate-eyed man did not betray signs of death, but instead turned to martial arts. "That may be," he conceded reasonably, "but as well *you* know, I spent my later years amongst the Sufis. I think I did my time out in the field... and I also managed to integrate the best of

Western tradition with the light of the East. You might have spent a while in Italy, Madam", he added pointedly, "but you didn't manage to salvage its most famous son."

"I've always felt that the knowledge possessed by Western Occultists of the Esoteric Philosophy, and their range of perceptions and thought of the Eastern Occultism, is very superficial[xxxv]. But!" she raised a hand before they could protest, "nobody could question your commitment and dedication to tradition, René". She paused to let him win the next hand. "Anyway, I think you might have misunderstood me. All I was *saying*, is that it's no wonder the missionaries failed in India. The most eloquent of Dante's descriptions of hell could hardly produce anything but a cooling effect on a populace who live perfectly contented[xxxvi] in the most infernal heat!"

This prompted another unified chuckle, triggering her to change tactic again, lest the atmosphere became too congenial. "At any rate, I think we can agree that the East is far superior to the west when it comes to the tradition."

Whilst the point was well received by its intended target, it did nothing to please either Alphonse or Joséphin, both of whom rushed to contradict her, the latter with an ardent stream of Catholic polemic and Alphonse with a muttered kabbalistic prayer.

René sighed as Alphonse won a hand with the ten of hearts – ten not nine, ten and not eleven – and realised he probably would not be champion of the 33rd game. Perhaps he would give a lecture instead:

"You are not wrong in what you say, my friends, both the Catholic traditions and the Kabbalah are essential limbs of the perennial tradition, but this is not the point. The point is that the degeneracy of modernity is emanating from the west and I have to say, Madame," he peered at her over the top of his spectacles, "that you *did* help to hasten the western demise when you opened Pandora's Box and took it upon yourself to entertain the masses!"

Allowing him to continue at length whilst she played five winning hands in a row, Madame Blavastsky remained silent, pretending to listen, confident that she would be winner of the 33rd Game of Bridge.

Failing to pay enough attention to the game, much to his partner's chagrin, René delivered his sermon with hauteur and grandeur. "I also must say that whilst your followers claim to be open-minded heralds of the 'New Age' - equally mindful of every religion - like all propagandists, the apostles of tolerance, truth to tell, are very often the most intolerant of men. It is strangely ironical, don't you think, that those who wished to overthrow all dogma have created for their own use, we will not say a new dogma, but a caricature of dogma, which they have succeeded in imposing on the western world in general; in this way there have been established, under the pretext of "freedom of thought," the most chimerical beliefs that have ever been seen at any time, under the form of these different idols, of which we have just singled out some of the more important."[xxxvii]

"Exactly." said his partner approvingly, having also resigned himself to losing the game. "And *you*, Elena", he wagged a stern finger at her, "did not merely succeed in distorting and undermining the Western way, but also the Eastern. Quite an achievement!"

"Oh, come on, Joseph," she said gamely, "it's not as bad as all that, surely! It's not as if 'the tradition", as you call it, was getting everything right. You weren't even getting it right yourself – a century or two earlier and you'd be hung for being a heretic before me!" He inclined his head a fraction in acknowledgement at this and Alphonse looked similarly chastened.

"Anyway, we needn't get into an argument about the Church," she continued with a smile. "We've all seen with our own eyes where things went wrong. Also where they went right," she added magnanimously. "I win by the way! Again."

Her partner beamed in pleasure whilst their opponents pulled faces. "Damn it, Madame," said Joséphin. "That's 33 games in a row. It seems that even 100 years in Kathmandu can't wean you off your old tricks!"

"You can't teach an old dog new ones, that's for sure." She countered, well satisfied by the outcome. You lot need to work on your poker faces!"

"Didn't you say yourself that one must set their goal according to their planet," said Alphonse cheerfully, before the others could speak, content to bask in the reflected glory of her continual triumph at cards. "Merodack[xxxviii] might be your personal preference, Joséphin– as it is for all French men - especially the current President - but this was a moment for Nebo[xxxix]!"

She scooped up all the cards and tapped them on the table. "Back to the subject of followers, René, I think yours are the best. Fewer of them," she said slyly, "but higher quality."

He gave a Gallic shrug. "Tres bien, of course, I 'ave to agree: Quality is better than quantity!" Every member of the quartet grinned from ear to ear at that, which served to egg him on to uncharacteristically risky humour. "I must admit there are also one or two Nazis in my set – much to my despair - but we've all got some of those. Except for Joe, perhaps, the reds prefer him!"

Joséphin snorted, "we should have just kept quiet and nothing would 'ave 'appened. Nothing else, that is, the western world was already over by the time I did my Salon, the swan song of a dying age."

Seeing he was about to get gloomy, Alphonse chimed in merrily. "We couldn't have just left it all to Aleister, he would have immanetised the eschaton by now and it would all be over for real, never mind any illusion! HA!" he added loudly as Madame Blavatsky squashed his foot under the table to indicate the shared joke that was coming.

René's eyebrows shot up his face. "Surely it's clear to everyone, by now, that "the end of a world" never is and

never can be anything but the end of an illusion." Both his Bridge opponents burst out laughing, causing his brows to raise implausibly further.
"What if *Rudy* had been given full rein, can you imagine!" Joséphin fired out passionately. "That would have been neither sensible *nor* fun". "Yes indeed," agreed Alphonse. "And just think what his people could have achieved if they hadn't kicked the heralded last Boddhisattva out of their Society and forced 'im to become an 'ermit!"
"Ssshhhh! For heaven's sake! If you carry on like this one of them will hear you and then we'll all be in for it!" said René melodramatically. "Rudy's followers are more partisan than Irish Republicans, what on Earth was he thinking when he converted them. 'His was probably an early case of neurolinguistic programming, don't you think?" he asked, looking around the table with a quizzical expression etched onto his patrician face.
"Anyway," he turned over the top card, revealing the King of Spades, "it's obvious it would have been better if George had become Master of the Universe, he could have kept all the stupid one busy digging 'oles and counting walnuts!"
There was such a roar of laughter at this that the White Room turned a warning shade of grey for a moment, forcing them to calm down. "Speaking of George, I saw him the other day," said Elena pleasantly, when the mirth had subsided. "He asked after you all, said he hoped your paths would cross sooner than scheduled". She turned to her right, pointedly gazing at René through the blindfold. He wanted to ask *you* about your theory that Brahman resides in the human heart."
"Well, it is true; with the proviso that one must bring that to full realisation[xl]" René corrected thoughtfully. "It's unlike him to ask a question like that. I thought his line was that the human 'as to *create* his own higher soul 'imself?"
"He was leading them astray! Maybe he's got fed-up of lording around the borderlands in his diamond body," said Joséphin darkly, gathering up the cards and starting to shuffle

them again. "Perhaps he will remember that magic is the act of the sublimation of man."

There was a collective sigh of appreciation and Alphonse gave a beatific smile. "One of your finer moments, Joseph, no wonder it keeps getting quoted."

"Very good, I must admit", agreed Madame with a nod.

This pleased their opponent so much that he mustered an apology. "You are very kind my friends. You know, Alphonse, I learned an awful lot from you – so many of us did – and I shouldn't really have nitpicked about the promises. People need a goal and inspiration, after all."

"That's very good of you to say, Joseph". Alphonse peered at him, mildly surprised at the unusual concession from a man who resembled an Assyrian deity, thanks to the cut of his beard. He decided to press his new advantage. "And I think we can *probably* all agree that there *is* a place for fantasy as long as it's channeled into art... and one doesn't get lost in the astral light," he added with a furrowing brow.

"Absolutely!" René agreed with feeling, whilst Joséphin broke the pack in half and deftly flicked them together again. "We can agree there 'ave to be symbols. Ones with real meaning, though, not stoopid ones with no foundation in spiritual reality."

Alphonse peered at him sternly. "There is only one dogma in magic: the visible is the manifestation of the invisible, or in other words, in the things that can be judged and seen, the perfect Logos exists in exact proportion with the things that cannot be judged by our senses or seen by our eyes."[xli]

"You have a good point, Alf", René admitted. "Let us recall that great occult secret, very seldom spoken - because it is embarrassing - that eternal truth perennially requires the creation of new forms that will reveal it"[xlii].

"And let us also please recall that some of us are stuck blindfolded in Katmandu and a good sense of humour is an essential prerequisite for survival!"

"And that the initiate stalks his – or her – opportunities;"

There is always some advantage that can be taken from even the worst of circumstances.^xliii"

"Oh you're a clever fellow, Joséphin," said Madame, once more appreciative. "This is the advantage of being an artist, it confers a certain sort of inspiration that can often be lacking in purely literary types."

"If I recall correctly, Madame, you have quite some form in the publishing field, yourself," said Alphonse indulgently.

"Oh my God," groaned Joséphin, "Please don't remind us!"

"Quite!" muttered René, looking pained.

She wasn't going to stand for this slight on her masterworks. "I'll have you know, young man, that The Veil of Isis was a work ahead of its time, it opened the doors to many seekers! I could have published many more editions in my lifetime and not had to scrabble around for money whilst those thieves and scoundrels bled me dry!"

Seeing she was getting upset all over again, Alphonse patted her hand and threw a warning glass at his countrymen. "Don't worry my dear, they're just teasing you."

"But we are not," said Joséphin through clenched teeth. "Isis is OK perhaps, for some people who know nothing, but the second one was an outrage!"

"As you should know I was being hoodwinked by one of the young men who helped me transcribe it!" she said hotly. "If you had to put up with even half of what I went through you'd have shaved off that ridiculous beard and sent yourself to a cave for the depth of eternity. In fact, seeing as you like Pythagoras so much, a period of vitriolic silence in the abyss might be in order!"

René gave his partner a stern glance. "There's no need to be cruel, Joséphin, we've already addressed the matter of the books. We all revealed too much and our followers are having to move at almost unfathomable speed as the Kali Yuga advances. What we really need to focus on," he paused for breath and gave her a searching look, "is getting rid of *your* abyssal blindfold so you can help reset the Russian chain."

His words reverberated around the endless white of the room as one of the veils fell completely aside. There was a collective inbreath whilst the Frenchmen wondered how Madame Blavatsky would react, whilst Madame Blavatsky herself appeared to have been frozen on the spot and did not move an inch, apparently wondering the same thing herself.

***

These are the natural and inevitable results of an ever more pronounced materialisation, for matter is essentially multiplicity and division, and this-be it said in passing-is why all that proceeds from matter can beget only strife and all manner of conflicts between peoples as between individuals. The deeper one sinks into matter, the more the elements of division and opposition gain force and scope; and, contrariwise, the more one rises toward pure spirituality, the nearer one approaches that unity which can only be fully realised by consciousness of universal principles."[xliv]

Stolichnaya

Most people after death stay in Kama-Loka, "fall asleep", that is, they lose consciousness, and with it the memory of the past incarnation

The Solar Way, Nina Pavlovna Roudnikova

Nicholas Roerich, Madonna Oriflamma, {{PD-US}}

As the door clicked shut

Behind him Marc was relieved to see there was some light coming from an open door to the right of the room. This enabled him to quickly find the staircase, though he still felt like an intruder as he creaked up the unfamiliar wooden steps. The door at the top was unlocked and he pushed it open a little so he could peep around the edge. The sight that greeted him was so enticing that he immediately opened it fully and stepped into Lost Continents, gazing around in wonder at the world's most famous occult bookshop.
"You must be Mr Marconi?"
The voice made him jump for he had not immediately noticed the ethereal-looking young woman with very long blonde hair who was sitting at the front desk, looking at him keenly. "You're not how I expected." She smiled. "I was expecting black wavy hair."
Marc stepped forward to introduce himself. "Forgive me the subterfuge Miss....Miss Morgan, I assume?" She nodded as she took his hand in her cool and slender fingers, which made him feel bashful. "You'll probably think this is stupid but I was worried about being followed. I'm way out of my comfort zone by now."
She gave an anxious glance towards the door of the shop. "You probably *were* being followed – or at least watched - they're watching me all the time. Stay where you are; in fact, step back a little if you don't mind, then look through the window at the café opposite. Do you see him?"
Marc had to crane his neck to see past one of the shelves in the window, but he had a clear enough view of Café de Paris. Sure enough, there was a fellow sitting there in the front window, ostensibly reading a newspaper, but even as Marc watched he peered over it and into the bookshop. As there were no lights on inside Marc assumed they were relatively hidden from view, but he still felt a chill running up his spine at the confirmation of his fear.

"I see him, yes. Youngish fellow with broad shoulders. Do you know who he is?"

Ana turned around to look at him in surprise. "Don't you see the man with the top hat and tails who's leaning on the wall. The one who looks like he stepped out of a Victorian photograph?"

Marc took another look. "I don't think so…are you sure he's still there?"

Ana sighed. He's usually gone by now but he's been there all day. I thought you might have been able to see them, too. Everything has gone a bit strange. You've heard about the Queen I suppose?"

Now it was Marc's turn to look startled. "What about the Queen?"

Ana checked her watch, which told her it was 2.30pm. "Oh it's still a bit early but the Queen will die today. Within the hour."

"*What!* Oh my gosh!" Marc put a hand to his mouth in shock. "Are you sure; how do you know?"

Ana arched an eyebrow at him. "My great-grandmother always knows these things. I also dreamed of the funeral last night but I didn't realise until granny told me what was happening. You should meet her as soon as possible. She's expecting you".

Marc felt lightheaded. "Do you mind if I sit down?"

"I'm sorry, where are my manners, please do!" Ana gestured at the armchair to the right of her. You sit here for a moment while I fetch your box. Then we'll go up and see granny and I'll make us some tea, OK?"

"OK". As she walked past him Marc put his head down on his arms, which were resting on his knees. How could the Queen be about to die and how did this girl know in advance! Was it even true? He guessed he would find out really soon and didn't relish that prospect. He felt somehow responsible. The death of the Queen (if, indeed, it *was* imminent) seemed weirdly linked to the snowballing scenario he'd plunged himself into like a classic Fool. He clearly had no idea at all what was really going on.

Ana was coming back now, humming a tune to herself. Seeing him in such a state she put the box on the desk and touched his shoulder, sounding concerned. "Are you alright Mr Marconi? I'll fetch you some water."

When she returned with the glass he took it from her gratefully and downed it in one. He would have done the same with wine or even vodka, which frankly might have been preferable. He puffed out his cheeks and looked at Ana properly for the first time. Fine boned and slender with porcelain skin and bright green eyes, she was certainly attractive, but also strangely fey, as if she wasn't quite there. Dressed in a long black skirt and black silk blouse with a white spray of flowers tucked behind one ear, he realised with a jolt that she was in mourning dress. How much weirder were things going to get before they came to a head?

She gave him a knowing smile. "I know how strange this all seems. Believe it or not, I've not quite got my head around it all myself. Come now, let's introduce you to my great-grandmother." She stepped towards the door and turned the sign to closed. "I'll shut up shop, I think, we can't risk anyone sneaking in while we're all upstairs. Take your box and follow me."

She tilted her chin to indicate that Marc should follow as she crossed the shop and opened the door to another staircase, this time heading upstairs. He hauled himself from the chair and picked up the box. "Wow that's pretty heavy", he noted. "Yes it is, quite", she called after him, already disappearing up the stairs.

As they stood in front of the door to Mrs Roudnikova's room, awaiting entry, Marc felt as if he was having an out of body experience and looking down on himself from the ceiling. Who was that crazy man, he thought ruefully, wondering why his previous boring life had seemed to undesirable of late.

The sound of the key turning in the lock from the other side jolted him back down to Earth and his heart gave a little leap. The moment of reckoning had arrived. Just before the door creaked open, Ana leaned closer to whisper to him. "No matter what happens, don't be scared, we're on the same side."

Marc looked at her in alarm as the door creaked open. An incredible scene greeted him inside the room. A strange sort of twilight prevailed through a dramatic combination of closed curtains and fancy candelabras. The atmosphere was electric and Marc was put in mind of antique photographs of Tesla experiments. Having stepped two paces inside he now found himself rooted to the spot. A woman who must have been very old but also appeared to be of indeterminate age was sitting on what looked like a throne at one end of a massive oval table which filled the back half of the room. She was looking right at him with bright blue eyes, which bored like gimlets into his soul.

There were several high-backed chairs around the same table and whilst they looked empty, he had an awful feeling that they were in fact occupied. In front of each chair there was an oblong picture where the placemat would usually be. They looked like tarot cards. Marc felt the space between his ears began to buzz and he broke out in a sweat as a sensation of unassailable terror began to take hold of him. He put both hands to his head and grabbed hold of what hair he had left on the sides of his temples, as if he were trying to stop his brain escaping. Just before he passed out on the floor of the room in a dead faint, he heard a feminine voice deliver instructions.

"Quickly, my dear, push that chair up behind him before he falls over".

Ana must have moved quickly indeed because - from his vantage point on the ceiling of Mrs Roudnikova's living quarters - Marc could see that he was slumped on a basket chair in the middle of the room. Now he was in an altered state it was also apparent that his earlier impression that the chairs around the table were occupied was, in fact, correct.

Alongside Mrs Roudnikova were a number of seated figures, all of them with their heads bowed, as if in prayer, but also (he sensed) to shield their faces from his view.

Away from the confines of his physical body with its unpredictable chemical reactions, he felt calmly curious. He was irresistibly drawn towards the table until he was floating horizontally above it. From this bird's eye view he could see that a total of five women were present, one of whom had eye-catching platinum blonde hair, beautifully styled. It was partially covered by a black lace veil, which formed a striking contrast with the pristine waves.

The wrists and hands of the same woman, extending from well-fitted black sleeves, were soft and white with perfectly manicured red nails and a huge solitaire diamond on the ring finger of her left hand. Between those elegant fingers she was touching the edge of what Marc confirmed was a large tarot card which depicted a woman holding the jaws of a lion in her hands. *Force. The subtle overcomes the gross*, he thought serenely. Looking around the table he could see that each of the figures had a similar card in front of them and he enjoyed looking at the marvellous painted designs, which were quite unlike any other tarot images he'd seen before.

Mrs Roudnikova was holding the High Priestess card, he noted, also observing that she herself, sitting as she was on the throne-like chair, was very much like the High Priestess made manifest. Like all the other women, Marc realised, she was dressed entirely in black with a lace veil covering the back of her head and hair. *Mourning dress.* As he recalled what Ana had said about the Queen he noticed a large framed portrait of the young HRH Elizabeth II, obviously taken after her coronation, standing in the middle of the table with candles either side of it.

There was an empty chair on the right of the blonde but on the other side of that there was a male figure. There was nothing unusual about the man's thick brown hair and square shoulders in their dark suit, but something about him was strangely compelling. Marc angled his body towards the man and was intrigued to see him take a notepad and pencil from the breast pocket of his jacket. The man wrote something onto the notepad in large letters, tore out the paper and then pushed it deliberately into the centre of the table.

ПРИВЕТ СЫНОК

This is for me, Marc thought, but what did it mean?
Before he could get completely lost in trying to decipher the note that was written in a language he didn't understand, something else on the table caught Marc's attention. Something so incongruous that he could hardly believe his disembodied eyes. Staring at it intently, he realised that it was some kind of animal head. *Well that's kind of gross*, he thought with distaste. *Why would anyone have that thing on the table?*
As if to answer his query, a pudgy white hand with a red ruby ring on one finger reached out and opened the top of what he now saw was a Siberian Fox Head. Somewhat to his amazement, the fingers removed a generous pinch of tobacco from the head and proceeded to roll a cigarette, as all the time the rest of the gathering looked reverently down at their respective cards.
Marc became focused to the point of hypnotism on the actions of this mysterious woman and was staring down at the top of her head, avid for any kind of clue as to her identity. Something about her was familiar. Who on Earth *was* it? He wracked his brains as if he were searching for the Philosopher's Stone but losing himself further in the process.

The Unpopular Philosopher's Stone!

It just popped into his head, stirring his consciousness enough for him to realise that he could no longer move, which alarmed him. He could not even turn his head. It was as if he were being pinned by an invisible forcefield that was emanating from the cards on the table directly below him. With a shock he saw that this woman had *two* cards in front of her. The Emperor and the Queen of Wands. Marc felt his mouth start to widen into a silent scream as she slowly and deliberately leaned back in the chair until he was staring in horror at the blindfolded face and sardonic grin of…could it be true, was that really *her?*

The terror of that moment was enough to send Marc back to his body in a split second. He groaned as he became conscious and put the palms of his hands over his eyes. "*Oh my gosh*", he said in misery, "*I don't know how much more of this I can take*." At that moment a key turned in the door lock – by whom, he could not see – and opened to allow Ana to enter with a tray of hot tea. Upon the silver tray were two handmade mugs and a plate containing huge chunks of shortbread, which she set it down on a nearby coffee table and gave him a warm smile. "There we are. This should make you feel a bit better!"

Feeling numb and not trusting himself to speak, Marc nodded and took the tea from her, sipping gratefully. She gave him a small side plate and held out the inviting-looking dish of shortbread. He took a piece and bit it mechanically. The buttery confection was truly delicious, producing an appreciative "mmm" from Marc as the sugar did its work and brought his brain back round a little.

Ana beamed at him. "Do you like it? I'm *so* pleased, I can never get any of Granny's friends to try it, can I?" She put her hands on her hips and turned to look at the table. "I can't believe that none of you will eat it; I've yet to find a single thing that any of you likes!"

The unwelcome reminder of the table full of ghosts triggered a grimace from Marc and he looked at the place opposite Ana's great-grandmother where Madame Blavatsky had been seated. He peered anxiously, stretching out his neck, but nothing could be seen except for the cards and portrait of the

Queen with its sentry candles.
A voice emanated from the head of the table. "Have we given you a fright, Mr Marconi?"
"Yes," he replied shortly, still lost for words.
"We should be properly introduced. I'm Nina Pavlovna Roudnikova." She extended a slim hand.
Marc put down his plate and cup on the coffee table and jumped up to take it. "I'm very pleased to meet you Mrs Roudnikova. Marcus Marconi. At your service."
"Good, good! Now sit! Join us." She smiled and gestured to a chair that was one place down on her left. Her eyes twinkled. "As you can see, we've kept a chair free for you".
He saw with relief that there was no card in front of his chair, whilst nervously spotting that The Fool was on his right and Force on his left. That would be the blonde woman, he remembered suddenly, wondering who she was. She also seemed weirdly familiar, but why?
Marc puffed out his cheeks as he exhaled and sat down slowly with clasped hands and hunched shoulders. He was well and truly out of his depth. He was also scared and the hairs all over his body were standing on end. Was she going to give him a card now? what if he got the Devil or the lightning struck Tower? Or the ten of Swords; any Sword? *What then!*
"Ana, my dear. It's for moments like this that we keep the Stolichnaya. Would you pour Mr Marconi a large double?"
Doing as bidden, Ana poured from the large bottle and set a heavy cut-glass tumbler in front of Marc a moment later. There were two thick fingers of vodka in the bottom. He drank it in one gulp - much as he had the glass of water earlier - and sat up in his chair with his back straight, pulling a face as the alcohol burned his throat and hit his stomach. He could have sworn he felt someone on his right give him a strong pat on the back and heard what sounded like *za zda-ró-vye!*[xlv] Uttered by someone, somewhere. "OK! I'm back. At least I think I am. It's possible. Aha! Here I am! Thank you

Mrs..."

"Nina", she said kindly. "Call me Nina." She looked to her right and murmured something to the now invisible Magician, which Marc just managed to catch. "Yes I know but look at the state of him, I had to do something...." There was a pause and then she began murmuring again. "anyway it's not the end of the World. Well it is, but.." She turned to Marc again. "I'm sorry for the so-called Baptism of Fire, Mr Marconi, but as I'm sure you'll appreciate, things are getting rather urgent; the time is at hand". She gave him an astute look.
Besides, I thought swords were your thing, being an initiate of the air?
"You're not kidding!" he agreed, buoyed by the vodka and starting to feel like a child in a sweet shop. "I hope you don't mind me saying this, Nina, but just then I swear I could have seen..." He gulped, unwilling to say the name out loud.
"You're right, but nobody else here can see her yet, only you have had that privilege and you are most welcome! But do forgive me Mr Marconi, it is almost time."
"Time for what?"
Mrs Roudnikova closed her eyes for a moment and placed her hands together. "My friends...The Queen is dead. God save the King!"
Marc reached for his glass to drain any last drops. "God save the King!" *Am I here?*
"Now we shall pray for the safe passage of her soul to the upper world". Mrs Roudnikova, Ana and Marc bowed their heads in prayer for a full fifteen minutes, during which time the atmosphere in the room became vivified with an intense spiritual force which, by the end of the meditation, made Marc feel as if he might levitate again."
"Ana-Maria, darling, would you pour Mr Marconi another glass, it's helping him...adapt."
As Ana placed another double shot of vodka onto the table in front of him, Marc's eye was drawn again to the note which the man – who he assumed was still sitting on his right – had

written. Strange that it was still there. A quick glance to the other side of the table informed him that the animal head was also still there.

"Thank you, Ana." He drained the glass again. "Mrs Roudnikova; I mean, Nina?"

"Yes?"

"What does this mean"? He turned the note so it was facing her and she glanced down at it before turning her penetrating gaze onto him again.

HELLO SON.

Swords

Vau; Knights; World of Formation; 2nd Initiation

Free yourself from the illusions of the lower worlds and reach a new spiritual birth

G.O. Mebes, Tarot Majors Course

In the Swords stage

The spiritual pilgrim no more has a master, not even anyone who could point the way. For him, it is a period of complete solitude. Internal growth is no longer encouraged by ceremonies or rituals. This stage also consists of 4 degrees, but these are purely esoteric and perceptible only to observers from the upper planes. The disciple himself knows nothing of His/her progress. The Swords stage can be crossed in two ways:
Firstly, on the path of faith, positive, aspiring and seeking to serve the Logos in His redemptive work. Secondly, in the negative way, sometimes called the "way of the strong", way of rebellion against the Logos and the state of the world. In this, the human being crosses the whole Sephirothic Tree, that is, the 10 degrees of the suit, fighting and isolating itself from the creative aspects of each Sefira. Rebellion against the external world (Malkuth), rejects the form (Yesod), negates the value of power and peace (Netzach and Hod), denies the possibility of harmony (Tiphereth), denies mercy and Justice (Gedulah and Geburah), reason and wisdom (Binah and Chokmah), arriving at denial of life (Keter).
These sufferings and the internal emptiness they lead to, reaching a peak, awaken in the pilgrim an immense thirst and need to satiate it with something perfect and totally pure: The passage to the World Cup suit.
Swords is the suit of the "psyche", that is, of the astral and the mental, and the experience is lived when these two principles of human beings achieve the greatest development. At the philosophical or negative aspect of Swords, reason predominates above feelings or the heart.
This step corresponds to the "Nasham" plane of Judaism or "Manas" of Eastern philosophy; in it, the mental, having not reached the upper plane "Haia" or "Budi", is not yet qualified for a creative synthesis, but only for an inexorable analysis that penetrates to the roots of existence.

The disciple, initiated in the hidden and magical aspect of Coins, already has a high degree of knowledge of his personality. Having developed his psychic centres and his magical abilities, obtained a certain power about the astral world and its environment, he became able to create new forms and transform existing ones. His activity is entirely governed by his personal will, which totally dominates the world of his desires and emotions. He achieved the maximum development of his personality.

However, simultaneously with these achievements, in his heart a dissatisfaction with the achieved, a depreciation of world values that, until now, have provided so much contentment. Wonders and doubts about one's usefulness do that. One starts to aspire to something different and higher, to become aware of the existence of a Light that permeates the world and desire to discover its nature and its source. One hopes to be able to meet God face-to-face, to understand the human being and his internal "I" - the reflection of God.

The Coins Initiate has the possibility to create something in the world, to offer you something, but nothing else can be received, because you already have what the world can give. It is still not understood that, continuing to give, one would continue to receive, maybe something unexpected and different. In the act of giving it is received.

Having reached the maximum of personal power, one begins to realise the illusory character of the world. One is knowledgeable of the forms but has not yet penetrated the essence that is hidden behind them, in the Source that creates them and, therefore, rejects them as only illusory. This can affect the initiate deeply because the world around him falls apart. He admits the existence of the Creator Principle - the Logos - but, at the same time, perceives the illusory character of every servant. He sees the sufferings of the world, notes that nothing can change, despite all the personal power he attained. He does not understand the purpose of such a world of suffering and injustice and a great revolt against the

Creative Power is born in him.

Swords, in their negative or philosophical aspect, is the stage of deep spiritual crisis that must be crossed and overcome, so that a magician, initiated from Coins, can reach the heights of the upper hermetic suits.

We present in this course the higher level of the human path, through the Minor Arcana, that is, the level that leads to Initiation. However, in many people's lives there are the same steps at lower levels and these also need to be overcome so that evolution can progress. Such steps are presented, sometimes, following the degrees and suits of the Minor Arcana, sometimes in a different order. They can be short and they can last a lifetime or even several incarnations.

Spiritual progress, most of the time, follows a spiral line, returning the individual to the same stages, but at a higher level. Generally, human beings do not have awareness of being tested by a certain suit or grade. On the other hand, one should not forget that not every deep revolt or scepticism is proof that the person is living the positive experience of Swords; most frequently it is the consequence of some failure in life, manifesting itself in revolt, scepticism and animosity.

Many people consider themselves "atheists" because their intellect rejects the exoteric presentation of God or because they are experiencing a painful crisis; others follow scrupulously the precepts of a religion, removing from the mind any religious problem, so as not to fall into doubt. It's possible for the former to be at the threshold of Swords, whilst the latter have not yet reached the suit of Coins.

The negative aspect of Swords is the source of almost all religious myths. The fall of the Angels in the book of Enoch, the revolt of the Asuras, in the Stanzas of Dyzan of the Secret Doctrine of Madame Blavatsky, the Prometheus sacrifice that stole the heavenly fire, the temptation of the Biblical serpent and many others have the same basis.

The negative Swords experience is expressed by a very complicated internal state. Being the mental aspect, in this stage, the most powerful, man intends to unveil the mystery of life and its own being, through the intellect. For him, the only criterion of Truth is his own mental power. He rejects any claim of authority, religious or philosophical. The limited and conditioned in the human being seeks to solve the problem of the Infinite and the Absolute. This results in failure and causes a revolt that can take very different forms.

This revolt and the active struggle against the Creator Principle of the manifested world, are gradually transformed into a search for the cause of causes and absolute values, that is, in a search for God. In each deep and widely lived experience of the negative stage of Swords, these two factors - the revolt and the search - are present.

In its evolution, on the way to the union with his higher "I", the human being must reject everything that was achieved (during the Coins stage) and advance solitarily, regardless of any law or order, without the assistance of Heaven, without an authoritative conductor, obeying only its internal criteria, refusing any limitation and even fighting against upper interdiction. It is the path of incessant struggle, provocation by internal loneliness and desolation.

In this darkness, man needs to find the right direction and follow it to the end. If one lacks the will to take it further, he or she may fall into the spiritual doldrums, into complete negativity or despair, from which there will be no way out. Aware of this danger, all the founders of the exoteric relics prohibit the knowledge of Good and Evil, hide the Heavenly Fire and prevent this shortcut to a set of laws, punishing the disobedience.

These protective measures have their reason for being. They were established for the vast majority of human beings who need to rely on the magic force of forms and authorities in order to evolve, that is, to carry out harmonisation; one's personality. For this majority, the absence of support points would result in internal helplessness. There are few who have overcome the need for such support and that, without falling into the internal void, are able to rise into a genuine spirituality, following the painful path of Swords, because suffering is the essence of this stage. However, without Golgotha, there would be no Resurrection.

Man, crossing this stage, rejects and denies everything, until the very beginning of life, for, finally, in the last degrees, finds God within the self. Progressively one free's oneself not only from the illusions of the physical world and of the astral plane, but also of the last illusion: that of the principle who, in himself, denied everything.

In the Minor Arcana, this path is symbolically presented as an ascent through the sephirotic system of Swords, that is, the progressive sublimation of consciousness as the disciple rises from Malkuth to Keter.

The Swords stage can be processed over the whole life or even during several incarnations. In very rare cases, the entire path of Swords can be traversed in an instant. It's the instant lift by cutting the card, a very dangerous alternative, since the human structure may not be able to withstand a spiritual change that is so abrupt. The transfiguration of Gethsemani, through blood, sweat and the acceptance of the "will" of the Higher Will, can be considered as the sudden passage through the suit of Swords.

The Swords experience is exclusively internal and deeply individual and therefore only the basic steps of the suit can be sketched. The rest depends not only on the disciple's individuality and personality, but also the level at which he is living his experience. Fully lived, it prepares and enables, in last degrees of Swords, the descent of the beneficial spiritual force, suitable for the Cup suit.

With regard to the next two stages – Cups and Wands - very little can be said, because the more the internal level rises, so much less can it be expressed by words.

***

A magic sword is always a sword, since its purpose is to serve the purposes of defense, or to be an instrument of destruction or dispersion of hostile vortex formations of undesirable power. Therefore, the magic sword, being coagulated by an adept in the environment of astral light, is an attribute inherent in the degree of his initiation and the degree of his magical power.

As for the religion of the sword, it is closely connected with the creed of the sword-bearing armour of Light - the armour of love. The presence of a sword in the environment of astral light (the possibility of projecting a vortex from itself of a certain direction and corresponding power) is of great importance in the process of becoming an adept, especially since such an opportunity is usually associated with obtaining knightly degrees of astral initiation.

The actualisation of the magic wand presupposes the undoubted hierarchical and lofty power of the adept in the physical and hyperphysical environment. Being a genuine attribute of power, the rod embodies the idea of an esoteric sceptre, it is a kind of ruler's staff, and at the same time it is an iron staff. Therefore, receiving the rod and updating it in the astral light environment is fraught with initiatory difficulties.

There is no doubt that you can be a magician three times, but still not get a magic wand.[xlvi]

Order of the Seven Sacrifices

"God knows who they were. I think they were some local peasants – Dostoevsky's 'holy Russia' in revolt. Ugh....motherfuckers".

Mikhail Bulgakov, The White Guard

Mikhail Bulgakov, 1928

"Assuming we can capture her

Tell me again why we can't drug her with mushrooms and perform sex magick like we did with the last one?"

"Like you did with *your* last one; mine didn't need drugs".

This was not supposed to be any kind of sick joke and the driver of the vehicle responded to what had been a genuine query. "You know why. This one isn't like the others. He wants to marry her".

There was silence in the vehicle as the four of them focused on the car in front that they were tailing. They knew where it was going but wanted to keep it in sight to be on the safe side. One of the four went over in his mind the well-worn incantations to his personal demon and considered the words of evocation he would dedicate to the dark Goddess. *First we'll need to remove the shield and Markers that Pixo will have set up*, he brooded, ever more sure that they would need to make a stop soon and hoping the driver of the vehicle was thinking along the same lines.

Ahead of them on the A4, the driver of the Land Rover looked anxiously into his rear-view mirror at the black Audi. There were a few cars between them but he knew they were tailing him and he had no idea what to do about it. Protecting Ana was his only goal but he couldn't shake the feeling that it was about to become an impossible task.

He was glad of the moral support offered by Marc, who was sitting quietly in the back seat and looking with interest at the dramatic scenery of the North Wessex Downs, but didn't honestly see how he could help. As soon as Ana had rejected the offer of sanctuary extended by the London branch of the Amilius Order, it felt as if they were on borrowed time.

Her presence beside him in the passenger seat was an agonising mixture of pleasure and fear. Pleasure that the woman he'd loved since childhood was close to him and fear that he would not be able to save her from the terrible forces ranged against her.

A close friend of Ana's father and fellow Glastonbury resident, Tristan had never plucked up enough courage to court the woman he'd loved since childhood. He loved her from afar throughout the years, never confessing his affection, which was nonetheless clear to anyone who knew them and saw how he behaved in Ana's presence. Now she was here beside him he resolved that it was finally time to broach the topic with her father and ask for her hand in marriage. It wasn't at all clear to him that she would accept – they had never even been on a date, he thought ruefully – but he had to try or he'd regret it forever.

As if she could feel his inner turmoil, Ana put a hand on his shoulder and gave it a squeeze. "Thank you for looking after me, Tristan. I still think you're all over-reacting but it's good to know how much you care."

Her cool hand burned like fire through the thin material of his t-shirt and he had to wrestle with his emotions before replying. "You know I'll do anything for you, sweetheart, but we're not overreacting." He glanced up at Marc through his mirror again and this time their eyes met, each reflecting the concern felt by the other. "I still think you should have taken up Marc's offer of help..."

The hand was removed and she gave a little sigh. "I've promised everyone that I'll think about it and I honestly will, but you must understand that the thought of being hidden away like that for the rest of my life is just...*mad*! I can't live like some sort of princess in a tower!"

The analogy was exact and Marc looked down at his hands unhappily. He could quite see where she was coming from. Ana was in the dreamlike stage of unreality that he'd experienced himself before finally waking up in the presence of Mrs Roudnikova.

Thick with emotion, Tristan's voice was almost breaking. "I know how it looks, but surely you realise that we wouldn't try to ruin your life or do anything other than act in your best interests." He didn't have the heart to tell her they were being followed, although it was getting to the point where he felt he had to. He considered by-passing Glastonbury completely and driving them straight to the police station in Bath. But what on Earth would he say? That a dark order was tracking them and whilst they hadn't actually done anything yet, he knew that they would at any moment. Hardly a convincing case.

"I know you don't want to hurt me, I just…. I just don't know what to do." To his dismay she started to weep. "I'll….I'll speak to daddy one more time and if he *really* thinks I need to do it I'll go with you." She gulped and blew her nose. "OK?" She turned around in her seat to look at Marc, who quietly murmured his assent. He felt horribly uncomfortable and also wished she had simply agreed to the proposal he'd put to her. His London lodge could offer powerful sanctuary for as long as it was needed and Ana was safely married. Everyone had agreed with the idea except Ana, but they couldn't force her to do something against her will.

Ana blew her nose loudly and then went quiet. When she next spoke her voice had changed to excitement, which took the men in the car by surprise and jolted them all out of their miserable mood. "Silbury!" she pointed ahead.

Marc leaned forward and whistled. "Oh my gosh, that's amazing!"

She turned to Tristan. "Can we stop and have a look at what Mrs Pixley did here?"

"No", he said curtly. "We can't do that." he stiffened slightly, anticipating a complaint but none came. Her quiet disappointment affected him more than a stroppy reply would have. He slowed down to at least give his passengers a better look at the spectacular grass-covered mound that was England's oldest ancient monument.

Ana wound down the window and twisted her neck to look at it from every angle possible. "It's so mysterious," she said thoughtfully. "I never get tired of looking at it. I *must* remember to ask Mrs Pixley what she can see there; I always forget to mention it when she's at the shop and then I remember again as soon as she leaves."

Checking on the proximity of the black Audi as the road ahead curved upwards, Tristan was perplexed to see it swerve to a halt close to the Hill. This raised his hopes that maybe he'd been overreacting, although it was more likely they were up to no good at the magical site. All the same, he could breathe a little more easily for the time being. He gave Ana a sidelong glance. "Do you not know the story?"

"No. Do *you*? Tell me!"

"It's a bit dark, I'm afraid," he started, thinking gloomily that between the Queen dying and the threats against Ana everything was darker than it should be. "This isn't widely known, but when she psychometrised the area she learned that many thousands of years ago the area beneath the hill was used for very dark magical practices – sorcery – involving human sacrifices and also animals. Over the years, when that old, dark cult waned, different peoples decided they should try to neutralise the bad energy of the site by building the hill on top of it to channel away those forces. That's the real reason they keep people off but at one point you could climb it. I went up there anything once just to see what it was like and it's very eerie on the top. It's deadly silent and the energy there is off the scale, I've never felt anything like it, even at Tikal."

His heart twisted as he felt Ana deflate, her earlier excitement killed by the less than positive story. "That's a shame," she said quietly to the passenger seat window. "I'd hoped it was something better…"

Hearing the sorrow in her voice, Marc couldn't help chiming in. "Hey, but at least the people tried to fix it."

Ana gave him a wan smile. "Yes that's true. Also, there are barrows opposite it, on the other side of the road. You have to walk a bit before you can see them, though. Somebody who came to the shop once told me that if you go there at midsummer you can hear the sound of music. So I went there with my dad and it's true. We lay down in the sun on top of the earthworks and after few minutes it was like we could hear a little party in the distance, it was like something out of Lord of the Rings…"

Marc leaned forward from the back seat. "That's so cool! What kind of music was it?"

"It's hard to say. It wasn't like I could make out flutes or strings or anything, it was just a sense of music and merriment."

She sounded wistful and Tristan glanced at her. It had only been a year since he'd last seen her but he was struck nonetheless by some change. Her delicate, pale beauty and gentle manner were the same, but was like she was slipping away from the world. Slipping back into the world of the fey from whence she came, back into the unseen world of ancestral spirts and hidden Masters.

Back in the black Audi a disagreement was taking place. The driver and the reciter of demonic incantations had insisted on stopping at Silbury Hill to "reclaim it while we're here", whilst the other two felt strongly that they should stay on the tail of the Land Rover.

Overruling them, the driver had put his foot down, but on the brake instead of the accelerator. "This is too good an opportunity to miss," he asserted, to a satisfied nod of agreement from the conjuror. "If we set our mark on this site now it can only work in our favour. Besides, we know where they're going. It must be obvious we're following them by now and I'd rather get an element of surprise back." This argument had helped win the other two around and whilst they were still doubtful, they agreed to participate in the suggested ritual on the north side of the base of Silbury.

They found a suitable parking space on one of the wide verges allocated for visitors to the barrows and took what they needed from the boot. The hill loomed over them like a living entity, shrouded by the September clouds which threatened rain at any moment. She dominated the landscape entirely, rising like the swollen breast of a dark green goddess amidst the ancient hills of Wessex.

All of them felt the chthonic pull from the base of the manmade mountain as they waded with purposeful strides through the fields of high grass – still yellow after an unusually hot, dry summer - to the north side, out of sight of the road.

It was unusually quiet, the silence palpitating as if were the emanation of a strange magnetic field from the centre of the hill. The radius of this force field held an indomitable sway, calling to the darkness of their souls and pulling them towards its own dark root with irresistible power. The closer they got, the more exultant they became, sensing the victory of chaos in the presence of the primeval goddess who thirsted for the blood of innocents.

It was against the rule of their order to succumb to any kind of emotion, but three of them were openly euphoric, jubilance spilling from their pores without measure. Only the driver – an initiate with over thirty years' training behind him – was successfully able to keep his heart cool, if not completely cold. Over the course of his life he had committed murder and at least one act of terrorism on his home soil, nominally in service to the Islamic State, but really in service to Baal, his preferred demonic entity.

To evade capture he had lived outside the UK for more than two decades, retreating to the depths of Eastern Europe. It was only recently, as the war in Ukraine made his bolt-hole unsafe, that he had returned to Britain undercover. The people smuggling operations around the UK were so well organised that it had been relatively easy to enter the country by illegal means and disappear back to his home turf in mid Wales.

Whilst he was keenly aware that the zeitgeist - with its wars, pestilence, societal unrest and other malign forces - was working in favour of his Order, the death of the Queen had been something of a wildcard. Not quite unexpected, but he cursed the timing. He knew that her death afforded the opposing chain a golden opportunity to perform an almighty ritual of passage, which would open long-forgotten magical doorways and help unite an otherwise divided nation. All of their efforts must therefore focus on the heir of their opponents, who was coming into her spiritual birthright.

Reaching the node of the leyline they stopped as one man and closed their eyes to drink in the aura of the goddess they sought to honour. After a period of meditation the driver crouched down to remove the marker from a canvas bag at his feet. The malefic object was already inscribed with dark sigils and stained with the blood of the last sacrifice he had made. A little old by now but it would serve its purpose. She would reward them for their tribute, he was certain.

Before they could proceed with their invocation, however, there was a not insignificant work of clearing to be done. As the driver suspected, Mrs Pixley had already been to the site and had placed a considerable shield around the portal of the Goddess. No wonder she had called to him so loudly. *I shall free you, my Queen*, he thought with grim determination, *and make the way clear for your externalisation*

.

Whistle Stop Tour

That timeless clock of all lunatics, which was so bright in the sky that night, may really have had some elfin luck about it, like a silver penny.

G K Chesterton, The Flying Inn

Gilbert Keith Chesterton, Appleton's Magazine

By mid-morning

On Saturday 9th September, the Land Rover was making haste, sailing past the Cherhill White Horse and on through Chippenham until they were on the road to Bath. Soon they could drop down to Glastonbury on the A39. It was not the best route from London by any means but Tristan had relented to Ana's pleas to drive her past Silbury Hill, which meant eschewing faster Motorways to the West Country.
Guessing the nature of the ritual taking place at the earthworks and gritting his teeth in fretful anger at the thought of the evil intentions behind it.
It would be a full moon that night and Tristan had a feeling they would either make their move then or – if successfully thwarted - would retreat and wait for another auspicious time in the near future. He wondered if they might over-extend themselves in an effort to capture her that night. Evidence of a real attempted kidnap would then give them sufficient cause to either seek police protection or convince Ana to find sanctuary with the Amilius brothers.
As the effectiveness of policing in Britain was, unfortunately, at an all-time low, with less than 1.5 per cent of crimes even undergoing some form of investigation, Tristan didn't hold out much hope that they would really help. Of the two available options he much preferred the second. Giving her a sidelong glance, his heart twisted to see that she was still quietly weeping, but in another respect he was relieved. If she understood the gravity of the situation, perhaps she could be persuaded to go into sanctuary until she was married and the danger had passed.
Sat alone on the back seat, Marc was also lost in thought. The events of the previous day had given him much to digest. One revelation had followed another but foremost amongst these had been the further unveiling of his ancestral connections through the figure of Vladimir Shmakov, one of Mrs Roudnikova's guests. The Fool. Or the *wandering* Fool, as

she'd put it.

The name was already familiar to him because it had featured in the papers he'd been given in the briefcase, but as most of them were written in Russian he hadn't been able to make much sense of them. Nor had he had time to do much research about his mysterious ancestor, about whom there was very little to be found on the Internet and certainly not in English. Only an English translation of The Holy Book of Thoth offered any clues, but he hadn't even seen a copy of that until Ana showed him hers.

A few hours spent with Mrs Roudnikova had shed light much light on the mystery and Marc was in awe of the 'magical chain' she described. She said it held the light throughout the Red Terror unleashed on Russia by the Revolution. She herself, he'd been amazed to learn, had escaped to Estonia alongside the retreating White Army of the crumbling empire and become a spiritual leader for the émigré community who gathered at Tartu in the years that followed. Renowned amongst her people as a healer and spiritual teacher, as well as a news reporter and poet, her secret life as a spy for the Imperial forces was still not widely known outside her immediate circle of friends and family.

Whilst Mrs Roudnikova, her beloved teacher, G.O Mebes, his wife, Maria and most other members of their chain had lived and worked in St Petersburg, Vladimir Shmakov had stood at the centre of the Moscow occult community. Finally accepting the inevitable and escaping to Czechoslovakia in the 1920s – thanks to the help of a friend, Tomáš Masaryk, who happened to be that country's first President – he had eventually found his way to Argentina and disappeared from view to all but the inner circle of his order.

The links with Edgar Cayce and foundation of the Amilius Group were less clear to Marc but he was informed that this came via Shmakov's son, Victor Vladimirovich[xlvii]. After moving to America in the 1950s, Victor joined forces with a small band of Edgar Cayce initiates, independent

Theosophists and Spiritualists, who'd set aside their differences for the sake of world peace and a strong shared interest in Atlantis. Marc had recalled the talk in Mysteries, which seemed even more significant now, with hindsight.

In 1932, Cayce stated that Atlantean souls were once again incarnating into earth and "are wielding and are to wield an influence upon the happenings of the present day world". Cayce taught that in a rapidly coming new age, all the powers and awareness known in Atlantis would return to us. These powers and awareness brought destruction back then. How will we use them this time around?

The contents of the box, which originated from the Russian embassy in Czechoslovakia, proved just as intriguing as the briefcase. Having placed it in the centre of Mrs Roudnikova's great table, he'd been fascinated to discover a treasure trove of magical regalia tucked within.

The contents were wrapped inside a heavy and expensive-looking woven black cloth, upon which was embroidered in thick golden thread an equilateral triangle inside a square with a dot in the centre. Within it was a silver chalice studded with different coloured gemstones; a mysterious blue and green rock crystal which fit perfectly into the palm of Marc's hand; a ceremonial triple-pronged fork upon which various words and symbols were carved; an icon of St Seraphim of Sarov; a small silver-framed portrait of Tsar Nicholas II and the Imperial family; seven silk cravats in different colours and – Marc was thrilled to find – an 'AGLA' disk, which strongly resembled the one he'd seen in Dr Dee's cabinet at the British Museum.

Mrs Roudnikova had told him that AGLA was a Kabbalistic word made up of the initial letter of the Hebrew words *Athan Gabor Leolam, Adonia*, which meant "Thou art powerful and eternal, Lord" and was used by rabbis for the exorcism of evil spirits. Christians had adopted the word in the sixteenth century and it began to appear in books about magic, including the Enchiridion of Pope Leo III.

"This will come in very useful," she told him, turning the disk around in her hands.

"I wonder why he didn't take it with him?" Marc had queried, only to be told that it had probably been left by Vladimir Shmakov as a magical gift for his protectors, who also faced difficult times as the Soviet Union expanded its reach across Eastern Europe.

"Your great- grandfather knew how to make these objects and if he left one with friends he would also have taken one with him. I'm a little surprised that you didn't find something like that in the briefcase that was given to by the Amilius group, but perhaps it was left to another ancestor or his wife."

The box had also contained a number of old books written in different ancient languages as well as a huge notebook, which appeared to be a diary and was stuffed with ephemera, including a signed photograph of Thomas Eddison pasted at the front. Lamenting his inability to understand Russian as he'd carefully peeled back the pages, he asked Mrs Roudnikova to translate some of it for him.

"All in good time," she'd replied. "For now you need to gather your things because tomorrow you'll be going on another journey."

***

The westerly journey drew to a close as they pulled into the driveway of Gareth Morgan's enviable home close to Glastonbury's ruined abbey. The golden-stoned Georgian house with beautiful mature gardens had been the scene of many a sacred gathering of souls. As a recognised centre for English Druidry the house was well-used as a meeting place for several occult and spiritual orders, as well as students wishing to learn the way of the wyrd from one of the Masters. Mr Morgan had clearly been waiting for them to arrive, for the double-fronted door was flung open before they had a chance to knock.

"Daddy!" There was a squeal as Ana flung down her bags and threw herself into his bear-like hug. He swung her off her feet and gave a little spin on the gravel-covered drive.

"It's so good to see you, Duchess!" his voice was muffled, buried in her thick hair and collar of her jacket.

Marc couldn't help being impressed as he entered the house. Like many Americans he had a fascination with antiques and the wonderfully maintained house with its sweeping staircase, high windows and museum-worthy items of décor, stirred his passion for the old and English.

Tristan gestured to the American politely. "Gareth, this is Marc Marconi. He's a representative of the American branch of the Order of Amilius and he's been most helpful, I'm very grateful to him. Marc, this is Gareth Morgan, Ana's father."

Gareth Morgan grasped Marc's hand in both his great paws. "I'm delighted to meet you, Mr Marconi and Tristan is right, we are *most* grateful to you."

The effusive welcome left Marc with a warm glow inside. It was a pleasant change to the chilly morning air and he smiled at the larger-than-life Mr Morgan with his thick white beard and long green housecoat with black cravat, liking him very much already.

"I'm very pleased to meet you Mr Morgan..."

"Gareth, please!" boomed the response before he could get any further.

"Gareth, yes of course, please call me Marc!" He opened his hands appreciatively. "This is a beautiful home you have here, it's just how I hoped an English country house would be. In fact, it's better! Glastonbury looks like a really wonderful place and I'm glad for the chance to be here, even under the circumstances."

The mood suddenly shifted and Ana piped up anxiously. "Daddy, shall we have some tea, "we could all do with waking up a bit after that drive."

Getting to the kitchen involved walking through the spacious front hall and a turn or two along the corridor, taking in metres of bookshelves, strategically placed side-tables, decorative lamps and fascinating pictures which Marc would have loved to linger over. The kitchen itself delivered a surprise, not because it was extremely big - verging on huge - but because there were several men sitting there around a massive oak table, one of whom was carving runes onto what looked like a magic wand. The men stood up to greet the new arrivals, lining up to give Ana a hug or kiss on the cheek.

A large Old English Sheepdog that was lying in front of the Aga stood up to investigate and Marc was relieved to note that it seemed friendly, greeting Ana and Tristan with a great wagging of its tail and sniffing Marc's hands without biting them off. A small Jack Russell which had been sitting on the knee of the man carving the wand was less friendly, yapping for a minute before its owner managed to quiet it down again.

One of the men there looked very familiar to Marc and he wracked his brains wondering where he might have met him. Only when the man finally spoke in a strong cockney accent did the penny drop. "John Eastern?! Oh my gosh, I went to the talk you gave at Mysteries in Virginia Beach three years ago – about the Glastonbury Zodiac?"

John was evidently very pleased and shook Marc's hand vigorously. "It's great to meet you, man, have you been to Glastonbury before?"

"No this is my first time and I'm pretty excited, I hope there'll be time to look around."

"It's full moon tonight so it's a great time to visit. Maybe I can extract you from here later on and we'll take a little tour, what do you say?"

"Wow, I'd love that!"

John gave him a conspiratorial wink. "I'll see what I can do; maybe we can acquaint you with the Aquarius section of the Glastonbury Zodiac while you're here."

***

"This is gonna be a whistle-stop tour – out of necessity as you probably won't be here for long – but it'll pack a spiritual punch, I guarantee it. Right now we're heading down Chilkwell Street". John pointed at a distinctive house on the opposite side of the road. "Over there on the left is an historic house, it was built in 1561. Like many of Glastonbury's historic houses it's done a stint as a BnB – that was in the 70s and 80s - but it's currently the residence of a Golden Dawn magician who think he's the reincarnation of Francis Bacon. Possibly also John Dee, although the timeline doesn't exactly fit for that. He might have multiple personality disorder. Lots of ritual activity going on in there". Marc peered at the house but it yielded no special clue about what might have been summoned within.

The monologue continued as they continued along Chilkwell Street. "In a short while we're gonna peel off left down the high street so let's cross over. Up here near the top we've got the organic chocolate factory. Their raw bee pollen cacao is the best thing in the shop; that'll give you an out of body experience or a bloody good trip at the very least if you eat enough of that. In fact, I'll get some for later. You wait here, they'll give me a better price".

After spending what appeared to be an inordinately long time in the chocolate factory, John emerged onto the High Street again and they carried on down the road. Raised voices on the opposite side caught Marc's attention. He wasn't the only one. A small crowd was gathering. "What's all that about?" he enquired, indicating the two bearded and dishevelled-looking men who were having a mounting set-to. They were practically chest bumping and the female companion of one of them (they were both attended by equally dishevelled, robe-wearing women) was grasping the arm of her mate in a futile effort to remove him from the worsening spat.

John levelled a well-practiced eye at the bumptious quartet.

"Yeah, bit much, but nothing to worry about. They both think they're Jesus and they don't often come face-to-face but now and again they have a Jesus-off or the women have a row about who's the true Magdalene."
Marc gave a snort of laughter. "You're kidding, right?"
John raised an eyebrow at him. "No, mate, this is standard stuff. Every oddball in England ends up 'ere at some stage."
"And here I am!"
"'Ere you are! Let's cross over now. Over on the right we've got St John's Church." Marc dutifully followed him across the street and entered the churchyard which was bound by a low wall. A few small gaggles of traveller-looking types had congregated on the pavement outside. One of them was strumming on a guitar whilst another banged a tambourine and two more danced a half-hearted jig. A couple of paces down were a trio of women with henna-dyed dreadlocks and musty-looking clothes selling ethnic Jewellery and crochet items from matts on the floor. A heavily bearded man wearing a very big purple velvet hat was asleep on the bench.
"If you look on the grass there," John counselled, "you'll see there's a labyrinth, yeah?" Marc nodded. "Good, let's go inside. St John's is an important sacred site, the church stands on a Saxon holy place although the first church on record dates from 1175. This present church dates from the 15th century".
As they headed inside Marc let out a sigh as he contemplated the light and airy space, expressing admiration for the beautiful stained-glass windows before John launched back into his historical monologue.
"Behind the pulpit is what's known as the Joseph of Arimathea window, in honour of the saint who brought the family of Jesus here following the crucifixion and founded the first Christian centre in England when he planted his staff on Wearyall Hill. The famous Glastonbury Thorn[xlviii] sprung up at this spot and can still be seen to this day. If we have time I'll take you up there later but it's quite a walk. In front

of the window is what may have been part of a shrine to J of A – that's Joseph of Arimathea in case you haven't twigged - and the case you can see on top of it is a funeral pall made in 1774 from a cope that was worn by Abbott Whiting, last Abbott of Glastonbury Abbey, God rest his soul."

"How did he die?"

"He was put to death on November 15th, 1539, by Henry VIII's forces of dissolution. On that date the elderly abbot, Richard Whiting was set up on a blatantly false charge of treason. Along with two colleagues, he was sentenced to death. The King's Einsatz Kommando hit-squad stretched and tied the old man on a hurdle. This was dragged by a horse through the town, past the Abbey, and up to the summit of the Tor, where gallows had been erected. There the three men were executed. Whiting's head was removed and placed above the Abbey gate. The rest of his body was cut into four pieces that were displayed in nearby towns.

Geoffrey Ashe raised some disturbing points about the ghastly scenario in King Arthur's Avalon. It would require considerable effort, in wet and muddy November, for a horse to drag a man tied to a hurdle up to the top of the Tor. The construction of the gallows there was no easy task either. The summit is renowned for the strong winds that often blow across it. If the sole purpose of the deed was to instill fear in the population then why not choose the front of the abbey, in the middle of the town, where everyone could potentially see it? There's an unsettling hint of impractical stranger motives amongst the executioners. The three bodies strung up on a hill suggest a blasphemous parody of the crucifixion and archaic sacrificial rites.

The Abbey library was trashed. Pages of priceless manuscripts were found as litter in the streets. The bones displayed as Arthur and Guinevere's were lost. Who knows what modern forensic science could have told us if they were still available? The monks were dispersed. Before long the majestic edifice of the building was pillaged for raw material.

One of its later owners used explosives to blow great holes in the walls to satisfy his materialistic priorities. The Grail chalice of British Christendom disappeared, leaving a wasteland behind."[xlix]

Marc shook his head in dismay. "Old Bluebeard sure has a lot to answer for."

"He does indeed. We'd better move on; I want to make sure you have plenty of time in the Abbey and Chalice Well."

As they headed back down the High Street John pointed out more local landmarks, including a bright purple shop called Yin Yang, a place known as the Goddess Rooms and an ancient-looking inn with a beautiful stone façade. The George and Pilgrim. "This is the oldest pub in town and home to several ghosts, some of which have been caught on film", Marc was informed. He also observed that every other shop – maybe even 3 out of 4 - appeared to sell crystals and things related to angels, unicorns or both.

By this point they were at the bottom of the hill. "Now we're at the Market square where there's our monument to the glorious war dead." It also appeared to be a gathering place for long-haired travellers. "This is the focal point for parades around important Glastonbury occasions like Beltane, when we have a procession of the red and white dragon's and presentation of the May Queen and King. The Maypole gets carted from here up past the White Spring to its final destination on Chalice Hill. I'll show you the White Spring at the end of the tour. The present guardians are a bit erratic and control-freakish about opening times and what you can or can't do in there, but it's well worth a look and it should be open around 2.30 today because of the full moon".

They walked around the war monument before John directed them to cross the road again. "Now we are approaching the heart of the matter - Glastonbury Abbey – or should I say the *ruins* of Glastonbury Abbey".

As they walked through the glass doors into the Abbey Grounds, Marc was struck with an overriding sense of the weight of history bearing down upon him, causing the atmosphere to shimmer and flex for a just perceptible split-second through time. "Wow..." he murmured under his breath, "this place really..."

"Packs a punch, yeah, it's very high voltage!" John steered his submissive and attentive tourist in the direction of the well-preserved remains of a small stone church. "This is the Lady Chapel - one of the finest 12th century buildings in Europe – which was built on the site of what's reputed to have been the first Christian church in England, dedicated to the Blessed Virgin Mary. A holy site was established here by the earliest Christians in Britain", John explained. "Joseph of Arimathea himself, in fact. The structure you see today replaced the original timber church which burned down in a great fire here in 1184. It once contained the relics of hundreds of saints.

"Being a sacred site of unparalleled import, work to rebuild the Lady Chapel commenced immediately after the fire. The four corner turrets are sort of like a shrine or reliquary and if you'll look up here at the doorway," he pointed at the exquisitely carved arches, "you'll see that it's decorated with scenes from the life of the Blessed Virgin. Look," he indicated one of the relief sculptures. "There's the Annunciation..."

After a few moments John led them towards a wooden bench in front of what had clearly once been the altar, watching intently as he took a small candle from his pocket, lit it with a plastic lighter and set it upon the stone altar. "Let's say a prayer for the departed Queen?"

The Tomb

The aim of the occultist is to organise and master phenomena and bring them into harmony with the eternal law of the Real.

The Training & Work of an Initiate, Dion Fortune

Violet Mary Firth; Dion Fortune

The skeletons of a royal couple

Were unearthed here in the twelfth century. The bones of the male were very large and the female had long golden hair, as the fairy queen Guinevere was reputed to have had.

"Evidence is a bit patchy but we learn about all this from Gerald of Wales, who in 1191 began to write *De Instructione Principis*, which included a history of Henry II's reign and good examples of kingship from English history. There it describes how Arthur's body was discovered at Glastonbury Abbey during his (Gerald's) own lifetime. He also wrote that the remains of Arthur and his Queen were found by monks between two stone pyramids."

...buried deep in the earth in a hollow oak and indicated by wonderful, almost miraculous, signs, and it was brought into the church with honour and deposited becomingly in a marble tomb. Here too a leaden cross, placed under a stone, not above it as is the custom in our days, but rather fixed below, which I have seen, for I have touched these letters carved there, not raised or projecting, but turned inwards towards the stone, contained: "Here lies buried the glorious king Arthur and Guinevere his second wife in the Isle of Avalon...

"Gerald also wrote that the bodies - one male, the other female - were buried sixteen feet down along with space for a third body. In this space was found

a blonde tress of woman's hair, with its shape and colour intact, which, as a monk snatched it with a greedy hand and lifted it up, immediately crumbled completely into dust.

Gerald was convinced these were the bodies of Arthur and Guinevere and describes seeing them with his own eyes. The male skeleton was huge:

For when his shin-bone was placed beside the shin of the

tallest man of the locality, whom the abbot pointed out to me, and set on the ground alongside his foot, it came three big fingers, width above his knee. His skull, too, was large and capacious like a prodigy or wonder, to such a degree that the space between the eyebrows and between the eyes was more than a palm's width. It showed signs of ten or more wounds, which had all been covered with scar tissue, except for one, greater than the rest, that seemed to have been the only lethal one.

"Some claimed that all of this was a hoax perpetuated by the monks of the abbey to help drum up money for a rebuild after the fire. Gerald, however, says that Henry II himself was responsible for the excavation, having become intrigued by stories of the unusual pyramids he'd heard from travelling minstrels - the troubadour mystics and wandering fools of the Middle Ages'. Gerald's isn't the only account from that era. In an 1191 chronicle Ralph of Coggeshall wrote:

This year were found at Glastonbury the bones of the most renowned Arthur, formerly King of Britain, buried in a very ancient coffin, about which two ancient pyramids had been built: on the sides of these was in inscription, illegible on account of the rudeness of the script and its worn condition. The bones were discovered as follows: as they were digging up this ground to bury a monk who had urgently desired in his lifetime to be interred there, they discovered a certain coffin, on which a leaden cross had been placed, bearing the inscription, 'Here lies the famous King Arturius, buried in the Isle of Avalon.

By this point they had reached the location of the purported royal grave and Marc read the sign above it with a good deal more credulity than he might have done a day or two before:

Site of King Arthur's tomb. In the year 1191 the bodies of King Arthur and his Queen were said to have been found on the south side of the Lady Chapel. On 19th April 1278 their remains were removed in the presence of King Edward I and his Queen Eleanor to a black marble tomb on this site. This tomb survived until the dissolution of the Abbey in 1539.

John explained that the souls of Arthur and Guinevere rested at the centre of England's Tree of Life in the mystical body of the Abbey, themselves forming the Middle Pillar - Pillar of Beauty – flanked on either side by Edmund Ironside – the Pillar of Strength – and Edmund the Elder, Pillar of Mercy.
Fully convinced by this point that Arthur and Guinevere were pretty much strolling around the Abbey Grounds a few steps ahead of them, Marc was now John's humble servant, brimming with the legends of Albion and ready to take up Excalibur himself in defence of the clan.
Satisfied with his work but far from finished, John guided them back out onto Magdalene Street and into the Catholic Church of Our Lady St Mary, where they sat for a while in silent contemplation then repeated the prayers they'd intoned at the Abbey for the Queen and Anastasia. This was followed by a brief tour of the atmospherically beautiful Almshouse and St Margaret's Chapel, which bore icons of both its eponymous saint and Mary Magdalene.
"And now," said John, "We're going to head up towards Chalice Well, one of the most important sacred sites in Britain, probably the world. The name Chalice Well comes from an ancient chalybeate spring, sometimes called the 'Blood Well', which has never been known to fail and is believed to originate deep within the earth, independently of rainfall. It's associated with blood because of the iron rich content, which also colours the water. It is one of two sacred springs which run close together down the hills: The Red Spring and the White Spring; the Grail Waters and the Faery

Waters.

"Even though the well has been in use for hundreds – maybe thousands - of years, the legendary reputation of Chalice Well is thanks to the English visionary mystic, Wellesley Tudor Pole, who in 1902 had vivid dreams of being a monk in Glastonbury. A couple of years later he intuited that there would be a stunning discovery in Glastonbury, which "would link the founder of the Christian faith with modern leaders of Christian thought".

Pole believed that a pre-Christian culture – a sort of prisca theologia - extended into Glastonbury via Ireland and was a wellspring of an authentic Western mystical tradition which prevails to this day, especially in the Celtic heartlands. His visions of Glastonbury began to incorporate 'three maidens', who would be instrumental in discovering what he claimed to be the grail cup of Christ at St Bride's Well. Bride's Hill, where the well is located, is between Wearyall Hill", John turned around to point at the hill in question, "and the River Brue. Around a 1000 years ago there was a chapel dedicated to St Bride that was built by the monks of the Abbey".

"Consultation with psychic seers who ranged from Annie Besant and A.E. Waite to the Swedish Princess Karadja, confirmed that the artefact was of immense import: The cup used by Christ at the last supper, inherited by Peter and which wound its way across Europe before coming to rest in Glastonbury. Pole would also come to believe that priceless documents relating to the Grail cup were to be found somewhere in the catacombs beneath the Hagia Sophia in what is now Istanbul. The search for these would take him on a lifelong quest, punctuated by the two World Wars in which he participated very actively.

"Glastonbury has been a holy site for thousands of years, with Albion described by William Blake as the 'Human Form Divine' and 'The Angel of the Presence'. Pole believed that the forces of the Holy Grail had converged on Glastonbury - site of Britain's first Christian church – which would become a world centre for spiritual healing.

"Around 1944, after the death of its then owner, a group of investors that included Pole and Alice Buckton bought the Chalice Well lands and the Tor School and founded the Chalice Well Trust. As he wrote in 1968: "Half a century ago, in the Women's Quarter of Glastonbury, from the depths of the Well of St. Bride, a Cup was brought out into the light of day. This vessel is the symbol of the heavenly and eternal Grail, the Chalice of Christ, the Promise of the Future." His ashes were scattered in the garden. And here we are!"

Marc pushed his glasses back up his nose as they walked past an inviting but mysterious-looking guest house called Little St Michael's and paid the suggested donation which would give them access to the public gardens. As he past through the turnstile Marc felt as if he was walking through a magical gateway to a sacred land that he had thought only existed in poetry and legends, fairy tales and songs.

VITRIOL

"Scientists have calculated that the chances of something so patently absurd actually existing are millions to one. But magicians have calculated that million-to-one chances crop up nine times out of ten.[1]"

Terry Pratchett

Photograph of Terry Pratchett by Luigi Novii

𝒜 sombre mood

Prevailed around Gareth Morgan's huge kitchen table. Several of those present, John included, were sat with head in hands and the Sheepdog was nestled close to its Master in silent and loyal support. Ana was sat beside Tristan weeping into his shoulder and her father had his arms stretched around both Ana on his left and John to the right.
Marc looked miserably into his cup of tea, not knowing what to say. He had just been marvelling at the beautiful vesica piscis design on the circular wooden cover to Chalice Well when John had taken a phone call which prompted a howl of "NO!" and sent him running to the bottom of the garden.
Scurrying after him in alarm – terrified that something had happed to Ana in their absence – Marc was informed that an act of great evil had just been committed, somehow in broad daylight. The Holy Thorn of Wearyall Hill, fruit of the staff of Joseph of Arimathea, planted on 'the holyest erth of Englande', had been savagely cut down and was no more.
The terrible news had truncated their tour and sent both men back to Gareth Watkins' house, where they'd already been informed of the tragedy. In fact, it was Gareth who had phoned John to tell him in the first place.
John raised his head to lament once again. "I can't believe those fuckers! What are we going to do!"
Ana buried her head into Tristan's shoulder. "I can't bear it," she sobbed, "why do people have to be so awful; who can have done such a thing!"
John poured himself another shot of whiskey from the bottle of Glenmorangie that was strategically placed in front of him on the table. "It's gonna be the Seven Sacrifices, innit!" He looked around at the others in outrage. "They got away with chopping the top off last time but we can't let this lie, it's clearly related to the other thing they're planning."
John glanced sideways at Ana and Gareth gave his shoulder a warning squeeze. "Careful, Eastern, we know who it is alright

but we can't let them get the better of us already".
An elderly but still robust-looking man spoke up. "Things are coming to a head, Gareth, we must convene a council this evening and meet with the elders. We can't face them alone, not when they're engaging in open warfare."
Tristan nodded at this. "I was telling Gareth earlier that they made a stop at Silbury Hill. They'd been tracking us since London and I was really starting to think they'd force a confrontation before we got here, but they suddenly swerved off near the barrows."
"I know exactly what the blighters were getting up to there!" the old man resounded angrily. "summoning the dark goddess to engage her power in their war against our lady!"
"I know, Colin!" said Gareth anxiously. "This has been a shock but it's not as if we weren't expecting them to move on us. At least now it's started we can plan a response. We definitely need to convene tonight as planned, but sooner than originally intended."
At that moment the doorbell rang, prompting the Sheepdog to jump to his feet and the Jack Russell to go belting out of the kitchen, barking like mad. Gareth leapt up. "Thank God she's here…" he announced, hurrying after the dogs. The sound of the door opening, followed by the dog's falling silent and Gareth's relieved voice, reached those sat waiting in the kitchen. A moment or two later he ushered in the guest.
Ana leapt up and flung her arms around Mrs Pixley. "I'm so glad you're here, have you heard the awful news?"
"There, there, it's alright my dear. Yes, I've heard. It's a terrible business." She gave the elderly Druid a concerned look over Ana's shoulder. "Good afternoon, Colin. I'm sorry we're meeting again under such difficult circumstances."
"You are most welcome my esteemed Mrs Pixley, we need all the help we can get."
"Of course, of course, I came as soon as I heard."
"Can I get you a cup of tea, Mrs Pixley?" Ana stepped back and hovered close to the stove.

"That would be lovely, my dear, thank you so much." She smiled warmly and then looked around the table, nodding at all those present, in turn, until she finally got to Tristan, who stood up directly and kissed her hand. "Together at last, I see!" Mrs Pixley told him with a twinkle in her eye. More quietly she murmured. "If she is to marry anyone, let it be you and not the other. For *him* to take her as his wife would herald the start of the worst of all worlds."

Tristan blushed and sat down, unable to even mumble the few words that were struggling to form in his mouth. He looked longingly at Ana, who was busying herself with tea, oblivious to either his plight or her own. Mrs Pixley put a hand to his cheek. "Don't worry, son, she *will* see you." Catching Tristan's eye, Gareth Morgan nodded briefly in assent.

Marc reached for the cellophane bag of confectionary that John had placed in the centre of the table as he listened to this exchange with great curiosity. His stomach gave a loud and plaintive growl. Marc was, by now, extremely hungry. He felt a bit guilty at taking yet another chocolate but they really were delicious and nobody else seemed interested. He stood 6ft 3 in his stockinged feet and although he wasn't especially overweight, he was broad enough and solid enough to need a lot of food. So far, the English portions had not quite matched up to his huge all-American appetite. At least, not since his first (and last) breakfast at the hotel.

Whilst he was thinking – also with longing - of sausages, hash browns, scrambled eggs and smoked salmon, Marc took a fourth chocolate, followed by a fifth. Just as he started to chew this last treat he realised that Mrs Pixley had turned her inquisitive, bird-like eye upon him. He felt his heart skip a beat before setting off again at a faster pace.

"Unfortunate recent incidents aside, have you enjoyed your trip around Glastonbury, thus far?" she enquired, with a mysterious emphasis he could not fathom and which reminded him of the out of body state he'd entered in the upper room of Lost Continents.

"Gosh, yes," he managed, "John is an incredible guide…" he glanced over at the expert, who now had his head on his arms that were resting on the table. Colin was patting him rhythmically on the back. Marc had been hoping for help with Mrs Pixley but everyone else around the table appeared to be otherwise engaged, leaving him in a peculiar void with the legendary mystic that somehow seemed to be deepening.

"He's guided you through Aquarius, no doubt," she asked, the twinkle morphing dramatically into a star-like gleam which suddenly reminded him of Formalhaut.

Why Formalhaut?

Marc wasn't sure if Mrs Pixley actually spoke the question out loud or was using telepathy. He decided it would be easier to answer her in thought. Took less energy. He felt rather dreamy. *I guess it's all around…Aquarius, that is.*

I know what it is. Mrs Pixley smiled knowingly. *Don't forget a token for the gatekeeper.*

As he gazed into the fathomless watery depths of the Southern Fish, Marc was peripherally conscious that the others around the table were stirring into a form of coordinated activity that somehow, just by sitting still, he was able to be a part of. Someone had turned off the lights and the dogs were stretched out in front of the Aga. The Jack Russell was already snoring. Candles had been lit. *Many candles; one for each soul of the knights and ladies.* In the kitchen, all was silent, but outside in the darkening emerald hills and brooding soldier-like trees, the owls began to call.

Somebody was telepathing more information to him. *It has been felt for long that Glastonbury has to become again the centre of a great spiritual movement and it has now been revealed that the first step towards it is to be taken*[li].

A hand was placed on top of Marc's right, which was palm down on the heavy oak table, angled towards the chocolate but immobile and compliant. It must have been the quiet young man, Percy, who Marc had barely exchanged more than a few words with but who had been sat beside him for the past two hours. Or maybe it was three hours. *What time does the sun start to set around here?* He wondered.

Another hand reached for his left, which had been clasping an empty mug and which was also now placed palm down on the table. *John.* Marc thought detachedly as his eyes drifted shut, at once becoming absorbed in delicate crystalline patterns that were blooming like strange flowers behind his closed lids. He was dimly aware that Mr Morgan, who was sitting opposite him, had begun to speak softly in an incomprehensible language that flowed like a silver stream and somehow seemed to merge with the star he'd just witnessed in Mrs Pixley's left eye. *How lovely,* Marc thought dreamily, *I wonder where the stream goes...*

Just before he blacked out the hands on either side increased their pressure over his own.

Brothers in spirit for the defence of the Kingdom and safety of our Queen, with long hair yellow as gold. Sword of air and cup of water, wand of fire and bowl of Earth, open your gates, the fellowship approaches.

***

When he next opened his eyes, Marc was surprised to find himself standing in line behind half a dozen grey and white-cloaked fellows. An even greater number stood silently behind him. The fellow at the front was carrying a lantern and held aloft a wand that Marc somehow knew was made of Rowan.

He wasn't sure how it had got there but Marc – who was also cloaked in similar garb - found that in his own hands was a sword, which shone most wondrously in the glorious light of the full risen moon, huge as a great white pearl in the inky velvet shell that was the sky. Its clear white light ran through him more surely than a shard from the midday sun, transforming his soul into a translucent mirror of light.

The line was moving slowly forward and those at the front

were disappearing through a brightly lit opening that was cut into the side of the dark high-sided hill, a cone of power that rose up above them with electrifying splendour.

In no time at all he was first in line at the entrance, sword pointing upwards with its blade almost touching his nose.

The sword reminds us that there is the law of Themis, even when conditioned by the times, places and environments and that the transgression of this Lex (-), will bring a punishment (+), due to the action of the equilibrium principle (n). Lex is the name given to conditional rules, which are evolutionary within time and space, but inevitable at every given moment[lii].

Standing at the amber-lit opening was a bright-eyed young woman with thick, shoulder-length hair, whose spirit seemed to extend all around her in joyous waves of light. She gave him a dazzling smile and without understanding what he was doing, Marc opened his left palm to show her the small white crystal that John had presented him with earlier that day.

As he stepped over the threshold of the land beneath the hill, the light became so bright that it seemed as if he was entering the heart of a flame. Those before him were moving at incredible speed and it took all his concentration to keep up the pace. He mildly regretted that he was unable to study the inside of the Earth he had entered, for it did not seem to be a cave, more like a radiant heart inside a vast, broad chest.

In no more than a beat or two of that heart, he emerged into the centre of the marvellous hollow hill, warm and ablaze with hundreds of candles and warmer still from the surprisingly large assembly of souls who were gathered there. As his own group was arraying itself into a wide circle, in which they were joined by many of those others present, Marc followed suit. He found himself at a natural position in the South of the circle.

Standing solemnly with his sword still upright, Marc observed the faces of the others present, recognising not only his fellow travellers from Gareth Morgan's house, but a few more besides. There was the wonderful older man – balding and bespectacled, with a too-large suit and English bowler hat which looked strangely incongruous on his Slavic-looking face who he'd first encountered in Mrs Roudnikova's upper room. His wife was by his side again. What were their names again? *Valentin and Maria.* Yes.

With a start he saw the face of Brother Saturnus, standing to the East with two other brothers who Marc did not recognise, but who he assumed were from the Order of Amilius. They locked eyes with him by way of acknowledgement, but other than that made no attempt at communication.

Familiar-looking others who he couldn't quite name were there as well, faces seen only in miniature on the back of old books, static black and white portraits brought vividly to life, sometimes bearing only a passing resemblance to the stiff antique photographs of bygone years.

Percy, who was still there beside him, handed him a long white candle, which Marc lit from an identical taper that Percy himself was already holding. Those who were not already standing in the circle began to silently range themselves around those who were, two or sometimes three behind each member of the company. All those in the inner circle were wearing the same style of hooded cloak, each carried a lit candle in one hand and some other object in the other.

Valentin, standing at the western part of the circle, was holding a gleaming golden chalice studied with pearls and other jewels. Mr Morgan – directly opposite Marc in the north – bore a large white cloth which reminded him of a shroud. Percy carried a sort of blade, which strongly resembled the heavily engraved three-pronged fork which Marc had found in his ancestral box. Some held musical instruments. One had an ornamental pipe, another a small but beautiful harp, a third a violin and a fourth a small drum, whilst yet another was holding a dark and gleaming glass, precisely of the sort he had seen in John Dee's cabinet.

Now they had stepped forward, Marc was better able to see

the distinctive faces and attire of some of the spirits that were standing behind his companions. Standing behind Valentin was a helmeted Templar knight wearing a belted white tunic which had a large black cross on the front. In his left hand he carried a long and shining shield – which also bore a cross on the front – and in his right was a great long sword with its tip pointing upwards. Beside the knight was an individual who Marc registered with a mild and distant shock as being Rudolf Steiner. Standing behind Maria were two ladies. One of them young and ethereal in Medieval dress with long flowing hair; beside her a reverent-looking person in the traditional dark robe and square headdress of an Orthodox Russian nun.

Standing behind the elder Colin with his long wizard's staff was a short and swarthy fellow with a very long beard who reminded Marc – though he knew not why – of Socrates. Alongside this philosophical-looking ancient was a tonsured monk with a huge golden crucifix around his neck and a Bible pressed against his chest by delicate white fingers. A sidelong glance told him that Percy was accompanied by a young soldier of the Great War, who stood with a bowed head and hands clasped in prayer. Others in the assembly also had soldiers beside them, or young women dressed in old-fashioned nurses uniform.

Becoming more absorbed in the eclectic cast of characters he had somehow found himself amongst, Marc was dimly aware of feeling awestruck at the sight of a youthful Queen Elizabeth II, who had not joined the circle but was standing towards the far north of the hollow hill, resplendent in her coronation robe and Crown jewels.

She wasn't the only one, for positioned behind Gareth Morgan was another legendary Queen, as Marc surmised from her dazzling appearance. A fabulous hooped gown adorned with an enormous ruby-studded crucifix at the hip, another in plain gold at her breast and a great white lace collar with matching bonnet and veil which framed her ghostly white face and copper red hair. More Kings and

Queens stood watching from the wings, flanked by monks to the North and poets to the South.

A change in atmosphere informed him that something was about to happen. The door to the outside world, it seemed, had closed, for here was the woman who'd greeted him at the entrance of the hollow hill. As she approached the circle she appeared to grow in both age and stature, until a solid, middle-aged but smooth-faced matron wearing a ceremonial robe in place of her simple pinafore dress was standing amongst them.

She took up her place in the western portion of the circle, where she was accompanied by a group of eight companions – all of them holding small silver chalices - who clearly formed a unit and stayed close together, just outside the main circle. As she greeted the assembly in the same unknown language he'd heard in Gareth Morgan's kitchen, Marc's soul began to lose connection with his mental centre. He was unable to do anything but watch and listen as the ceremony unfolded. He would barely even remember what took place.

As the woman continued to speak, two springs of water bubbled out from different parts of the hollow hill and came together in one enchanted stream, which ran through the centre of the circle. Four individuals stepped forward, each from a different quarter, and held aloft whichever magical instrument they were holding. Gareth Morgan – stood opposite with his mysterious shroud - was one of them. Marc stepped forward himself with the sword held aloft.

There was a sudden and dramatic ringing of bells, by which clear signal all those present fell to their knees with eyes cast down, to await the arrival of the Master.

BEHOLD THE LAMB OF GOD!

Back in the Georgian house on Chilkwell Street a golden silence prevailed between the walls. On the outside, police constable David Wilby, a member of Colin's order who'd been persuaded to stand guard over the house that night, was stationed on the drive in his police car, listening to Jazz FM on low volume. Whilst he had taken seriously the threat posed to Ana – especially in light of the desecration of Glastonbury's Holy Thorn that afternoon – he had nothing to report and was regretting that he hadn't been able to participate more fully in the Mysteries that night.

Tristan had alerted him to the nearby presence of the Order of Seven Sacrifices, whose actions already spoke volumes, but PC Wilby had not seen anything suspicious take place at all. Not with his own eyes, at least, excepting the pitiful state of the legendary Thorn. In fact, the night was unusually tranquil, as fruitful with stars as could be hoped for during the full harvest moon, which followed a long, hot summer. It was approaching midnight and Jupiter, shining like a beacon lighthouse, was sailing close beside Selena like a faithful sentry to his mothership.

Upstairs in the prettiest (but not the largest) of the many spare rooms in Gareth Morgan's magnificent home, Ana was sleeping peacefully. She was starting to dream of Silbury Hill, walking towards the monolithic earthwork with silent intensity, drawn by a powerful magnetic force that she did not fully understand, though she felt it in the depths of her womb.

A couple of doors down Tristan lay awake, gazing at the glorious full moon which was shining through the open curtains. Such was his degree of happiness that he no longer believed that anything bad could happen, either to Ana or anyone else in his world. For the first time in his life, everything was as it should be.

Not only encouraged by Mrs Pixley and Ana's father, but furnished with the square cut emerald engagement ring which had belonged to her mother, he had proposed to her by firelight a few hours after the others had set out for their ritual. Ana had accepted the ring that her father had discreetly bestowed upon Tristan shortly after Mrs Pixley's arrival, returning his kiss with a greater joy than he had dared believe was possible.

Unable to tear his gaze away from the victorious moon in all her glory, Tristan was elated by the knowledge that his love was sleeping soundly under the same roof, PC Wilby was outside the house and there was a guard dog in the kitchen. Their closest friends and her father would return before dawn. The illusion that all was right with the world allowed him to succumb to the sweet embrace of Nyx, lover of darkness, daughter of Chaos, mother of hypnosis and death.

Persephone

I was upon the threshold and changed life

Dante, Purgatorio, Canto XXX

Elkan Persephone

No man witnessed

The radiant, white-robed lady as she stepped bare-footed over the dew-sodden grass, her long golden hair appearing silver in the moonlight, her wide-open eyes unseeing of the Earth and compelled by her dreams to head forth to God-knows where. With an enchanted hand she had caressed the whimpering dog, commanding him to stand down with that one silent gesture.
It was an hour before the pink fingers of dawn would trace Aurora's portrait in the sky, but already the sentry was sleeping. The fellowship and wider pageant was yet to return from the Mysteries of the Hollow hills. Even the eyes of the hill itself were turned inwards, as every gaze averted from the passage of their sacrificial Queen.
Her feet trod so lightly that the earth barely grazed her soles. She passed unseen, not even by the night fox, as she crossed the grounds of Abbey House and passed through the secret gateway into the grounds of Glastonbury Abbey. The black wrought iron swung silently open as she approached, the bolts drawn back by the invisible hands of an unknown spectre.
The hem of her nightgown was soaked as it trailed the moonlit grass, a gliding white lady on the lawn which led into the temple. The passage took her straight across the High altar and along the centre of the choir, over the grave of Edmund ironside and past what used to be the Under Tower. On she glided through the Nave until she floated like a dove beyond the ancient West Door of the Great Church and turned left in the direction of the Abbott's Kitchen.
From their place in the shadow of marshalled trees behind the ornamental square building, four members of the Order of Seven Sacrifices had their dark eyes fixed upon her. Their blood rose by degrees with every fairy-footed step that she made. Within the folds of black cloaks they clasped their ritual objects: A twisted knife still stained with blood; a gnarled wand of yew inscribed with a hex and bound at the

base with cat skin leather; a cup formed from the horn of a sacrificial stag and a flat clay disk engraved with an invocation of the dark goddess.

The four of them were ranged around an inverted Pentagram which had been scraped out of the earth and grass. Each had swallowed a desecrated host, stolen from the Church of Our Lady St Mary by one of their local associates. A minor scandal had ensued following the theft and an article in the local paper had expressed dry surprise that neither local Jesus had come out in protest. their female disciples also stayed silent, not least of all because one of them had been involved in the theft herself.

Intoxicated by the stunning success of the summoning spell they had cast upon the sleeping Princess, each of the four men was wrestling to hold down his personal demon. Already over-inflated with pride and glory, now they were enflamed with lust and avarice, drawn by the immense latent power of the prize.

With Anastasia less than 50 paces away and their car parked nearby in Magdalene Street, her capture was now certain. Each anticipated a great reward from the leader of their Order and all of them hoped to be gifted a girl for the gratification of their pleasure and, ultimately, to be used as sacrifices to the same personal demons that were hounding them at that moment.

She was almost within grasp. Five more paces and she would be standing in the centre of their inverted pentagram, symbol of the Lords of Death. The moment she reached the dark heart of their magical vortex the whole of time seemed to stop for a broken instant. Ana halted abruptly and uncertainty flickered for the first time in the glassy pools of her hypnotised eyes. Somewhere behind their surface her consciousness was struggling to rise, helpless in the presence of blackened hearts and leaden grips. Where were her allies now?

The nearby shriek of an owl almost shook her free and she flinched on the spot, prompting the largest of the men to scoop her up in his arms and stride off in the direction of the car, closely flanked by the rest.

Taking care not to drive off too quickly, lest they attract attention in the otherwise oblivious town, they carefully pulled away from Magdalene Street with Ana trapped between the two men on the back seat. Already injected with a powerful sedative, she was limp and dead to the world, her head lolling back against the seat and her eyes now closed. They rolled smoothly out of town in the direction of the A39, from which the driver intended to pick up the M5 motorway and eventually bear West towards their stronghold in the Shropshire hills.

They could hardly believe their luck. Never had one of their hypnotising spells been so successful; they generally had to use brute force from the outset. Just as they were driving past Crispin Hall – about a kilometre out of Glastonbury – the man sat on Ana's left spoke out.

"Well, well, what have we here!" He held up her limp left hand. "Our princess appears to be engaged."

The man in the passenger seat swivelled his head around and the driver had to resist doing the same

"That's a turn up for the books, I wonder when it happened?"

"Must have been sometime yesterday, I wonder if they've done the deed yet?"

"I doubt it. A girl like this probably will wait until she's married."

"Let's hope so because she'd remember any sex alchemy. All being well, the combination of our spells and the sedative will wipe out her memory for a good 24 hours, but we'll need to have a contingency plan in case she gets triggered by anything…"

"I wish we hadn't got out at Silbury," the second man in the back seat grumbled.

Before anyone could agree with that the driver spoke up. "It's a good job we *did* stop or we'd never have dismantled Pixo's shield and the spell wouldn't have worked."

With that, the four of them fell into a moody silence that lasted for most of the next 100 miles - almost 2 hours - as long as it had taken to get past Worcester.

As they started to pull away from the main roads and further into the countryside, the westerly turn put the newly risen sun behind them and all breathed a little more easily. They had succeeded in capturing Anastasia and that was all that mattered for the time being. He would know what to do with her. He always did.

In the Upper Room of Lost Continents, Mrs Roudnikova was sitting still as a statue, pale as a wraith. She had been in that position for an indeterminate length of time, frozen by an uncharacteristic despair akin to that which she had felt when news of the Tsar's assassination first reached her.

This time, however, she lacked the imperative call to action which had forced her and her first husband to abandon Russia, escaping across the Gulf of Finland to Tallin. In its place was a dull sense of impotence which verged dangerously close to hopelessness. Her great-granddaughter – the youngest and undisputed favourite, her chosen successor, an irreplaceable link in the unbroken magical chain, was lost.

Those who'd remained with her were gazing into the past, recalling the catastrophes of a century ago. Butator was staring into the distance with a haunted look, recalling the dreadful day in 1926 when the extent of the betrayal by his former pupil became clear and he was arrested by the OGPU.

The infamous case of the Leningrad Freemasons had been reported widely in the press and consisted of so much scurrilously, slanderous, ridiculous, dishonest and dangerous information that he'd struggled to take the interrogation seriously – despite the fact his life was at stake. This had resulted in his imprisonment in the notorious Solovetsky Island prison camp in the Soviet Arctic.

It was known then as Solovky and conditions in the gulag were so violently bad that none but those who'd lived – or died – there could believe it possible. Maria put a troubled hand to her brow as her husband began to relive the awful memory, as happened on rare occasions when he was especially anxious.

First were sent to the Metekh prison at Tiflis, a detention place for political prisoners. There were about 2,600 'White Guards and many of the Georgian Mensheviks. Every week, on Tuesday nights, from 60 to 300 persons were shot in the prison. This mean that Tuesdays were a veritable hell for the whole of Metekh. We did not know who was Marked down to be shot, so everyone expected to be shot. Nobody could get a wink of sleep till morning.

The ceaseless bloodshed was torture not only to the prisoners, but to the people living in freedom outside. All the streets around the Metekh had long been uninhabited, the population of this quarter had abandoned their houses, unable any longer to listen to the shots of the executioners, the shrieks and groans of the victims.

The Tchekists in the Meteky were always drunk. They were regular butchers....On 'shooting nights' from five to ten men were taken from each room. The procedure of reading out the list of those doomed to die was drawn out by the Tchekists to an average minimum of a quarter of an hour in each room. There was a long pause before each name was read, during which the whole room shivered with terror.

Even people with strong nerves could not withstand such torture. On Tuesday nights half the prisoners in the castle sobbed until morning came. Next day no one could eat a morsel of food; the prison dinner was left untouched. This happened every week. And prisoners from the Mountain Republic who came to the Solovky in 1925 told us that it was still happening then. Many people could not endure the prolonged nightmare and became insane. Many committed suicide in every conceivable manner. I spent four months and a half in the Meteckh, and prepared myself for death every Tuesday. Everywhere was the same total suppression of human personality, the same torture by nocturnal interrogations, starvation and blows, the same lawless, indiscriminate shootings.

The concentration camps were never heated, even at the height of winter, when in these far northern latitudes the thermometer often falls to -50 or -60. The prisoners were given the following ration: one potato for breakfast, potato peelings cooked in hot water for dinner and one potato for supper....driven by hunger to eat the bark of trees, unable to stand from exhaustion, compelled by torture and shootings to perform hard labour.

The Solovky camp was built on the site of the original Solovetsky Monastery, which had been founded in 1429 by Saints Sabbatius and Hermann and Saint Zosima built the first church in 1436. The island is only about 17 x 11 miles in size. There are five other large islands alongside the main one and several smaller ones, all in the White Sea and close to the Western coast of the Archangel district and Gulf of Onega. It was a wonderful place, a high point of Russian culture, but the Soviet power destroyed this highly cultivated and advanced post in the Far North with characteristic violence and cruelty. In 1922 all the wooden buildings of the monastery were burned and half the monks murdered, including the Igumen[IIII]. The rest were sent to labour camps in Central Russia. The treasures were stolen by Tchekists, the icons chopped up for fuel, the bells melted down in Moscow.

Besides a multitude of objects that were precious in a religious and material sense, the Soviet Huns destroyed treasures of immense historical value. The Tcheckists pillaged the library of the monastery, which during the five centuries of its existence had been filled with unique works. They heated the stoves with rare books, old documents and chronicles of the greatest antiquity....The ancient building was reduce to a heap of ruins.

Grigori Ottonovich gave a short, bitter laugh and looked around the table. "You know, a writer called Juan Antonio Llorente once described the Spanish Inquisition in great detail, the interrogation methods and torture. The book was called The History of the Inquisition in Spain. It should have been terrible reading but compared with what we saw in Solovky it was trivial.

Maxim Corky was one of the most evil of the guards. He forced people sent to the Serkirny Hill part of the camp to perch on poles. Terrible, tall thin poles; The perches they were called. Prisoners were made to sit there for days. If someone fell they beat him to a pulp with sticks or threw him down 375 steps. Dead or alive, they'd bury him on the spot.

Of course, we had our own form of resistance. We'd hold the papers given to us for re-education upside down on purpose!
"To the Mosquitoes" is a form of punishment very popular with the Solovetsky Tchekists. The manner of its infliction is as follows. The prisoner is stripped naked and made to stand on a particular stone opposite the commandant's office. He is ordered, with threats of " stone sacks " and shooting, to stand absolutely still, not to move a finger and not to drive away the mosquitoes, which cover the poor wretch's body as with a thick black crust. The torture is continued for several hours. When the punishment is over, the victim's body is one huge sore from the bites of the poisonous insects. The weaker prisoners die, and the stronger cannot sit or lie down for many weeks after the punishment.
The White House in Kholmogory was named because it was a white painted building. For a two-year period shootings took place a very day, but the bodies of the executed were never removed. All the rooms were filled with corpses - right up to the ceiling. 2000 sailors from Kronstadt were shot there in three days. About 100,000 were shot in total and the smell of the bodies poisoned the air for miles. The stench never abated. It hung over the prisoners day and night. All people in the town abandoned their homes. Drowning was another method used to kill us and the small islands were also heaped up with the bodies of those who'd tried to escape via the sea...[liv]
You know, Even the hospitals of the Solovetsky Islands are in themselves almost a guarantee that the patients who enter them will die en masse... the camp punishments, like the

camp medical arrangements, are based upon no other calculation than that of sending the largest possible number of prisoners, more or less swiftly, to " the other side…

"My God, Grigori!" Vladimir Alekseevich groaned in anguish, "those fiends! "It makes me want to strangle the devil Trotsky and demon Lenin a thousand times over, then send the legion of Stalin to the bowels of hell! If I could only drink that Stolichnaya I'd be calling for a second bottle!"
He slammed the table, which shook, and Vsevolod held up his hand in gentle protest. In his lifetime he had been known as the Moscow St Germain and was still revered in the hidden occult circles of his Motherland. "You are quite right, Vladimir, the horrors are unending. Let us not bear further needless torment. Dearest Grigori Ottonovich– teacher to us all - I fear we can take no more. The story of your plight is so dreadful but let us spare a thought for Mrs Roudnikova and the poor lost Anastasia. This is a disaster we might perhaps resolve, so – with your blessing - let us dwell no more on those unhappiest and worst of all times?
Butator at once snapped out of his harrowing reminiscence and apologised profusely to his friends and compatriots. "My God, what on Earth was I thinking. Nina Pavlovna, please forgive me! You bear the light, Vsevolod Vyacheslavovich. It is imperative we focus on the time at hand.
"Good; we are agreed", Vsevolod approved, "so, let us examine the facts. It is true that she has been captured by agents of the Djinn and will soon be subject to his terrible powers of seduction. It's imperative we find out their location as soon as possible. At present it is still strongly shielded but I think I'm right in saying that there is still some hope that Mr Marconi can locate her. As long as Elena agrees on their mutual cooperation?"
Mrs Roudnikova gripped the scrying glass before her and remained staring resolutely ahead. "Yes, that's right," she said uncertainly. We must hope…" "Where there is hope

there is life," Vladimir said gently, clasping Mrs Roudnikova's free hand by way of support. "I have faith in my boy and Anastaia might be innocent, but she has a lifetime of magical training. I believe she will be able to steer a course through this and that Elena Petrovna will come to our aid when matters really demand it. She has already chosen to communicate with Anastasia and we know how useful she can be when she puts her mind to it."

He leaned further towards Mrs Roudnikova. "This does give us an opportunity we haven't dared dream of in a century. We can finally set aside whatever differences may once have divided our brothers and sisters in diaspora and those who were made to suffer at home. From this point on, nothing should come between us – no ideology or religion, no occult rule or societal allegiance - no matter how small or how trivial, nor how large or seemingly intractable.

"Henceforth we are to be as *One*. We must use all the powers we have at our disposal in service of the chain". He sat up straight in his chair and took a deep breath. He looked around the table. "Vladimir Alekseevich is closest to Madame Blavatsky and can assist with her materialisation, but we're going to need more help. It is time to bring forth the Stone of Cintamani. Serge; you were the last one to touch it. Will you take our petition to the Maharishi?"

By holiness in life, guard the precious Gem of Gems.
Aum Tat Sat Aum!
I am thou, thou art I — parts of the Divine Self.
My Warriors! Life thunders — be watchful.
Danger! The soul hearkens to its warning!
The world is in turmoil — strive for salvation.
I invoke blessings unto you.
Salvation will be yours!

***

In creation realise the happiness of life,
and unto the desert turn your eye.
Aflame with love for Christ,
carry joy to Him[iv].

Aleph-Mem-Shin

Three mothers: Aleph, Mem, Shin: Their basis is a scale of innocence and a scale of guilt and a tongue ordained to balance between the two...a great mystery, concealed.

Sefer Yetzirah, from Saadia's commentary

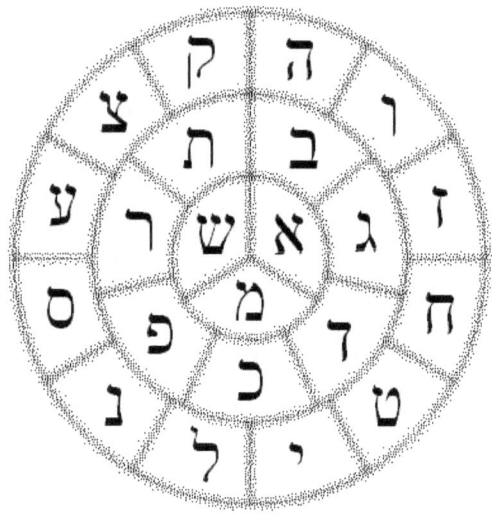

Elena Petrovna

The time is at hand for you to hear us. The threads of the Mother of the World stretch from top to bottom, from the centre to every point of the periphery and, in this centre, their unity is confirmed, which determines the connection between them. Therefore, you cannot love your neighbour without loving God.[lvi] Or vice versa"And we know how you love God and your neighbour, Elena Petrovna! Vladimir Alekseevich added fervently."
"Is it possible to assert a connection between the forms of the periphery and not establish the Principle of the Common Good, whilst rejecting their deep Unity; God? Only by seeking the Truth, by striving for the centre, that is, by loving God, can we vividly and directly feel the connection with our neighbour and work for the Common Good.[lvii]"
Sensing but not seeing her raised eyebrow, he gave a winning smile. "Elena Petrovna. For the Common Good you must prepare to exit Katmandu and end your feud with the Brothers of Amilius. They have sent their emissary – one of my own heirs - to help secure your release. We beg of you to summon whoever you still wish to speak with and say your goodbyes. You will then be free to either move to a higher plane or return to Earth to assist us". He extended a hand around the table. "Your compatriots".
Madame Blavastky reached for her tobacco and rolled a cigarette. She had chosen to remain invisible and all they could see of her was the repugnant animal head and the glowing cherry of tobacco that was dangling at the level of her lips. The pungent grey smoke curled slowly into the atmosphere, framing her massive form in a most disconcerting manner that reminded Vladimir Shmakov of exteriorised ectoplasm.
It wasn't a pleasant sight and he groaned in exaggerated torment, his composure momentarily frustrated. "Madame, I beg you; My nerves are shattered! You know I never quite

recovered from being holed up in that pitiful basement eating nothing but potatoes. If I were American or British I'd – how do they say it – ask you to give me a break".

His words became cajoling. "We just want to *see* you". He looked hopefully around the table and opened his hands again. "We *all* do! You are the mothership - the one who inspired us all – she who opened the doors to the mysteries and brought magic from the East to our Motherland! Look how many of us have stuck together – how the chain has grown – with so many more in perpetual prayer in the Assumption Cathedral. More than 100 years have passed since the critical time. It is time to set things to rights and for us all to make peace with Christ."

His words at that moment proved so persuasive that Madame Blavatsky's bejewelled hands suddenly manifested in response, the ruby shining like a drop of blood by the light of the still-glowing ember.

Vladimir pressed his advantage. "My God, finally! You have no idea how long we've waited. It's over 100 years for us, Elena Petrovna, and even longer for you, I know. The Motherland has missed you. The things that have happened in your absence, I cannot begin to describe. We need you now, more than ever. I suppose you already heard that another madman has seized the city – the entire nation, no less! He would reform the unholy empire; if ever there was a time for the White Guard to reconvene, this is surely it!"

"Here here!" Butator broke into spontaneous applause, the forceful cymbal of his etheric hands accompanied by the sweet contralto of his wife voicing fulsome agreement.

Vladimir Alekseevich smiled appreciatively. "Yes indeed, my friends. It isn't just our Duchess we must save, but all of Russia and all of England. The world, in fact! Let us Renéw our vows! We have waited our appointed years with the patience of saints. Watched as bloody hell was waged with powers that were meant to aid the forces of salvation. We must reassert our control of the EMESH Redivivus[lviii]. Let us

invoke the Astral Lords and Bringer of Light!"
This startling statement was so well received that all those visible stood to their feet and joined in the applause, which steadily built to an enormous crescendo as the souls of their ancestors, the lost and abandoned, the tortured and abused, those who had been starved and fell dead upon the most fertile soil on earth, the armies of the Emperor and elemental energies of Russia's artists and actors, her dancers and musicians, monks and shamans, poets and dreamers, brought together their hands by the dazzling spiritual light of the golden chain which had finally arisen – like dolphins leaping in the ocean - in the upper room of Lost Continents.

Chekov and Marilyn – glorious as Aphrodite in the mesmerising radiance of her singular feminine splendour - returned to the table in a flash, shortly followed by Maria and Valentin. The latter had brought with them the Templar Knight and Medieval lady, who stood behind them as silent sentries. Valentin was so enlivened by the surge of unified piety that he delivered a brief lecture.

"My friends. The time has indeed come for full reconciliation between the Churches of John and Peter, the doctrines of East and West. May we also remember who the redeemed bringer of light is meant to herald," he added gently, peering over his spectacles at those around the table with a kindly smile.

His gaze fell onto Butator. "Lest we get a little too carried away by our reunion, we should acknowledge that your disciples Vadim Karlovich and Evgeny Karlovich – devoted though they undoubtedly were - went too far in pursuit of their goals".

Grigori Ottonovich sighed and nodded slowly. "It is true, Kyot. Those most evil of days took their toll on our boy." He looked around the table. "Vadim Karlovich was a devoted Christian in his youth, he wanted nothing more than to dissolve into blissful union with Jesus Christ, but then the terror came, the men grew older and started to become desperate", he explained to the serious faces and one or two sympathetic nods. "Our arrest hit them very hard". He turned to his wife and they clasped each other's hands. "It became clear that the devils had consolidated power with the help of the American lodge which hated the Tsar and their thoughts turned to revenge. My boys." He sighed again. "Their hearts were in the right place, you know, but their heads were just too strong".

Valentine put a comforting hand on his shoulder. "The circumstances were terrible and I am not here to judge. Even Doctor Steiner was unable to steer their course by that point, for he had already passed over[lix]."

At this point Vladimir Alekseevich could not help but intervene. "It is all the fault of Evgeny Karlovich; it is he who got involved with the Bolsheviks in October[lx]. Vadim Karlovich, on the other hand, rightly understood that they were the antichrist!"

Vsevold Vyacheslavovich held up his hand at this. "Let us speak from experience. I was introduced to Evgeny Karlovich for the first time in spring of 1923. Him and Mr Verevin invited me to participate in their mystical effects in regard to the theory and practice of western and eastern occultism. Prior to meeting with me they were occupied with this task along with Larionov, an engineer-chemist who was also a mystic and specialist in the sphere of symbolism. He likewise had tight and friendly relationships with Sidor – also a Mason, as you know – and some other men known to us. I accepted their proposal and just prior to the new year of 1924 we began to resolve certain mystical questions, until a fracture occurred with respect to the question of how to learn occultism. I then left the Teger-Verevin group."[lxi]

"Really Teger was more of an atheist than a theist and was neglectful of truly spiritual theory. That said, in practical terms he achieved great things and I was able to follow their experiments when Feodor Petrovich Verevin joined EMESH. I cannot help but wonder what the Chekhovski might had achieved if Teger's influence had not polluted their efforts.

Maybe nothing at all, for it was Teger who was able to create the scientific breakthroughs which made that work so effective."

Valentine smiled again. "God forgives all and he also works in mysterious ways. We here are friends and must not judge the actions of others whose circumstances we may not fully understand. One point upon which we are all united without question is our calling to be guardians of tradition:

To be a guardian signifies two things: firstly, the study of a practical application of the heritage of the past, and secondly continuous creative effort aiming at the advancement of the work. For the tradition lives only when it is deepened, elevated and increased in size. Conservation alone does not suffice at all. It is only a corpse which lends itself to conservation by means of mummification.

The great spiritual work - seen always on the historical plane - takes place under simultaneous action stemming from two contrasting sources: from above and from below, ie, under the action of continuous revelation and that of the effort of human consciousness. In other words, it is the product of the collaboration of revelation and humanism, or of Avatars and Buddhas - to say it in terms of the Indo-Tibetan spiritual tradition. This latter awaits both a new wave of revelation, the culmination point of which will be the Kalki Avatar, and the manifestation of a new Buddha, the Maitreya Buddha. At the same time, esoteric Islam (batin) - Shi'ism and Sufism - awaits the coming (parousia) of the twelfth Imam "who, at the end will bring the full revelation of the esotericism of all divine revelations" (Henri Corbin, Histoire de la philosophie islamique) and believing Jews await the coming of the Messiah. We need hardly mention, also, the widespread expectation of the second coming of Christ.

Thus, there is a climate of expectation in the world - expectation sustained, contemplated and intensified through the course of the centuries. Without being nourished and directed from above this energy of human expectation alone would have exhausted itself long ago. But it is not exhausted;

rather, on the contrary, it is growing. This is because it aspires to a reality and not an illusion. And this reality is the historical accomplishment of the great work of uniting spirituality and intellectuality, revelation and humanism, on the vast scale of the whole of mankind.

.....The Avatar is imagined in Indian 'mythology' as a giant with the head of a horse, ie, as a being with the human will of a giant and, at the same time, intellectuality placed completely in the service of revelation from above – the horse being the obedient servant of its rider.

Thus, he represents in prodigious measure three activities of human will: seeking, knocking and asking – conforming to the saying of the Master of all masters, "Ask, and it will be given you; seek, and you will find; knock, and it will be opened to you." (Matthew vii, 7)[lxii].

There was silence for a time whilst those gathered digested the profound words. Serge was the first to speak up. "How good it is to hear from you Valentin; too long you had been silent! You are right to remind us of where the heart of the matter lies and ultimate salvation for all can be found. The astral and mental struggles are not over, but the omnipotent, omniscient and omnipresent Creator in the Holy of Holies cannot be defeated.

"Now I must turn to a task of immense import which affects us all. The wish-fulfilment jewel of Cintimani. May I ask you all to assist me in calling to our gathering the Mahirishi and Elena Ivanovna and praying that they are inclined to fulfil our request for unity between us?

To my Friends - Andrei Bely

He believed in a golden radiance,
And he died from the arrows of the sun.
He measured centuries with his thinking,
But could not live his life — this one.

Don't laugh at the dead poet:
But come, bring him a wreath.
On the cross — winter, summer
There bangs my porcelain wreath.

Its flowers now are broken;
The icon faded gray.
Such heavy stones. I'm waiting
For someone to take them away.

He loved ringing bells and the sunset...
Only this...
Why is it so painful, so painful!
The fault is not his.

Have pity; come — think of me.
I'll rush with my wreath toward you.
O love me — love me.
Perhaps I'm not dead... and I'll wake anew
And come back!

The Castle

My dear friends, it is not the Osiris, but the Isis legend that has to be fulfilled in our time.

The Quest for Isis-Sophia, Rudolf Steiner

Rudolf Steiner, c1882 {{PD-US}}

It was a death-like sleep

That Ana struggled to awaken from. She became dimly aware that she was in a strange bed in a strange room, far from home. A foot wide crack of light entered between long curtains which framed a huge window with great stone lintels on one side of the side of the very large room she was attempting to wake up in. Where in God's name *was* she?
With an even greater jolt of surprise she realised there was a ring on the fourth finger of her left hand. Her wedding finger! Blinking in the half-light she held it up in front of her face and saw that she was wearing her mother's square-cut emerald engagement ring. How strange! She wondered how the ring had got there and decided her father must have given it to her because she was upset. So had her father, Tristan and Marc brought her to this place for safe-keeping?
In that case, why could she not remember anything? Perhaps something had happened during the hollow hill ritual, which she dimly recalled had been discussed over lunch the previous day. She stretched out inside the bed, a luxurious but clearly very old four-poster whose bed linen smelled of lavender. There were more questions. How she'd arrived there? Everything which had occurred since some time yesterday afternoon was lost to the void of hypnosis.
Sighing with frustration at the blank space of her memory, Ana sat up and reached for a tumbler of water that was in easy reach on one of the bedside tables. She took a few sips, then set down the glass and swung her legs over the side of the bed.
Looking down at her feet as she wracked her brains, she was surprised to note – a little startled, in fact – that the hem of her long, white night gown was stained. She pulled on her right ankle to examine the sole of her foot and was shocked to see it was filthy. Clearly she had been outside in the middle of the night in just her nightgown! But why? She suspected it had something to do with the hollow hill but forgot about it

for a moment as unfamiliar sounds began to creep into her ears. She sat still, trying to hear what was happening. There were muffled voices beyond the closed door. Male voices. Ana's body tensed as they paused outside the room and dropped to a whisper, then relaxed again as they moved along without entering. She allowed her toes to touch the rug beneath the bed and padded over to the huge window, wincing as her toes reached the stone flags the rug did not cover. She drew back the heavy embroidered curtains and looked with interest through a second veil of cream antique lace. It was an idyllic scene which greeted her.

Flanking the sweeping arc of an immaculate gravel driveway, which curved around a larger-than-life stone statue of Venus de Milo in the centre of a circular fountain, were jade-coloured strips of perfectly manicured grass and bushes. All this was encircled by a moat of fresh water filled with bullrushes and water-lilies, over which a surprisingly narrow and rickety-looking footbridge stretched towards the statue of Venus. Beyond the moat were acres of green pasture surrounded by tall, broad-leaved trees to the South and East and a wide, dark lake to the North and West. Two beautiful horses – one black and the other pure white - grazed peacefully in the meadow close to the moat, surrounded by a small flock of same-coloured goats. Further beyond, close to a grove of ancient apple trees she spied a few shy deer.

Ana turned back to face the room, which was so completely to her taste that it could have been made for her. Tapestry-covered stone walls with ornate moulded corners swept up to a high ceiling crowned with a magnificent chandelier. Opposite the bed, a huge dressing table topped with an elaborate triple mirror was flanked on either side by floor-to-ceiling shelves. These were stacked with beautifully bound books and a treasure-trove of exotic knick knacks which rivalled Nina Roudnikova's impressive study and drew Ana like a magnet.

She was just examining an exquisitely crafted copper oil

lamp, which appeared to be of great antiquity when the sound of voices elsewhere in the house caught her attention again. She strained to hear what they were saying, the gleaming lamp still nestled in the bowl of her hands with one thumb stroking it thoughtfully, but could make out nothing of either the conversation or identity of the speakers, beyond the fact they were male.

She placed the lamp back down, suddenly feeling apprehensive. Something wasn't right, she decided. Whilst unusual occurrence were a regular feature of her everyday life – and had been for as long as she could remember – a wholesale physical displacement to an unknown place was previously unheard of. She moved uncertainly towards the door but fell shy of actually opening it, unsure of what she would find.

No, she would bide her time a little longer before leaving what felt like the sanctuary of the beautiful bedroom. *Her* bedroom. Removing her hand from the gilt door handle, Ana walked over to a smaller door to the right of the bed – one of two that were on either side of it – and threw it wide open. She caught her breath when she saw what was inside and wondered, not for the first time, if she was inside a waking dream. She was certainly inside a gorgeous walk-in wardrobe. With eyes that had widened in a peculiarly feminine sort of wonder, she feasted on the treasure trove of jewel-coloured silk slips, spotless lace edges and seed-pearl-studded seams. Rows of faintly-scented dresses, skirts and blouses hung above neatly-stacked shoes and slippers, whilst gloves, scarves, handbags and hats nestled in a back-wall of polished square shelves. A peep inside a wide but slender mahogany drawer revealed a metre of exquisite silk underwear separated by tissue paper and clearly brand new. The drawer below it was full of pristine cotton socks and airy silk stockings.

As she closed the closet door behind her thoughtfully, it crossed her mind that she might even have died and gone to heaven. The door on the left of the bed revealed an equally

pleasurable scene. Behind it lay the sort of bathroom that Ana had only ever dreamed of, for ladylike though her great-grandmother undoubtedly was, the apartment above Lost Continents had nowhere near the space for such luxury.
The idea of taking a hot bath while she thought about what to do next was such a tempting prospect that she immediately turned on the taps of the free-standing roll-top tub, which stood on gold paws towards the back of the room. Luxuriating in steam and scented bubbles a short while later, she leant back and closed her eyes with a blissful sigh. Retail was a tough business and Ana couldn't remember the last time she'd lazed around for so long on a Sunday morning.
From somewhere deep within the castle came the strains of a piano – a Chopin Nocturne – which enticed her into a dream-like reverie. The exquisite music pulled her out of her body and towards it with an irresistible magnetic force, until she saw in her mind's eye the man who was playing, as if through a tunnel, or a glass darkly. After an infinite moment of bewitchment he looked up at her and smiled.

Come to me Ana.

***

In Gareth Morgan's house a terrible awakening had occurred. All the occupants were excoriating themselves for having failed to prevent the loss of Ana. There was total confusion about how the kidnap had taken place and the house was in a state of near panic.
There was no sign of forced entry; neither PC Wilby nor the dogs appeared to have noticed her leaving the house. Tristan had slept through the entire thing until almost noon, whilst her father, Marc and Percy, who had returned at dawn, exhausted from their night-time excursions, had slept like logs for the rest of the morning.
Thoroughly enchanted by the miracle of love he had

experienced, Tristan had fallen deep into a lucid dream of sitting alone in a pine forest, communing with nature.

It was, by this time, in pure pleasure and idleness that he picked up a pine-needle to philosophise about it.
"Think of sitting on needles!" he said. "Yet, I suppose this is the sort of needle that Eve, in the old legend, used in Eden. Aye, and the old legend was right, too! Think of sitting on all the needles in London! Think of sitting on all the needles in Sheffield! Think of sitting on any needles, except on all the needles of Paradise! Oh, yes, the old legend was right enough. The very needles of God are softer than the carpets of men."
He took a pleasure in watching the weird little forest animals creeping out from under the green curtains of the wood. He reminded himself that in the old legend they had been as tame as the ass, as well as being as comic. He thought of Adam naming the animals, and said to a beetle, "I should call you Badger."[xiii]

At a certain point in the dream he had been even more overjoyed when the love of his life – his future wife – had emerged from the forest like Eve herself, but a thousand times more radiant. He jumped to his feet and took her up in his arms, spinning her around with a joyous cry.

When they sat down again upon the carpet of needles she plunged right into a conversation as if they'd been speaking of such things all along, as if she had thoroughly read his mind and was now debunking the contents. She held his hand as she spoke, the light of the moon shining brightly in her emerald eyes, which matched the ring she now wore on her finger.

"...It is all very well to talk about love in our narrow, personal, romantic way; but there is something higher than the love of a lover or the love of love."
"What is that?" [he asked] looking down.

"The love of Fate,"....In the Arabian tales, the most perfect prince is wedded to the most perfect princess—because it is fitting...The Turk rides out to wed the fairest queen of the earth; he conquers empires to do it; and he is not ashamed of his laurels." [lxiv]

"Is that not what I did, my love; ride out to win you and claim you as my wife?"

"Alas", she said sadly, tears trembling like dew drops on the upper lashes of her eyes. "Another has come for me and staked his claim. I am lost forever, my love, lost like Scheherazade and now I must survive the night with suffering the same awful fate of the noble virgins of the scorned Sultan's harem."

A terrible sense of horror began to creep over him as she spoke, staring deeply into his eyes as if compelling him to recall the most terrible of memories, the sort that should be banished forever to the pit of hell and guarded by Uriel, lest they tried to come true again. Why was she speaking like this, what was she trying to tell him?

And when he awoke nor spirit nor existence was left him, because of the maiden whom he had seen in his sleep[lxv]

The sound of Tristan shouting had woken the others and all four men met in the landing of the first floor of the house, stumbling into the sound of terror with sleep-stunted incredulity.

Tristan grabbed Gareth Morgan by the shoulders and shook him fiercely. "SHE'S GONE, THEY'VE TAKEN HER!"

Marc clutched his hair in shock. This couldn't be happening. "Am I here?"

He'd unthinkingly said it out loud and Tristan rounded on him. "Yes you're damn well here but Ana-Sophia has *gone*!"

Thus ensued a frantic search of the house and garden, a phone call to PC Wilby and lightning consultation with everyone else they could think of who might have seen something, including the owners of two guest houses which stood opposite the Abbey grounds on Magdalene Street. The mystery only deepened. It was if she had vanished into thin air, like Guinevere kidnapped by faerie folk.

By four o'clock in the afternoon, Marc was feeling as if he'd been hit by a truck, the amazing events of the past week having well and truly caught up with him. The stress of Ana's disappearance and after-effects of the night-long ritual were not the only reasons for him creeping off to have a lie down while the others held a conference. A scratchy feeling in his throat, unusual loss of appetite and slightly feverish feeling were most unwelcome heralds of something he could really do without but had a terrible suspicion.

Coronavirus.

He didn't have one of those annoying tests to hand but he knew in his bones that the dreaded rona had finally caught up with him, just when he'd relaxed his guard and decided it was all over.

After managing to avoid catching anything other than a few house-spiders for over two years, Marc was apprehensively curious to see how the most talked about illness since the AIDS epidemic would affect him. He thought back to his fake vaccinations. Paranoid that the mandatory covid drug was something sinister rather than helpful but forced by his corporate employer to take it or face being sacked, he had managed to find a nurse who was secretly administering saline solutions instead of the proscribed treatment.

Just as he was working himself up into a panic attack in case he died of covid despite – or maybe because of – his lack of an official vaccine, he noticed something sticking out of The Secret Tradition in Arthurian Legend, which had been left on the bedside table. To his surprise, it looked like a letter.

Extracting the folded up note from page 238-9 he read it with mounting incredulity, sat up a little straighter in bed and read it again five times in a row.

Beloved M

SOS!

For heaven's sake, M, I'm in a real flapdoodle and desperate to know when you might be coming. I'm stuck up here with the French doing nothing but play Bridge and frankly I've had enough. The latest thing is they want to get together to remove the blindfold but I won't hear of it. As you and I know full well, the only one who can remove this blasted aberration of occult law is you. Please hurry!

Your devoted servant, E

PS. Don't forget to bring the stone with you.

Marc was thunderstruck by the letter. Who the heck was 'E' and why was she his devoted servant? Who were the Frenchmen and why were they playing bridge? *Where were they* and what did she mean by blindfold?

...

The Musician

Man's greatest wisdom is to choose his obsession well.

Éliphas Lévi, The Book of the Wise[lxvi]

Éliphas Lévi, c1864 {{PD-US}}

Ana stood facing the pianist,

Trying to catch her breath. Her heart was racing wildly and despite the coolness of the spartan room, her palms had become clammy with sweat. A moment earlier he had swept towards Ana like a whirlwind, flashing his long, dark wing ahead of him before swooping down to kiss her on the lips for a great, long moment.
When he stepped back again it was to gaze at her with slightly puzzled expression on his handsome face. It was framed with shining black hair which curled around his ears and neck.

Binsica mors osculi

She felt herself flush as the thought reached her. Not knowing whether to be angry, afraid or something worse, she stared at him dumbly. He had completely taken her breath away. "Have we met before," she murmured, "you seem familiar somehow, I don't know…" she trailed off uncertainly and looked beyond him to the room around them for something that she knew wasn't there.
Having brought her to him, his associates had withdrawn to the back of the room in the ground floor of the castle, which was dominated by a vast stone fireplace, above which hunt the head of great stag. Ana looked up at the beast, which seemed to be watching her with its black eyes, antlers extended, as if ready to charge. She felt extremely vulnerable – naked, even – in the presence of Mr O'Ryan, but did not feel the fear that she knew she should. At least, not fear for her physical safety, though she did fear for something else.
The astral field of the man was the most powerful she had ever experienced and she was disturbed by the realisation that she was strongly attracted to him, as if the knowledge put her at the edge of a precipice. She touched the engagement ring thoughtfully and for some reason her mind drifted to Tristan.

She had always thought she would one day marry him. He was a good man and she knew he loved her and her family, but he had never so much as kissed her. The kiss from this stranger had brought her at once to a new side of life, which excited her as much as she feared it.

"Miss. Morgan…" His voice was like a lover's caress as he fixed a beam from his dancing eyes upon her. "I've been waiting for you for a very long time." He took her left hand in his own and touched the emerald ring with his thumb, twisting it gently. Noticing at once that the ring was a little loose on her finger, Ana felt an inexplicable urge to cry. She pulled back her hand and stepped back a pace.

The man opened his arms. "You must be hungry? Or perhaps you'd like a drink?"

She *was* hungry and she *would* like a drink but she didn't want to tell him that and instead gave him a sharp glance, confused by the maelstrom of emotions now coursing through her veins. The tears dried at the last moment. Ana felt as if she would like to pick a fight with this man.

"How did I get here?" She said quietly, struggling to master the intense shyness which sometimes overcame her. Where is my Father and who are *you*?

Cool and vibrant, without any hint of an apology, the man turned his back and returned to the piano, which he began to quietly play. "My name is O'Ryan. Uilliam O'Ryan." He looked up at her and smiled. "There's no need to worry, Miss Morgan. Your family want you to be safe and I've offered the use of my house. I hope it is to your liking, we took great care over the bedroom."

"It's a lovely house but I don't know why I'm here alone. And who is we?" Ana was dimly conscious that she should have been terrified by the situation, but her rising attraction to Mr O'Ryan – and something else she could not define - was effectively overcoming all other feelings.

"There are six ladies who help me. They are very eager to meet you. It is they who decorated your room and choose some clothes we thought you'd enjoy wearing. I see you are wearing one of the dresses now; you look beautiful.

Ana looked down bashfully at the full length, grass-green silk dress which made her look ever more as if she'd just stepped out of a pre-Raphaelite painting. Clothes, she knew, were a weakness of hers and hardly a day of her life had been spent without somehow dressing up. The music was having an hypnotic effect and Ana suddenly felt like sitting down. Daintily settling down onto the nearest armchair, her eyelids drifted shut as the music washed over her. Mr O'Ryan was an extraordinarily good pianist. "Are you a musician?" she couldn't help asking, although her voice already sounded distant and somehow disembodied, as if it were coming from a place outside her.

He smiled broadly, looking even more dazzlingly handsome than before. "The Pleiades – those seven stars which appear in the sky close to Orion – were the seven daughters of Atlas and the Oceanid, Pleione. When their sisters, the Hyades, died, the Pleiades went mad with grief and killed themselves to form a companion constellation".

The music had become infinitely mysterious, blurring the edges of reality with an unearthly melody. Ana wasn't sure how long she sat been listening, for at a certain point she went through a vortex of time. When she returned the sinking sun was setting the sky ablaze, casting great golden eidolons of Aurora through the windows of the room. The gateway of twilight had opened wide to the world of magic.

***

Propped up on a stack of cushions, sipping at a mug of hot honey and lemon water, Marc opened the Skype programme on his computer and video called his wife. It was mid Sunday morning in America and he expected her to be drinking coffee with a newspaper in the kitchen before taking the twins out for lunch with her parents and sister.

Alice Marconi answered the call on her phone after a few rings. "Hey stranger…" She sounded cheerful. Marc broke the news that he was sick in bed and greedily sucked up the predicted sympathy. There was a pause. "So, I have some more bad news" He put a rueful hand to his head. "They got Ana."

"*What!* Oh my *God!*" the shock in her voice was palpable. First you talk about the weather and your man flu and *then* you land this!"

"I know, I'm sorry," he snuffled miserably. "I'm in denial. It's like I'm in the wrong universe and can't leave; things just keep getting crazier – as if the Queen wasn't bad enough!"

"Yeah you're not kidding," Alice agreed, "it does sound like some kind of parallel universe out there. Kind of like one of the CERN experiments, huh?

Marc groaned. "Oh my gosh, you're right. Wow. I thought I hadn't got that far with the Mandala Effect Module but maybe that last test triggered something…" His eyes began to dart around as his mind raced wildly over the project parameters. He clutched his hair with both hands and started to pant for breath, at which point Alice intervened, sounding a little concerned.

"Relax, honey, I only said it seems like it. Obviously it can't be it, you've not even finished. You guys don't even have the full contract yet, do you?

Marc began to calm down a little. "I guess, yeah. It's just nothing would surprise me now; if you only knew what I went through last night, the things I've seen! Oh my gosh." He groaned again.

"C'mon honey, don't lose it now, I think you are in denial. Surely Ana is the priority for now. Have the police been informed?"

Marc nodded vigorously and tried not to cry. "Yes, yes, we all talked to them and her father and fiancée are downstairs now going through next steps. Meanwhile I'm stuck up here with Rona."

She peered at him. "You don't look really *that* sick to be honest"

He grimaced. "To tell the truth, I've had worse flu, but I need to explain why I can't come into work next week when I call them tomorrow..."

His wife gave an abrupt little laugh. "Well, covid will let you off the hook alright but they're not going to be happy..."

There was a pause while Marc looked down, twiddling his thumbs, waiting for Alice to ask him.

"Is there anything else bothering you?" She could read him like a book.

He sighed dramatically. "I got a letter."

"Oh yeah...what sort of letter?"

"Well, have a look". He produced the note and held it up in front of the camera whilst Alice squinted at it.

"Honey, I can't read it like that," she said. "Except for the E. Who is E?"

Marc puffed out his cheeks and exhaled again. "Meh..."

"What's that supposed to mean?"

"You're not going to believe it." He scratched his head.

"Try me?"

"I think it's from Madame Blavatsky"

.

POKER

By a route obscure and lonely,
Haunted by ill angels only,
Where an Eidolon, named NIGHT,
On a black throne reigns upright,
I have reached these lands but newly
From an ultimate dim Thule—
From a wild weird clime that lieth, sublime,
Out of SPACE—Out of TIME.

Eidolons, Edgar Allen Poe

عبد الواحد يحى

René Guénon, Thiago Maia Verdum

I don't know why

We put up with this sheet," Joséphin muttered under his breath.
Dressed by now in traditional white Bedouin garb, complete with fez, René sighed but remained calm. "Let's just concentrate on winning shall we."
Alphonse nodded ponderously but remained silent, gazing at the cards in his hand.
Joséphin scowled at them both. "You are becoming as bad as 'er, I can't understand it. Remember what she said about you in the Philaletheians, Abbe!"
That earned him a direct stare. "I've told you before, Joséphin, Elena and I are quite reconciled". He looked back at his cards deliberately, "we united over our shared interest in gender equality."
René and Joséphin snorted with incredulity. "I 'ave to 'and it to you, Alphonse, your unabated 'umour and patience are superb.
The Abbe was dressed in his most extravagant ceremonial gear, as was Joséphin, both to startling effect. The latter's beard and hair looked more enormous and luxuriant than ever, whilst the robe of the former was so elaborate it gave him the appearance of Balthasar. Had the three of them been spotted in Café de Paris – anywhere, in fact – people would have stopped and stared. *There go three Magi*, they would have thought. They would have been right, in a way, although it had a long while since any of the three had lit incense, carried out an act of healing or transmuted gold. This was the extent of Madame Blavtasky's sadly inescapable dominance over their schedules at the present time.
They awaited her with varying degrees of annoyance, ranging from almost extreme to almost non-existent. Whatever they were feeling about things, the situation was the same. After recovering from her initial shock, Madame Blavtasky had addressed their request to remove her blindfold in typically

obstinate but also contradictory fashion:
It was *absolutely out of the question*!
Well, in fact, she would *think* about it.
No, she *had* thought about it. They would be allowed to remove the blindfold if – between them - they succeeded in winning 22 out of 33 hands of poker against her as dealer. Also, to make things *a bit more entertaining* for all concerned, they must all come in their best ceremonial dress and she would do the same.

Having entirely lost the power of the moment, which had been rather strong, the three Parisians had, for some reason agreed to another Sisyphian task. Whether out of surprise, resignation, hope or some mysterious occult factor which they did not yet recognise, none of them could say. Sat there now in the White Room – waiting for her to return from her encounter with Ana-Maria-Sophia – each man kept his innermost thoughts well hidden.

Despite – perhaps even because of – this effective cloaking, their thoughts were running along the same path. Something along the lines of
How on Earth are we going to do this;
we're going to have to trick her somehow or we won't win 1, let alone 22.
22 is an interesting number of course, what can she mean?
22 Hebrew Letters.
22 Tarot majors.
22 Arcana.
I agree it has to be significant.
Maybe it isn't, though. Maybe is it just another blind?

Joséphin and Alphonse both considered whether they might employ the powers of the Arcana in service of their cause, whilst René – in a variant on the theme - wondered whether the Magician or the Wheel would be stronger archetypes with which to identify if the test was to be cards.
One transforms work into play and holds the initiatory spark,

but the other might tip the balance of fortune in one's favour.
"Look, this is a team effort, perhaps we need to each take command of an Arcanum and work a little...you know....magic" Alphonse eventually suggested, somewhat furtively.

René spoke up. "If this is really her game she's certain to take the High Priestess, don't you think?"

"Actually, I think she is The Emperor right now, impossible thought that seems", said Joséphin gloomily. "Mrs Roudnikova was very clever in her cut of the cards last week and had a very clear intention in mind by the look of things. The Emperor is the Door, Daleth. In any case, we should convene with their chain for a proper update, we've been stuck here for far too long going round in circles with *Madame*."

"Yes, yes, you are quite right, a revival of the French-Russian alliance is long overdue. Well, one of us must be The Magician, that is clear."

"I'm not sure he's available either, Grigori Ottonovich has adopted that Archetype and I must admit...."

"For heaven's sake! Do you think she's just been distracting us so her people can get all the best positions?"

"You're getting paranoid now Joséphin, they have much bigger concerns than that. We all know she can be wily but Madame has a good heart and you should be more patient."

"I wish I was *playing* patience; I 'ate poker!"

At that moment - just before they got fully distracted by their tarot musings and bickering – a shape began to materialise in the rocking chair that faced them across the table. They watched in an increasingly pained silence as Madame Blavatsky took an inordinate amount of time to fully appear. That she was testing the limits of their patience – and not for the first time – was abundantly clear.

"I'm so sorry to keep you all waiting!" she said cheerfully, as if to rub salt in the wound. "I had a little business to attend to with the Maharishi and Elena. It must be a while since any of you saw them, they said...."

"What kind of business?" said Joséphin, unable to keep the irritation from his voice. "Could it not have waited until we finished this hand?"

"Now now, Joseph, it's a little too early for that isn't it? You know everyone always has to fit in with their schedules, they're always moving around so much."

"It's supposed to be the French who are late," he retorted stiffly.

"I have to admit that it's not ideal to simply disappear without a word immediately after dealing," Alphonse concurred, peering at Madame Blavatsky with mild disapproval. "We've hung around so long that we were starting to inhabit the major Arcana. Not that there are many of them left to claim."

Her eyes twinkled in delight at that. "Oh, how marvellous! You see, if I hadn't left you alone all this time you would never have had such fun. Anyway, we need to start over again."

"And why is that?" countered René hotly, looking down at the three of a kind he was holding.

"I'm expecting another player," she said and then looked down shiftily, as if embarrassed, when they all stared at her in amazement.

"Who!" René eventually managed.

"Oh, you know...." She replied, taking a pinch of tobacco from the fox's head.

"NO!" they all chorused.

"Well never mind you'll soon find out. In the meantime let's think a bit more about those Majors shall we?"

Before they could deliver an adequate response to this new trick of the Madame's, a dramatic alteration in the energy field of the White Room caught their attention. The three mages got to their feet and took a step back from the table as a large male form shuddered in and out of view, before disappearing entirely for several long moments and finally reappearing with an astral flash which took them by surprise.

Who could this newcomer be?
As he lay in bed wracking his brains and thinking about blindfolds, Marc had a sudden epiphany. He recalled with Eureka-like triumph the intensely disturbing sight of Madame Blavatsky grinning up at him from Mrs Roudnikova's round table. Far from making things clear, however, the discovery of the author of the letter only served to intensify his confusion and raise more questions. Most importantly, why did she think that he was the one to remove the blindfold and how was he to do it?

At a loss as to how he might even approach these questions he began to aimlessly search the internet for inspiration. The online newspapers, which gave the impression that nothing whatsoever was happening on Earth apart from the Queen's funeral, soon had him approaching a zombie-like state. Perhaps Youtube would offer up something different?

As soon as he opened the video sharing website he remembered something: Hadn't Olivia said that her show was on Youtube? He closed his eyes and tried to remember the name of it. The large 'X' that was printed on her business card appeared before his eyes and he reached for his wallet on the bedside table. He soon found the card and turned it over.

X

Dark Journalist

Following a quick search easily found the channel, which was also distinguished by a prominent 'X' on the profile picture and many of the video thumbnails. He scrolled through the show titles with mounting excitement. This was his cup of tea:

The AI Transhumanist Nanotech, Antarctica UFO Secrets & Alien Invasion Op; The Bearer Bonds Mystery: Secret

Finance & The UFO File; Nazis in Space: Von Braun JFK and the UFO Invasion; Secret Systems & Hidden Forces; The JFK Assassination: 57 years of Deep State Deception; Russel Targ SRI Star Gate Remote Viewing Revealed: Psychic Surveillance; Corporate Media goes full Big Brother; Robert F Kennedy Jr. Medical Tyranny Big Pharma Bill Gates AI Immunity Passport Surveillance State!

All in all it was quite a list and Marc had quite had trouble deciding where to jump in. Eventually settling on the Russel Targ interview, he pressed play on the video and lay back to listen, hoping that some blue-sky thinking would reveal the path to Madame Blavatsky's mysterious blindfold.

Aaand we are live; you're watching the Dark Journalist show, what a fantastic crowd we have out there in the idea's room – and we are of course joined by the lovely Olivia..."

"Hi everybody!"

...I'm always happy to talk about the remarkable work we did at SRI during the Cold War....Remote viewing is a kind of psychic phenomenon, I can do quite a lot with your local awareness....you can find a lost bracelet, you can describe a weapon's factory in Soviet Siberia, you can look at atomic dimensions as the Theosophical Society was interested in doing. At the end of the 19th century it gave the first accurate description of what a proton would look like. The Theosophical researchers Annie Besant and Charles Leadbeater described protons and the triangular form of quarks and 100 years before they were described as quarks and gluons. I published that in the Reality of ESP, photographed it right of the 1895 magazine called Lucifer[lxvii].

......Madame Blavtasky was a pioneer....she was aware of the periodic table which had just been discovered in England and said 'we should get a psychic periodic table'.....

....The more you hide something the more it shines like a beacon in psychic space....[lxviii]

... We now know that every day Price would meet with his Scientology auditor, or on the phone or by mail, and tail that auditor what they had done. The reason we know this is that two years later the IRS broke into the Scientology celebrity centre and found a file folder of documents from Pat Price describing the top secret things he was doing. So we know absolutely that every day he was doing these top secret spying things for the CIA he was handing this in to Scientology[lxix]*...Pat definitely died mysteriously; he was on his way to see us.... The Russians knew this was going on.*

His great fascination with the contents of the Dark Journalist show did not prevent Marc, in his Covid-weakened state, from drifting off into another state of consciousness. He didn't exactly fall asleep but he certainly left his body – and not for the first time in the past week. This time it was different, though. In place of a wondrously lucid, magically unfurling realm was nothing much at all.

At first he flickered between states, zoning in and out of the interview playing on his computer, back into his body and then out again into the *other* place.

Gradually the other place took prominence and pulled him into it entirely. If only there was something to see in there, some way of getting his bearings. Strange, Marc thought, everything is just...*White*.

René, Joséphin and Alphonse believed they were well acquainted with all the mages of the past few thousand years – from Pythagoras and Plotinus to Wellesley Tudor Pole and Gareth Knight via Raymond Lull and John Dee – but this was a first-timer, to be sure. As the astral whirls subsided and the figure came more fully into focus they stepped forward half a pace and as one man leaned forward to get a better look. Their first impressions weren't wholly positive.

Looks untidy; What kind of clothing is that supposed to be? [Marc was barefooted and wearing his dressing gown]*; His beard is a mess; he's disorganised; I think he might be American...*

The second impressions were rather more favourable to their critical eyes, which nevertheless sought out the positives in the spirit of honest enquiry.*This man has a great ancestor. He is well meaning and open-minded. I believe I see the mantle of the Fool somewhere in his aura. Nice ring!*

"Welcome Mr Marconi. Or should I say: M.

The Mem Key

For the majority of human-beings the Tifaret-to-Da'at pathway (ie, the Mem pathway) represents a spiritual hiatus in human consciousness. Activating Tifaret's link with Da'at bridges the gap that currently exists in consciousness between Humanity and the Creator. Without the covenant of Da'at we're lost in exile on planet Earth, unaware of the divine Prescence (Shekinah) in our lives.

Patrick Mulcahy, Sefer Yetzirah Magic

M 1

There was an universal exclamation from the Frenchmen, who stared at Madame Blavatsky in outright incredulity.
"How can he be M, I thought M was Moraya!"
"Alois Mailander, the Germans said![lxx]"
"M___', surely…"
Marcus Marconi was also amazed at the claim and not for the first time wondered: "Am I here?"
Delighted at the sensation she had caused, Madame Blavatsky grinned broadly. "Isn't it fascinating to consider all the great Ms there have been over time; it's something I've often reflected upon. I even made a list; would you like to hear who's on it?"
Before they had time to either accept or decline her invitation, HPB launched into a startling consideration of all the Mages in history who heralded from the Mother letter Mem:
"I have a special name for all this, you know, it's called The Mem Key".
Recovering from their earlier reluctance, this kabbalistic reference piqued the interest of all four members of her audience, one of whom inquired: "I must admit that sounds rather interesting, where did you get the idea from?"
"From another M of course!" she cried triumphantly. "Patrick Mulcahy, who is alive and well in Australia and also rather good at horoscopes. His book, Sefer Yetizrah Magic is simply marvellous; he brings a unique insight to the structure of the Tree of Life through his new interpretation."
As they silently digested this unusual nugget of information she proceeded through the list. "So, there are the ones you already mentioned of course – Moraya, Mailander, M___, Mahachohan, Manu, Maitreya and the Maharishi - but a better starting place would be Melchizedek," she began with great confidence.
"But that's not all," she continued, "We've also got no less than *Moses*, Jacob's first son, Manasseh, Esther's guardian,

Mordecai, the messenger Malachi and Archangel Michael, the Blessed Virgin Mary, Mary Magdalene and Martha, the Mage Melchior and Saints Marc and Matthew. Also Mary the Jewess and Mary Queen of Scots. Marilyn and Serge, of course - and Marie Antoinette."

She paused to ensure they were listening, which they were, with all four men now seated across the table with their eyes fixed on her. "Good, now there are more we could name from the Old and New Testaments but I won't go into all those right now, I'll jump straight onto the modern era. You've already named one of them and we also have Martinez de Pasqually and Louis-Claude de St Martin, Gustave Meyrink Samuel Liddell MacGregor Mathers and Moina. And let us not forget the Titan of my Fatherland, Mebes or his contemporary in England, Theodore Moriarty. Or, indeed, Franz Mesmer, Arthur Machen, Mary Heath, Stainton Moses and my esteemed compatriot, Anna Rudolfovna Mintzlova". "Despite her many faults", she added sniffily.. In the Middle Ages she would of course have been burned as a witch in a bonfire, but not one person that once is drawn to her remains the same as he was before[lxxi]."

"Sounds very much like someone else I can think of," Joséphin muttered balefully under his breath.

"Well she *did* try to copy me, Joséphin, you're right about that," HPB admitted. "Albeit not quite so successfully. It would have been better for her if she'd stuck to my system instead of following Dr Steiner up the garden path. Her abrupt vanishment from Moscow was a masterstroke nonetheless." "Michaelangelo, Miro, Moreau, Mondrian," interjected René before she could swing further off on this tangent.

She gave him a penetrating look from beyond the blindfold. "Yes indeed. Nor should we forget Marduk or the one we shouldn't mention, otherwise known as the Black Alchemist. Which brings me onto Morgan, Morgawse and Mordred. I toyed with the idea of admitting Karl Marx" she raised her a finger in warning before they could protest, "but decided against it. On the other hand, we should probably accept Charles Manson as a candidate on the dark side. And Malo, of course," she added fondly. "Not that he's in any way dark. Ana-*Maria* and the rest of the Morgan clan also fit the bill, as does Maria Dorogova."

After going on in this vein for a short while longer she finally put down the paper and began to roll a cigarette.

There was a brief pause before Joséphin spoke up, sounding pained. "Is that it? It is an impressive list of names, to be sure – and I suppose there must be something in the 'M' theory - but we could do a good list for the 'As, and Ss', as well – not to mention the Ps and Js - most letters in fact! What's the *point* of all this, Elena?"

"The *point*, Joséphin, is the Mem Key!" she said passionately. "And the fact that we finally have Mr Marconi here with us. I thought that if I mentioned that there were other Ms out in the field it would help him rise to the challenge".

As Joséphin put his head in his hands on the table, Alphonse and René turned towards the new arrival. Alphonse greeted him first. "Welcome Mr Marconi, I'm pleased to make your acquaintance."

"Likewise, thank you," Marc managed.

"I assure you this is a shock for us as well, Mr Marconi. Who can predict the ways in which the Spirit will blow!" said René politely, but with more than a hint of irony. "What do *you* think about this 'M' business."

Realising with instantaneous alarm this was his cue to say something brilliant and thereby justify his existence, Marc blurted out the first thing that came to mind. "Yeah, it's interesting, I can't help thinking of the, uh, Mandela effect."

"**AHA!**" Madame Blavatsky exploded, making them all jump. Noticing that the mouths of the Frenchmen had all fallen open, Marc assumed he had said something stupid and tried to row back. "What I mean is, it's been on my mind because of work and, err…"

"No, no, no, Mr Marconi, you should trust your inner guide,

you've hit upon something that none of us would have thought of, which is precisely why you are 'M'!"
"Tell us about the name, Marconi; are you any relation to the Marquis?".
Another curveball. "Gee, I don't think so, although I have to say he's a hero of mine because there's so much *magic* in the radio system. Mercury got it right when he sang: '*I heard it on my radio.*' I heard it on mine too!" Marc gave a chuckle, pleased with himself for holding up a conversation, and was surprised again to see that the eyes of Frenchmen showed a new respect. Their silence egged him onto what were hopefully new heights of brilliance.
"Marconi demoed the system in 1896 for the British government and managed to transmit signals for several miles across Salisbury Plain. Over Stonehenge, how cool is that! The year after he sent the first wireless communication over open sea. Do you know what it said?"
They all shook their heads
"It said, '*Are you ready*'" Marc replied with a grin, thoroughly enjoying himself by now.
"After sending the world's first radio message across the Atlantic, in January 1903 Marconi sent greetings from President Roosevelt to King Edward VII in England. When his invention was used to help rescue survivors of the sunken Titanic, his star really started to rise. By 1914 he was a Senator in the Kingdom of Italy and Honorary Knight Grand Cross of the Royal Victorian Order in Britain.
"In later years Marconi began to wonder whether his invention was a force for good or evil. His device became an essential part of the Great War effort as Italy joined on the side of the allies. He rose through the ranks of the Italian army and was ultimately made a marquess by King Victor Emmanuel III.
"Then, even more interesting, perhaps, we have the connection between developing radio technology and the Spiritualist movement."

There was a collective intake of ether when Marc made this statement and the dazzling location of the White Room flexed and shimmered in sympathy.

"To put it in context: by the late 19th century, new communication technology made people think about devices which might enable contact with the spirit or alien worlds. Long-distance communication by electrical means was seen as somehow analogous to spirit communications. As happened in Morse code, for example, spirits at seances gave messages via encoded knocks and raps.

"To put the icing of the cake we have the fact that many of those involved in the creation of telecomms were also involved in the investigation of supernatural and psychic phenomena. Phenomena such as telepathy, telekinesis and teleportation were also taught – as I'm sure you're all aware – within occult lodges worldwide, especially in Russia, where there is a native affinity for psychic arts.

Poor Vadim Karlovich, thought Madame Blavatsky mournfully, though not forcefully enough to divert attention from Marc's amazing monologue.

"Sir Oliver Lodge published a book about séances held with his deceased son Raymond, whilst Edison said that he wanted to create 'an apparatus to see if it is possible for personalities which have left this earth to communicate with us'. I discovered recently that my great grand-father kept a copy of Edison's autograph in his notebook[lxxii]," Marc added proudly.

"So, Marconi's invention arrived in the midst of the Spiritualist and Theosophical movements, which brought a very special context to the notion of communication over long distances; as if from out of nowhere or thin air. The logical progression was to attempt communication with aliens and especially Martians. By the 1920s there was a lot of speculation that Martians were trying to make contact via radio signals. In fact, there was even a Hollywood movie about that quite recently, called Contact. You know the one, starring the Scientologist, Jodie Foster? I love that film!"

Met with an unsettling silence, Marc felt he had no choice but to keep spilling beans, as if he'd been simultaneously hypnotised and triggered by the question itself.

"Even Marconi claimed to be receiving strange transmissions resembling Morse code, which he said could have been from outer space. This is similar to a claim made by Tesla in 1899 after he interpreted a series of long-distance wireless signals as originating from outer space, maybe even Mars itself. By the mid-1920s there were multiple attempts to reach Mars from Earth using radio technology. A Martian woman called Oomaruru was apparently discovered and spirit trumpets or mediums were used to channel messages from Martians."

The thread was getting too long and Marc began to trail off. "I think that's it. Boy, I feel like I've been talking for ages."

A slew of questions immediately followed his pause:

Is radio technology facilitating communication between humans and beings of the subtle realms?

Have you contacted Martians?

Didn't Valentin have something to say about the electrical agent being a vehicle of the anti-Christ?

Yes, he contrasted electrical devices with the true astral light, indicating that it amplified the false light. He was in a position to know this for sure, of course, as he spent so long intercepting radio messages sent by the communist propaganda machine.

Before this conversation (which all the men found rather interesting) could continue, Madame Blavatsky waved her cigarette to get their attention. "That's very good; thank you Mr Marconi. You can get rid of the blindfold now."

They all stared at her with mouths agape. Joséphin recovered first. "What, just like that; are you kidding me?!"

René raised his eyebrows again. "We do have to wonder what all those games were about, Madame!"

Alphonse twiddled his thumbs and gave her a searching look. He had long since given up trying to make sense of her method, although he continued to suspect that she had one,

chaotic though it might appear. "That's good news Elena, we're glad you're finally ready. He turned to Marc with a quizzical smile. "I assume you know how to proceed?"
Even in his disembodied state Marc felt his eyes widen. He was still puffed with confidence from his surprisingly successful lecture and didn't want to lose the advantage. Perhaps this was one of those moments when winging it with bravado was the best solution.
"Sure," he said lightly, reverting to the mode he adopted with his team leader at AstroLink. As he got to his feet he had the uncanny sensation that an unseen force was guiding him. "I'll just go right ahead. Yep."
The Frenchmen, who were staring at him with inscrutable expressions, nodded together, as if their heads were joined together by a single string. This was a test alright, he thought. Madame Blavatsky, on the other hand, had her blindfolded eyes angled down towards the table and appeared distracted, nervous, even. He had the feeling that she was vulnerable and needed his protection, which made him feel as if this was his personal quest in life and there was no possibility of failure.
He began to step around the table and behind her chair, moving slowly in case the extra time brought some new revelation. It didn't. He looked curiously at the blindfold. So curiously, in fact, that the pressure of the moment left him completely. As he leaned forward to get a better look he was unaware that the expressions on the faces of the Frenchmen turned from a mixture of scepticism and annoyance to one of astonishment and mystification.
As he scrutinised the unutterably arcane bind, which resembled in its blackness the depths of a black hole, he became strongly aware of the ancestral signet ring on the forefinger of his right hand. He had the distinct impression that the ring was somehow connected with the blindfold and he held up his hand to look at it. To his surprise the stone was also shimmering, as if it were alive, with just as much intensity as the blindfold but a very different kind of energy.

The amazing stone seemed to embody all the elements in volatile shifts of light-flame, light-water and light-air, flashing within the circle of finely wrought copper, embraced by a mysterious substance, brighter than lightening.
"You've got it…good". HPB's voice was unusually calm and serious, the tone she normally reserved for her Master and very rare moments with her most trusted confidantes. It was the tone which brought Marc round again, for he had just begun to slip into a form of hypnosis, drawing him further into the ring. He dropped his hands and stood up straight again. "Yes."
"Good." She repeated meditatively. "And I've got this…" She reached into a pocket of her voluminous dress and extracted an object which she held up in the palm of her hand for all to see.
The others present gasped involuntarily; the three Frenchmen because they knew exactly what it was and could hardly believe their eyes; Marc because he didn't' have a clue what it was but it bewitched him entirely. René, Joséphin and Alphonse leapt to their feet and leaned over the table to get a better look, exclaiming their astonishment:

"*Mon Dieu! C'est la pierre de Cintamani!*"
"*Manœuvre de genie!*"
"*La victoire est assurée!*"

Madame Blavtasky reverted to her usual acerbic tone. "It's very impressive, I know, but I'm surprised you had nothing to say about the fragment of Tuaoi that M just produced!"
The Frenchmen gawped at him as Marc took his right hand from his pocket and stretched it out to show them, somehow masking his own surprise and resolving that he would henceforth act as if all this were normal. A stir of imperiousness prodded him, at which moment Madame Blavatsky raised her voice a little.
"That's enough now, can we get on with it please?"

"Oh yeah, sure," said Marc, a little embarrassed by his own pride. Reaching out experimentally, he lightly touched the knot in the hollow of the base of her skull. Whatever bizarre material it was made of felt unutterably strange between his fingers and he tried not to notice that the others were all frozen to the spot. He closed his eyes but could still see both the blindfold and the stone through the back of his eyelids.

At that moment the words of his great grandfather, Vladimir Shmakov, echoed in his mind:

"Using the method of 'conscious ignorance', you can completely concentrate the power of your will and all your cognitive abilities on one particular problem....and it is quite clear, of course, that the more perfect a person's instantaneous consciousness is, the more information he can gather in a unit of time."

Marc had the definite sensation that a wave of light which began at his feet was washing over his body like a second skin, driving all thoughts or emotions from his consciousness, as if perfecting his will. The words *I AM HERE* popped instantly to mind, as if it was the first objective thought he'd had about himself in his life. He was conscious of the intrinsic balance inherent in every single atom of his being. A being comprised of *Protons, Neutrons, Electrons, Quarks, Gluons, Astral Light, Ether and Spirit.*

An image of Anastasia came strongly to his mind, smiling with shining eyes. She was wearing a long, white-green robe with embroidered sleeves and her hair was swinging loose about her shoulders.

In the periphery of his inner-eye vision he saw a white and apparently disembodied arm hold aloft a great sword. With its blade flashing brilliantly like a light sabre, Marc tracked the path of this sword with a sense of finality, as it was first lifted high into the air and then brought down with devastating force upon the crown of his head.

The effect was akin to the splitting of the atom, as if he had been struck by lightening. As white light exploded everywhere in his skull it felt as if a previously unused part of his brain - the whole of the left half, it seemed – suddenly came awake – was *activated* – and that this was his *female* side. Not female in any kind of sexual way; in fact, all sense of sexuality was obliterated in that moment. It was more like the two polar sides of his entire inner being were balanced and as one, both unifying and multiplying his being at precisely the same moment. It was as if the splitting of his mind had resulted in the balancing of the poles within him.

The effect of this seemingly miraculous change in condition was experienced as an infinitely and very rapidly extending fountain of energy. Kind of like a nuclear reaction.

Realising with mounting fear that he was being mind blown, Marc gave way to the rising fear that his body – *even his soul* - might spontaneously combust, until the urgent sound of Madame Blavatsky's voice brought him round.

"M! The Blindfold!"

AAAH, THE BLINDFOLD!

Her words were like thunder in his mind! Marc had just enough time to see his ring flash with an unearthly sort of blue-white-lavender-green as he pulled his hands – each of them grasping one side of the blindfold – open, up and away from Madame Blavtasky's head.

"LIGHT IN EXTENSION!" chorused the Frenchmen, which stunned Marc even further as he stood there with his arms akimbo, the abyssal ribbon stretched out between his hands.

What do I do with it now! He wondered, at which moment the astral form of a dove, or maybe a pigeon, swooped down from out of nowhere, took the thing in its beak and disappeared back into nothing.

"Thank you Henry!" Mrs Blavatsky said in satisfaction, followed by. "My oh my, I'd forgotten about *this*…"

A Miracle

All saints revile her, and all sober men
Ruled by the God Apollo's golden mean –
In scorn of which I sailed to find her
In distant regions likeliest to hold her
Whom I desired above all things to know,
Sister of the mirage and echo..

Robert Graves, The White Goddess

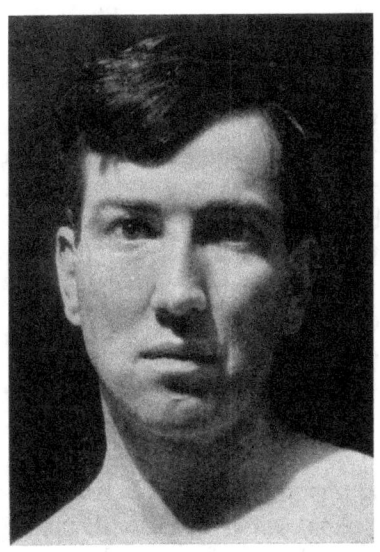

Robert Graves, 1929 {{PD-US}}

It's a miracle

I'm even here at all. Ana. I believe my views on Spiritism and communication with astral shells are widely reported to this day! I must admit, though – especially given the present circumstances - that I *may* have been a bit off the mark as clearly it IS possible to communicate with the deceased." She paused whilst she considered this further. "It's just debatable whether ALL the deceased can do what myself and the others – you know, Alphonse and that lot - are capable of. It depends on the crystallisation of your astral shell, you see. Hmm, yes…"
Madame Blavatsky was saying a bit more than she'd intended because Ana – currently perched on a window seat in the bedroom – was staring at her in white-faced shock, apparently unable respond. It was surprising, really, as Madame Blavatsky would have thought Ana was well-used to seeing ghosts. Or was she?
The wide-eyed clueless look was starting to annoy her. HPB didn't have much patience at the best of times and this was getting silly. "For heaven's sake, Anastasia, pull yourself together! it's not like this is the first time you've seen a spook! What do you think all those people in your great grandmother's upper room are?"
Stop it you'll frighten her! The urgent whisper in Mrs Blavatsky's right ear came too late, for Ana had collapsed on the floor in a dead faint. *I told you we should go easy; she hasn't got over whatever it was they hypnotised her with!*
Marc, who was present in his astral form and therefore invisible to Ana, experienced a disturbing combination of irritation with the newly freed Madame and anxiety for Ana's plight. He was ill at ease in the Castle and did not want to contemplate what might happen if O'Ryan or the other Necromancer caught him there.
Madame Blavatsky nodded as she leaned over the prostrate Anastasia. "Yes, I know, but we're running out of *time*; she

has to *wake up*! Go and rattle that wooden stool around, will you, the noise might rouse her?"
Tutting in displeasure, Marc did as bidden, kicking over the stool in frustration and surprising himself at the force he was able to exert in his astral state. There was a loud clatter followed by a soft moan from the feminine heap on the floor beneath the window. He rushed back across the room as Ana sat up slowly with her eyes still closed and leaned against the window seat. "Just give me a moment please," she murmured. Mrs Blavatsky manifested the fox head and retreated to an armchair beside the fireplace to roll a cigarette, whilst Marc became absorbed in the fine collection of antiques and ephemera which adorned the beautiful tower room. There was a knock on the door which made all three of them jump.
"Are you alright in there?" Nobody recognised the suspicious-sounding male voice which came from behind the door.
"I'm fine thank you!" Ana called back anxiously. "I just bumped into the stool while I was getting dressed."
There was an uncertain pause and then the sound of footsteps walking away. Ana stood up and tiptoed over to the door. After a while she turned back to Madame Blavatsky. "Can you please not do that again, I don't want to make them suspicious, I'm in enough trouble as it is!"
"That wasn't me," she corrected, blowing a smoke ring and ignoring the small explosion of tuts and sighs from the direction of the bookshelf.
Ana gaped at her. "Who was it then?"
"That's Mr Marconi," answered Madame Blavatsky with satisfaction, before she could be silenced.
"Marc!" Ana gasped.
"Yes. He released me from occult imprisonment a short while ago, so here we are! You're lucky you know, this is my *first real outing* since the grand unveiling. Mr Marconi's great grandfather has been begging me to show myself for years but here I am with you, entirely unbidden."

"Why can't I see him?"
Madame Blavatsky wafted smoke around. "Oh, you know, it's because he's in his astral body but he's not yet passed over. He'll have to go back soon. Anyway, he says hello and that he hopes you're alright. He's here to help," she added, hoping it would calm the younger woman.
Ana sat down on the bed and gave a wan smile. "Hi Marc, I'm glad you're here, this is a lot to take in. I know this will sound bizarre but I actually feel at home here. The castle is awesome and Mr O'Ryan is so…"
"Attractive?" said Mrs Blavatsky with a raised eyebrow. She stubbed out the cigarette and started to roll another.
Ana blushed and looked down. "I suppose he is, yes. I've never met anyone quite like him before and Mrs Pixley told me to look out for someone with dark wavy hair."
"It's not the first time you've met him." Madame Blavatsky's voice was heavy with irony as she lit the second cigarette.
"What do you mean?!" Ana heard desperation mingling with hope in her own voice and wondered where it was all coming from. She didn't think she had been quite so keen to find a man but maybe Mrs Pixley's talk of a mysterious dark haired 'someone' had affected her more than she realised.
"You two have quite a past…" HPB began recklessly, although she soon began to row back as she sensed the intensity of longing which emanated from the younger woman. "But it's nothing for you to worry about. Well, you *should* be worried actually, but…oh fiddlesticks, I'm getting this all wrong, it's so long since I've been out you know!"
"I do feel connected to him in some weird kind of way," said Ana dreamily. "I've been sat here thinking about him, it's like he's in my head." *I've even been fantasising about him* she thought guiltily, knowing this was extremely dangerous.
Good God! HPB and M thought simultaneously. The situation was worse than anyone could have imagined.
"Hmm", HPB managed. "You need to be very careful there, you wouldn't want to generate larvae, they can be horribly

powerful and damned hard to get rid of." She fixed Ana with a penetrating stare. She kept hoping to somehow dehypnotise the girl, but she insisted upon staring into space at Mr O'Ryan. "Can you remember anything about how you got here," she added carefully.

Still avoiding her eye, Ana stood up and walked back over to the window, wringing her hands. "I keep trying but I can't remember anything that happened after lunchtime yesterday. You know..." she turned to look around the room for where Marc might be. "Around the time that you, daddy and the others had the ceremony?"

Mrs Blavatsky nodded whilst Marc whispered something in her ear. "Hmm, yes....OK." She turned again to Ana. "I don't suppose you remember whether or not *Tristan* went with them?"

There was something so pointed in her tone of voice that it triggered the start of a memory in Ana, who twisted the Emerald ring unconsciously. "I'm not sure," she began uncertainly. "Didn't he go with them?"

There was another pause whilst Madame Blavatsky nodded along to whatever Marc was saying to her. "No, it seems that Tristan stayed behind with *you*. That's a beautiful ring, my girl, where did you get it?"

Ana stared at her hand. "It's my mother's...."

"Yes it was your mother's; God rest her soul". She leaned back to take a long, hard puff of the cigarette before flicking the end into the fireplace. "How did you *get* it?"

A penny finally dropped and Ana put the ring hand up to her mouth in shock. A flicker of memory had returned. The warmth of the fire, Colin's Jack Russell snoring peacefully, a glass of her father's excellent claret, rose-scented candles. "Tristan!" She exclaimed, looking up at Madame Blavatsky, who nodded back slowly. "Yes, Ana...Tristan. The knight in shining armour who picked you up in the early hours of the morning to drive you to Glastonbury. Your childhood friend. Your father's faithful helper. Mrs Pixley's favourite. The man with dark wavy hair. Your *fiancé*." Goodness gracious, the girl was a perfect dolt!

Ana sat back down with a haunted look in her eyes as the trickle of memories turned into a flood. Marc sat down beside her for moral support. As the father of adolescents who weren't much younger than her, he felt intense compassion for her plight.

Allowing a moment for things to fall back into place, Madame Blavatsky rolled another cigarette and smoked it in silence before speaking up again. "I know this is difficult Anastasia, but we're here to help you through this. I didn't spend 150 years in psychic limbo for nothing; I'm here to ensure that the Chain remains unbroken. Which means I'm going to get you out of this pickle. Your karma is *not* to be stuck in a jar for souls!"

Her eyes bored into Marc for a second. "When M wakes up from his fever he's going to tell your father and Tristan exactly where they can find you. All you and I have to do is sit tight until they get here, which is going to require a bit of intelligence given how determined your suitor is. You must carry on as if you know *nothing*. As if Mr O'Ryan's magical seduction technique is still working a treat."

She gave Ana quizzical look and won a heated blush by way of response. "He IS using magic you know; it should be blatantly obvious that he's cast a spell on you!" Ana merely looked starstruck in response to this and Madame Blavatsky felt increasingly concerned. *Its worse than I imagined,* she thought in silence, *the girl is completely smitten. Those past life ties can be damn hard to break. Thank God I never had to go through anything like this and goodness knows everything else was thrown at me.*

She broke off her reverie and bored her eyes back into Marc. "Your work here is done, M. You have served us both remarkably well and I shan't forget. You are most definitely in for a promotion! If I need you again I shall write but now you must rally the troops. You have to get them here before the Queen's funeral. I have a feeling the Necromancers will bring forward their Equinox rite in an attempt to divert the energy of the folk soul of the nation along their dark pathway. It's a risky gamble on their part but with Pluto in Capricorn the rewards are so great they will find it hard to resist."

Marc stood up at once. His astral body was already starting to flicker as his physical self began to awaken from its heavy slumber.

Goodbye Ana; goodbye Madame Blavatsky. Please take care. Our thoughts will be with you...and don't worry:

I'll be back.

Night School

In the astral plane there is to be seen an emanation of the eternal, having neither a beginning nor an end, as it is timeless and spaceless. The adept who sees his way about this plane may find everything here, no matter if the point in question be in the past, the present or the future.
How far this perception will reach depends on the degree of his perfection.

Initiation into Hermetics, Franz Bardon

Franz Bardon, 1948

It's almost time

To go to bed, Anastasia. We can't have a re-run of last night, you had rather a narrow escape."

Ana blushed and stared ahead, not trusting herself to speak in case she uttered the truth: She *wanted* a re-run of the night before, although she also permitted her rational mind to answer to this desire. How often had she been warned about the Realm of Maya, Zone of Delusion and Belt of Lies? She knew that spiritual tests came like this but still the thing she knew to be a lie was presenting itself to her as the most profound truth, as if it were exactly what she had always sought, without even realising it.

Madame Blavatsky sighed, reading her thoughts, and rolled a cigarette. O'Ryan had made a very determined approach into Anastasia's dreamworld in the guise of a magical eagle, but she had mounted an effective resistance by reverting to the invincible state of childhood. It had been a wholly spontaneous response to the astral proximity of her soulmate, which had thrown him off course through the power of innocence and casta powerful shield. As the sword of Ana's Guardian Angel smashed into him O'Ryan had metamorphosed into rather a ridiculous black anaconda, which had sent Anastasia scurrying out of his reach. It had all been rather thrilling and Ana could not forget the unmatched experience of encountering her male soul. She wondered what might have happened if the Eagle had captured her Child.

HPB took a big puff of her cigarette. "He's going to up the ante. You need to be mentally prepared for your past life recall. He's got all his people working on it so I've decided we need some reinforcements." She fixed Ana with an icy stare. "It's time you went to Night School. I have summoned a teacher to your dreams and the course will be tonight. As well as strengthening your mind, the presence of a Master teacher will prevent O'Ryan from attempting to capture you in a dream. They're even harder to resist in the astral, as you're starting to discover. You'll have a devil of a time when *that one* next comes calling!"

Ana looked at her plaintively. "Why won't you tell me what I was and why I'm here?"

"It's against the law" said HPB with regret. "Karma has decreed that you shall be recalled, so all we can is try to make sure you don't repeat the same mistake again. It changed the course of history, you know?" she added conversationally.

How maddening! Ana thought, wondering what on Earth might justify the extent of the drama that surrounded her.

"Don't worry," HPB added, reading her mind. "You'll find out soon enough.

"Have you ever had anything like this happen," Ana asked her. "You know, some kind of soul mate thing that turns your life upside down?"

The question transported Madame Blavatsky back to the steppes of Russia and a handsome young cavalry officer, galloping with her across the endless plains, the wind in their hair and laughter on their tongues. "Only once," she murmured, "but it was different for me and temptation was swiftly removed from my path. I had to marry very young, you know," she added ruefully.

The strange old lady's energy had shifted into shades of sorrow and Ana put a hand out, as if to comfort her. "Are you alright Madame Blavatsky?" she said tentatively.

"What? Oh, yes, it's nothing..." HPB waved her hand as if to dismiss the question, but her gesture was half-hearted and Ana couldn't helping thinking she seemed sad.

"Anyway, it's not me we need to be worrying about," Madame rounded decisively. "You're the one who needs fortifying right now and there's no substitute for proper face-to-face time with an ascended Master. I have invited Serge to lead the first class. He'll speak to you in French but he's from Ukraine. Be sure to pay attention as he's got so much to do and is going out of his way to help you. You must download as much information from as possible before he gets called back to the war in his Fatherland. The chances are I will have to go with him so let's not waste time. Have a bath and then get to bed early. He'll be here at a minute to Midnight.

***

Bon soir, Anastasia. I am Serge. Let us begin.

"What do you see when you look at the world around you?" The question took Ana by surprise and her mind momentarily went blank. Then, for some strange reason, the picture of the gentleman in the top hat popped into her head and she blurted his name out. "Stainton Moses!"
His quizzical smile widened. "Ah, yes, you *do* see Mr Moses, don't you! Your response was honest but let's not get caught up in the ghostlands just yet, there's plenty of time for that. We'll start with more basic facts.
"The present day – just as it was a century ago – is a time of crises and dead ends in so many fields of life. Everywhere we see that men and women have lost spiritual courage and renounced their joy of life. Divisions between peoples – fear and mistrust – possess nations and individuals. Narrow puritanism and sickly debauchery are signs of our time.
"It is precisely because of these crises that the Initiate must stand up as a defender of the very fine nuances in what we call the art of living. In ancient times this art was practiced with mastery, but it is almost unknown in the modern world, especially here in the west[lxxiii].
"I have always thought that in order to understand the development of the history of human thought, we could not ignore humanity's effort towards the limits of the unfathomable, which leads the thinker to the source of the traditional mystical knowledge of the Initiates.
The conception of the Universal Mystery – Mysterium -
Present in the formative hour of the world and its
Creator, Great Architect of the Universe and Divine Individuality, is at the very origin of the research of
all Initiates. Our existence represents only a faint, sometimes altered reflection of this Mystery, which is the basis of Life.
Always opposing the established principles, these researches tend towards the knowledge of the eternal Truth. Awareness of the high predestination of man is the guiding star of Initiatory Teaching. Higher than personal desire and far above the chthonic pull of fate," he added carefully, seeing how she blanched at his words.

"A thick forest of dark prejudices and confused superstitions surround the ancient Teaching, as well as imbalance and immoderate enthusiasm from the weak-minded and mediocre intelligences. It becomes more important, therefore, to properly reveal the simple, classically pure Wisdom tradition that is hidden behind the symbols of a distant past. One of the essential formulas that can be deduced from the Initiatory Teaching is recognition of the strength of the human will and immeasurable possibilities of the human psyche. That is why, following Initiatory Teaching, the fundamental purpose and justification of our ephemeral existence lies in the study and development of human psychic life.

"It is possible that for some people the Initiatory Doctrine appears only as a series of opinions or interesting beliefs. It will move others more deeply, perhaps as a form of strong protest against crude materialism and the lowering of man to the level of the anonymously acting forces in the multitude struggling for daily existence. And, perhaps, the Initiatory Teaching will cause a shy spark to spring up in some souls that will grow into a holy flame of the Human and the Beautiful. For these souls this Doctrine will confirm what the higher instinct - intuition - dictates to them: That life is the struggle for the consecration of the supreme ideal in the inner universe as in the outer world. According to the word of the ancient Sages: "Life gives to them and will inspire admiration and veneration, for the life is beautiful".

Serge paused and smiled, warmth radiating out of his infinitely wise and compassionate eyes. "Now Anastasia, I will not pretend to give a definitive presentation of the Initiatory Doctrine in one class, but I do strive to express the synthesis of it: Rather to indicate the problems than to solve them!"[lxxiv]

"Let us consider thought; the workings of the Mind. Initiatory Teaching is interested not so much in the concrete content of thought and its modes of expression, but, rather, the paths which thought follows, the conditions and means used for the direction of thought and the practical conclusions to be drawn from it. Thought is imperfect; sometimes the verb does not serve other than to make it confused or to free oneself from it by a meaningless formula. The practical action of an idea or the result it brings in life is the measure of its value, because the law of life is in constant generation.

"It is not necessary, from the initiatory point of view, to define Divinity, Satan, good, evil and other principles. It is only necessary to grasp the very fact of the existence, in man (or woman), of these ideas and of the moral rule which proceeds from them matters[lxxv]. If the thought has passed its practical test - that of the material criterion - then we can only deepen it, work on it from the angle of speech, form of the nervous or astral degree and of perfection of logic, the mental form. Any initiatory idea must be lived by the Initiate and put into practice. Its definition matters less.

"Therefore, the Initiation remains above all utilitarian in its natural transformation into a practical school of enhancement methods. The essence of this improvement consists in the penetration into the sub-conscious, which must manifest itself more fully in our consciousness, through the way of the superior states of the human mind.

"In the active character of Initiation, the legacy of the past, lies its profound distinction from the modern scientific and philosophical systems that tend to remain in a play of mind, without any influence on the organisation of human life. In the vital drama of human reincarnations, Initiation aspires not only to recognise the inner link of these incarnations, but also to bring the separate acts in the successive lives of man into a coherent whole. This totality, according to the Initiatic Doctrine, must become the realisation of the ends of Initiation, which are: Deliverance or Reinstatement[lxxvi].

"I must also admit that a great deal of *receptivity* is necessary for a truly initiatory education. This receptivity becomes the channel of all the contacts of the initiate with his or her point of attachment. The developed receptive virtue is what helps to create the *enlightened human*, as it is called by the Elders. The enlightened human has a definite possibility of communication with the Higher Forces. It is thanks to receptivity that one manages to fully know, find and fix the present image of our own subconscious. We call this subconscious the interior man – or woman - or, from a much deeper ritualistic term – the stranger.

"Let us also note that the inner life of a human and his or her thought are directed by the different stages of the interior, by the various planes where the human is while they are meditating. By studying the human soul, esoteric practice over the millennia discovered several states of the soul - astral, psychic and higher states. We must, therefore, first learn to discern the plane we inhabit and then, if we want to fix our reasoning on the great cosmic problems, universal and other, to study the higher states of the soul. The more accessible these become to us, the better we can illuminate our conclusions in their light and the more we can enrich our inner experience.

"During Initiation training it is always necessary to start with the rational. Whilst we refine and illuminate our states of mind, we simultaneously refine the rational. And in a regular way we arrive at the so-called irrational states that govern our psychic life, just as the Irrational directs the Universe. Science proves to us that it is not arithmetic which governs our life, but the law of great numbers, the astronomical law, the law of infinity - inaccessible laws that are incomprehensible in the light of the rational alone. Thus, during the Initiatory Path, one raises one's rational faculty by transmuting it into the irrational, that is to say, by putting it in direct contact and in co-vibration with cosmic laws and the divine laws. If the control of the training of the initiate must be severe and his advancement very careful, it is precisely to avoid the slip of his reason in the astral currents of whimsical imagination. Something that you are starting to experience," he added.

"We can say that the initiatory logic is positive, because it is based on the possibilities possessed by man to develop himself during these educational practices. If a well-trained acrobat shows us the miracles he can accomplish with his physical body, an initiate who properly trains his psychic body discovers a world of abilities unsuspected in secular existence. These abilities allow him to give a character of certainty to the conclusions of his boldest meditations.

It is in this work of transmutation of his rational in an

irrational state that man attains to the knowledge of the content of his subconscious.

"So, we might say, the conscious and the subconscious may act together in full harmony. This irrationality is the true atmosphere of the great unknown. Of the unknown, which is often discussed during the Initiation, the question will be asked of us: Where does your certainty of the transcendental value of the unknown man come from? We can answer: The value of the unknown man imposes himself in all the movements of our internal life, which are centralised, and that we feel comprise a living set. The unknown is the axis which centralises all movements of the inner life around him.

"The outer man, penetrated by the light and knowledge of this light, comes to understand in an absolute and palpable way that the goals formulated by Initiation are the only true ends of life, the sole realisation of our human evolution. Thanks to his intimacy with the unknown, man learns the ultimate truths about life. This achievement is called the "second birth", the one that causes the closest contacts to be obtained with his unknown, who now directs life. Exterior Man, hand-in-hand with the inner being, the unknown, then becomes a conscious instrument, instructed in the true ways and destinies of humanity. Likewise, through his unknown, man realises his rapprochement and intimacy with the divine plan.

"It is curious to study the various trainings of Hindu initiates and Christian oriental hermits. In their practices, which require years of perseverance via the contemplative way, they manage to reach the states the highest of their souls and, therefore, the possibility and real feeling of contact with the divine.

"If, as current science says, we can transmute our bodies in the physical plane into other bodies by way of disintegration of the atom, we can likewise transmute the different states of man up to a joyful higher state. We disintegrate in him all the weight, the whole set of mistakes and sins gathered during the incarnations of his monad. We also know that the illuminated pentagram receives the direct light of the divine plan and sometimes becomes radiant, almost physically, as the prophets and the great saints radiated divine light.

"The pentagram blazes – that is, acts - when it renders and sows the Light with the same detachment as that of whom the pentagram received it from. The mission of sowing, of instructing, of indicating the true ends of evolution, becomes the nature of even this flamboyant pentagram, of this "Man of Desire" of which Louis Claude de Saint-Martin spoke.
The Man of Desire, as it is said, is above all imbued with dynamism, for evolution and for participation in the work of integration and universal transmutation of our Saviour. First of all he is an instructor, a fisherman of souls or, rather, a birther of souls: he draws them out of the animalistic dependent state and leads them to the conscious and free state. It is in this Man of Desire that our unknown manifests itself in its fullness, when intimate contact and inner harmony are established and man loses his dualism, when the unknown man and the exterior man are united.
"When the unknown man, freed from the great darkness that the secular life imposes on him, receives the Direct Light - not reflected and independent of the astral plane - then this unknown becomes the dynamic, constructive, man of desire.
To be a Man of desire, an instructor, what a serious destiny! Immediately in front of him stands the wall of astral resistances and external contingencies".
Seeing that a question had arisen in his pupil at this talk of the Man of Desire, Serge paused his monologue. "Is there anything you'd like to ask me, Ana?"
"Is it possible for someone to become – or simply to be – a Man of Desire – but in service to darkness rather than light, to himself rather than humanity or God?"
"Oh, beautiful girl. You are discovering that love changes everything! Magic is in the will of the Adept. If his intentions are pure his magic – his *desire* - will serve God, but if he is corrupted then so will be his desire.
"The inner struggle, the dualism of man, finds its end in harmony and constructive efforts, when the astral plane, conscious or unconscious, *no longer has any hold*. Any negative egregores may try to break this harmony, this momentum, to re-establish dualism in order to retain their point of support in man and weaken him. The pressure of

astral forces can imprison or liberate man.

"The physical plane in its innumerable manifestations - society, state, race, customs, etc - maintains an animosity towards the inner man that is often incomprehensible to those who suffer it. Throughout human history, the teacher has been persecuted and slandered: there is a vacuum around him, his efforts are discredited and, suddenly, with infinite sadness he sees the Cross of Golgotha ascend to him. He sees the assassination of Master Hiram by his collaborators - those closest to him - just as Christ was betrayed by a disciple of the inner circle of the Apostles.

"Hiram's capture is very instructive in its image and assertion: The Master is always killed by his student, who suspects a hidden power, a hidden treasure and wants to seize control of it, being unfit to follow the generous ideas of the Way of this Master. In reality, this disciple is simply driven by the resistance of astral egregores and envious earthly enemies.

The insider knows the inevitability of these incidents because the more he rises, the more he lights up, and the more the sacrifice becomes his, emerges, solidifies and gives importance to his achievements.

"On the Way, the initiate must be protected by the Higher Forces against the unleashing of the powerful astral and physical waves, because, very often in training, the neophyte weakens and appears momentarily vulnerable. Hence the symbol of the protective mantle, always linked to the one that follows the way.

Louis Claude de Saint-Martin, interior man and writer of value, after participating in the symbolic brotherhoods (called initiatory) and after long experiences, understood that the true basis of Initiation is the initiatory contact between the initiator and the initiate." He paused again to ensure she was listening carefully. "One who is truly receptive is capable of initiatory contact with many Masters."

All occult groups or lodges are formed around insiders endowed[1] with the talent of animators, which the Master Mebes and his initiates call 'The Shin Element' and which others call 'The Magnetic Centre'. These groups always tend to fixate on the adoration of their Master and to form chapels of small religions around him. This adoration, always fake, causes desires and tone-deaf animosities. These ephemeral organisations have become a hindrance, a trial on the Way, instead of serving it. This is the individual life of man in the depths of his inner experience, which is central to Initiation. Proselytising is not compatible with the initiatory Way. We "give birth" to the soul while it insists: we give her the spiritual bread because she strikes and perseveres.

"The key to the evolution of man, of his infinite possibilities, is to be found within himself. Or herself, in the case of woman. When, as a result of a certain series of efforts, training and transmutations of his mind, he will find himself in front of his unknown being, he will realise the unity of his own inner self. Following the esoteric expression, he must find the third binary term (arising from the dual poles of the exterior and interior man) and rediscover the lost Word; then the symbol of the acacia, of the evolution towards the immortality of the soul, will be known to him.

"Regardless of the strictly intimate and individual character of the Initiatory Path, the initiate who follows it is always obliged to instruct, that is to say, to make others benefit from the light he has received. This mission is linked to the initiatory progression. Not having an organisation in the strict sense of the term, the initiate works either in different symbolic brotherhoods, as the Rose-Crosses did, or in different religious, social, scientific or other communities. His duty, without proselytising in the direct sense of the word, is to spiritualise his environment, to raise its level of culture with broad and generous ideas born from the conceptions and conclusions of initiatory esotericism.

"Except for a few insiders who have reached the highest stages of contemplation, others must always realise the parable of talents, always working for human progress. This is the social mission of the initiate. It is in this continual effort to support and purify the collective man that, for an initiate, the possibilities of truly participating in the work of Christ are opening up: Purifying the world from the Fall.

"Of course, it is necessary first of all to strengthen yourself, to become a master of oneself, to return to the secular world and influence it towards the Good, without being crushed by this world, by Evil. It is also one of the aspects highlighting the real character and, at the same time, the great problem of sacrifice, the basis of the conditions of the moral climate of the Initiatory Path. There, the initiate joins the Love of which Christ speaks, Love that must become universal, natural, in the Kingdom of Elias the Artist, that is to say in the future world reintegrated[lxxvii].

Dinner

What the Fool exhales, the Fool inhales.
There is no feminine for Fool.
In the Descents, the sex of the Fool alternates.
The inner strives to become the outer.

The Outworld others are self-reflected.
Seeing others as Self, the soul seeks to make amends.
Balanced again, the Fool descends.
New thoughts become wrought deeds.

All below is image, and names perish.
The Virgin in the Fool's eye does not perish.
The Virgin Waters generate their own light.
Without separation, there is no illumination.

The Zelator, David Ovason

She looked like a statue of Hathor,

Sitting very still and straight in the high-backed chair, a golden curtain of hair about her shoulders and her emerald eyes fixed on the man sitting opposite. As the deepest core of her being strained against the bonds imposed upon it, her mind's eye focused on the words of Madame Blavatsky and Serge. With an unshakable certainty she knew she must resist the cries of her lower being, whilst an urgency of equal strength to this resistance threatened to engulf her.
"Would you prefer red or white?" he asked politely, as if oblivious to this drama. Her hesitation was barely perceptible but telling all the same. Her higher self, that knowing genius, did not wish to agree to anything he might offer, but her innocent flesh wanted pleasure and her mind could use a little relaxation after all that highbrow tuition".
"White."
Albedo. Perfect. He reached over to the ice bucket and dispensed a measure of Riesling into the crystal glass before her. For himself he poured red and then raised the goblet. "Come, lift the cup, and in the fire of Spring, the winter garden of repentance fling."[lxxviii]
"It's not spring," she murmured, sipping the Riesling and allowing herself a moment of reflection. *That is very nice wine*, she thought appreciatively, glancing around the oak-panelled dining room. This place is *beautiful; he must be rich. I AM.* He leaned forward. "In some cultures it *is* almost Spring. Rosh Hashanah is at the end of this month and we're about to enter the season of the Greater Mysteries of Eleusis, which isn't exactly Spring but it is, of course, initiatory."
Ana blushed and looked down. Out of her depth and feigning sophistication she had betrayed her weakness with the comment of a fool.
There was a twinkle in his eye. He wasn't nervous it he slightest. "I thought you would have known things like that after all those years at Lost Continents."
She took a slug of the wine. "Yes, I know, but if you happen to be Zoroastrian or even English – anywhere in the Western world, in fact - it'd be the opposite time of year to Spring

now. Persephone would say that winter is definitely coming." He ignored the fact this was another rather stupid thing to say and instead topped up her glass. "I like your dress; that colour suits you". The empire-line gown was of golden silk embroidered with small crimson flowers around the deeply cut neck and edges of the capped sleeves. The ends of a crimson ribbon that was tied beneath her bust hung down her spine to its base.

Food was already on the table and she bit into a sliver of the heavenly white crab, creature of the moon, which had been her own choice of dish. The man across the table cut into his rack of lamb. This action proved too much to resist for a large black hound, hitherto dozing beside the open fire. It raised its head, got to its feet and arrived at Mr O'Ryan's side in one energetic movement. "Somebody's awake!" he said indulgently, feeding the first piece of meat to the huge animal.

Whilst she liked all animals, Ana was more of a cat person and gave the powerful beast a wary look. "Don't worry," he told her, "Monsieur looks a bit scary but he's fine when he gets to know you. Besides," he added calmly. "He likes you."

"How can you tell!" protested Ana, who had not gone near the ominous-looking creature.

"Because you're still alive," chuckled Mr O'Ryan. "I'm kidding," he added in response to her alarmed face. "Now go and lie down, Monsieur, before we frighten our lovely guest."

Out of sight behind her chair again, the dog was soon out of Ana's mind. The next two hours passed in a gradually deepening dream, until the fire had settled into a comfortable mound of glowing embers.

By the time the clock struck 11.00 he was topping up one of her glasses from a tall silver flagon of water and another from the bottle of pink champagne which had manifested with dessert. Beyond the heavy curtains and leaded window came the sound of rain, which merged with the blackness of night to form a dark cocoon around the firelit Castle. Ana, by now, was smiling, the words and warnings of her teachers having slipped from her mind as easily as the wine had slipped through her mouth, past her heart and into her belly.

"Why don't you sit on the sofa while I play for you?" O'Ryan pushed back his chair and took a violin from its case, which was resting against the wall beneath the window and was one of many musical instruments she'd seen in the Castle. There was even a collection of antique flutes made from swan bones and hollowed out reeds in a cabinet near the entrance hall.

She saw no reason to refuse, though she couldn't help regretting the greater physical proximity it put between them. She wished he would sit beside her, but the memory of Tristan and her great-grandmother struggled with desire from the refuge of her heart.

Anastasia was lulled into the space between waking and dreaming with the gentle caress of Orfeo ed Euridice. It seemed as if no sooner did she recline against the deep red velvet than she was drawn before the entrance to the underworld with a force so invincible that no alternative route appeared to exist. He met her at the gateway - his dazzling countenance the only source of light - and knelt before her with this spirt self. He put a hand to her face and hust before she fell into death-like sleep, he kissed her on the cheek.

She would not remember him gently gathering her in his arms and carrying her upstairs to the bedroom, where he lay her between the sheets, golden gown and all, before leaving the room and heading back into the night. She would not recall anything of her dreams, only the most sublime of waking moments she had ever experienced, enveloped in the twin light of the rising sun and an endless astral kiss, more real than anything she had felt in waking life. In this life, at least.

Arcanum 8: Orientation of the Mystery to the Constellation of Cancer[lxxix]

From the materials of V Belustin, Circles of the Mind of Hermes

And then we saw the semi-circular platform of a bare plateau and in the centre of it a source of blue water, a powerful jet gushing out from the rocky soil.
There was a priest at the spring. He was dressed in a knee-length yellow robe with alternating vertical stripes, wide black and narrow blue. The priest's head was topped with an openwork bell-shaped ivory tiara. In his left hand, he held a long, flexible branch, which he quickly rotated from left to right around the water gushing from the stone.
The priest rotated the flexible branch more and more quickly, and when he twice exclaimed "OR-AKSHATRA!", the jet began to spin after the movement of the branch, and the water radiated in small splashes in all directions. 22 people who were standing around the spring tilted their heads and each of them was touched by splashes of sparkling blue water. These were The College of 22 Priests, Secret Servants of Atlantis and Servants of God.

***

Matter in the hands of the adepts of Darkness is a powerful weapon of struggle against the triune god of Light. They call on the naked matter to vice and crime, to fight against purity and innocence, believing that matter is the temptation of the world, that flesh is a golden harp promising incarnate
pleasure and happiness. Hunger is a magical creation of the supreme initiates of Darkness, who send humanity its pale ghost to remind of the imperious voice of matter. And this voice never sounds so loud as during the famine.[lxxx]

Sphere of Eros

The nature of this world is ecstasy, and it takes the soul on the wings of sweet madness to the bizarre halls of Love, where at the moment of the highest tension of sweet fusion with life, it simultaneously drinks the cup of Death, burns in these fiery embraces. This is the world of a wondrous and terrible fairy tale; it knows no value except its ecstasy, in which all living things blossom in all their splendour and through the death of their identity they join the immortality of unconditioned existence. And this world attracts a person to itself, fills his spirit with great longing, counts him to inner beauty, constantly pulls him out of the chains of cosmic dreaming

Vladimir Shmakov, Pneumatology

Vladimir Shmakov, from Rosicrucians in Soviet Russia, A.L., Nikitin

The atmosphere

In Nina Roudnikova's room at Lost Continents was one of sorrow and solidarity, a state with which they were all familiar. Both individually and as a group they were well used to tragedy and hardship, with all but one of them having lived through the Bolshevik Revolution and most of them also surviving the Russian civil war and Hitler.

Whilst Marilyn had not faced those particular challenges, her personal circumstances and the sacrificial manner of her death meant her comprehension of suffering was at least as profound as theirs. Her presence in the group was thanks to the favour of her initiator, Mikhael Chekhov. All those seated at the table greatly admired the personal magnetism that was a hallmark of her innate spiritual light.

As a rule, they held that God - divinity, acme of truth – has five main properties and these are: Goodness, Love, Justice, Wisdom and Beauty. All of these properties, Marilyn possessed in great measure. At that moment she was tightly holding hands with Mikhael on her right and Valentin's wife, Maria, on her left. Her beautifully made-up eyes were turned down towards the table, a position she had not moved from in hours as she struggled to contain her anxiety and grief.

Under ordinary circumstances the reunion of soul mates – such as had occurred between Ana and Mr O'Ryan - was considered a miracle greater than the parting of the Red Sea, but these were no ordinary circumstances. As a woman who had both lived and died for love, Marilyn felt Ana's dilemma with acute empathy. More than feeling, she was also thinking – thinking very carefully and deeply – to recall in detail something Vsevelod had told her many moons ago. Something about the Sphere of Eros. He had called it "the supreme centre, the driving force, the vital principle of the manifested universe, around which, in accordance with the Kabbalistic heavens, the remaining nine spheres of the Sephiroth Tree revolve[lxxxi]."

Valentin, for his own part, had revealed that the esoteric name of the Fool is Love – Amor – and thereby analogous to Eros, which constituted a great height and depth of lofty and abyssal knowledge. As all lovers know. The sphere of Daath. Marilyn was an excellent pupil and Vsevelod had further instructed her – with the aid of one of the countless diagrams which he, like the others, used to illustrate his works: "The initiatory path of the androgynous column is the Middle Pillar…it is the only integral path that leads to the ultimate reintegration of the entire manifested universe. For the Adamic monads, this is the way of the sword and the struggle; the way is magical and strong-willed. In the highest aspect it leads to magic, in the lowest, also to magic.

The entities walking the androgynous column of the Sephiroth Tree do not reject the signs of the right and left columns of this Tree, but, marching upward, they are armed with the censer of faith and the rod of knowledge, but their main weapon is the sword".

Eros – Love, 0 - is a universal matter, whilst Uranus is1, Salvation via the Saviour of Environmental Resistance and Neptune is 2, for Goodness and Hermetic Balance. Saturn is equal to 3, the Union of Love and Harmony of fluids, whilst Jupiter is 4, the Power of Good Materialisation of fluids. Mars - 5 – was considered the Cognition of Love and Victory of Matter and the Sun was 6: Patience and Balance of fluids. Venus as 7 was Love of Justice - Embodied Justice- just as Mercury was 8, for the Marriage of Love and Merging of Opposites in Netzach and Hod. Luna was 9, the Synthesis of nine previous values.

The union of love is a union with Christ, she knew. *The marriage of love is the highest love as an initiation.* And yet, *Hermetic equilibrium is the balance of plus and minus forces at the point of their synthesis and the harmony of fluids is like a union, marriage, sympathy of the fluids of individuals or sympathy of the fluids of astral streams. The materialisation of fluids is the materialisation of astral light streams*[lxxxii].

Moscow's St Germain, who was a great admirer of beauty, had explained that the victory of matter is the separation from the primary trigram visible on the Tree of Life, the Turner of Eros-Uranus-Neptune. The fusion of opposites is a fusion in the act of a complex flash in the astral environment…"

There must be some way of resolving this, she murmured

imperceptibly to anyone but those whose hands she held and whose grip now tightened in response. Handsome Vsevolod, who was sitting directly opposite, was staring at her with his clear blue eyes. She had always understood him; Mikhael had taught her well.

Nina Roudnikova, who was on a similar train of thought to Marilyn, was also searching for the solution, a way to resolve the dramatic conundrum of the binary forces at work. The more she considered the problem, the more the solution became clear: A Sacrifice was needed, something which evoked the Soul of the Messiah.

"What was sweet as honey in the mouth becomes bitter in the stomach; I am ready to make the exchange."

A deeper and more mournful wave swept over the table. Giving it a moment to pass, Grigori's wife, Maria, was first to speak. "We have dreaded this moment. You are very brave, Nina; it has ever been thus. It is a definite route available to the Chain, though it is also by far the most costly."

"Not the *most* costly," Mrs Roudnikova corrected her sadly. "The greatest price – the one that isn't worth paying – is the fall of Sophia in our Ana."

There was a long and gloomy pause and then Vladimir spoke. "What about Ana's father and the Circle of Avalon, Tristan?"

The last word hung like a raindrop of grief in the vivifying ether of the room. Valentin finally answered. "He is a pure soul but called to the path of suffering. Renunciation may be his trial."

"He shall be the next," spoke Butator with resolve. "He has already proven himself worthy. Ana's father has shown him the old ways and Mrs Pixley has instructed him in her techniques for many years now. He would be a worthy match for Ana, but fate has intervened, despite our best efforts to stop it. Perhaps we should have known better…"

"You mustn't think like that, Grigori," said Vladimir with feeling. "Look at what has happened in the past 100 years, it is precisely as we feared. In fact, it is worse. We cannot be blamed for hoping that the latest in our line might prove capable of the sacrifice of love required to help defeat the most monstrous of egregores."

"If only O'Ryan were a better man," said Mikhael with a grim expression. "I cannot tell you how it galls me to see him playing the Knight and deciding to fall in love. He thinks he can wash away a lifetime of cunning self-service and blood sacrifice with the spiritual credit of his blameless soul mate. Again! He has learned nothing throughout all those lifetimes, no matter the degree of his initiation."

His words sparked a glittering wave of anger in all those present, who allowed themselves to think of vengeance rather than sacrifice for a moment. "There must be another way," said Vladimir with a beseeching look at Mrs Roudnikova. "After all we've been through in the past century – silently watching and waiting, always renouncing, praying without ceasing – can we not, after all, at this hour of great need, avail ourselves of the sword of vengeance and finally destroy this beast. If we fully merge our forces with the Circle of Avalon we must stand a chance of defeating it." He pulled himself up straighter in his seat. "And if we fail, we shall die the second death with honour and pass across together."

His words had the effect of a bell chiming loudly and a fierce new light manifested in all of their eyes whilst they weighed all possible outcomes to such a radical course of action.

Maybe, maybe…
Let us try to formulate a rite…
It is worth the risk…

With a tremulous voice which betrayed the humility she always felt in their assembled presence, Marilyn finally spoke aloud her thoughts. "Forgive me if I'm mistaken", she began hesitantly, but it is my belief that Ana will overcome fate and rise to the occasion if we rally to her side at the right time. She need not relive the tragic event at Delphi."

Vladimir leapt to his feet. "Aphrodite has spoken!" he said triumphantly. "And let us not forget she has Madame Blavatsky by her side – if anyone can talk an impressionable girl out of merging with Eros it's her!"

His earnest face and pithy observation, delivered with customary passion, triggered a wave of such hilarity in all those present that it effected a ripple in the ether. They suddenly saw how the tide might turn. *Who dares, wins,* they remembered, recalling that the power of will, knowledge and long years of silence was also theirs.

"There is something else to consider," said Nabusar thoughtfully. *"The measure of conscience is the highest stage of consciousness that a person is capable of, but Ana has not had the opportunity to test hers fully. Even now, she has only had a taste of that which she must renounce. The test she faces is very great, for it speaks to her body, mind and soul with a force so great she might perceive it as the light of the Lord, rather than the false light of deception.*

"The higher the stage of consciousness, the greater the mental tension between zenith and nadir, the stronger the voice of conscience sounds and the tighter its lynching[lxxxiii]. I do believe that the rallying of those she has loved and the reminder of all she has long-held dear will serve to overcome the spell of Nyx cast upon her".

Valentin nodded slowly. "We shall prepare for the worst but hope for the best. The unthinkable cannot be allowed to happen. We must avert another World War. Let us pray."

Lord Jesus Christ, Son of the Father,
Send out your Spirit over the Earth.
Let Your Holy Spirit fill the hearts of all nations,
That they may be preserved from degeneration,
disaster and war[lxxxiv].

"We have to get our myths straight," Grigori's wife, Maria, urged later that evening, so let us rectify the terms of the rituals without delay.

"As we see it," she gestured to her husband and Mrs Roudnikova, "O'Ryan will try to re-enact the full Orphic Mysteries with some form of sacrifice, so *we* shall proceed with the Greater Rite of Eleusis, three days prior to the exoterically appointed fall date. The Queen herself will bear witness in her Archetypal aspect as Imperatrix at its point of

greatest potency – at the dawn of her funeral rite. I have dedicated Arcanum III to her already and the pageant will befit the Imperatrix, I'm certain.
"The Orphic channel is most dangerous," said Mikhael tensely. "The piano and violin were powerful enough but he's not even moved onto the wind instruments, just imagine what effect the pan pipes will have on her astral sheath…and he's begun the Dionysiac. Cupid will reach Psyche."
Vladimir could not resist a wry smile. "It is fortunate that Madame Blavatsky, in her infinite usefulness, had the idea of distracting her with Night School. It has hampered his ability to reach Ana's naked soul and opened some channels for us. She is a good pupil, Nina, a credit to you, but the Supreme Arcanum is achieved through life and cannot be taught in class. *The world is the schoolroom of God*[lxxxv]."
Nabusar nodded. "We must petition her Guardian Angel to bring the music of the Spheres to her dreams," he said carefully. Then we might counter his subversion via the higher Orphic plane and her angelic contact will be strengthened by our prayers. As long as her angel is her guide, she will prevail in the test and secure her release." He paused before finishing, "even if it is only partial", finally saying out loud what all of them had been thinking.
All the while they had been talking, Marilyn had felt a stirring of her inner self which grew exponentially with every word until she felt an incredible force well up for the depths of her being. The suffering of women roused the love of Mars in her soul, although this sympathetic anguish was not betrayed by the measured tone of her voice, which contained a hint of menace.
"It will not be a 'half-life'; winter is not coming to Ana's soul. I shall be that man's Nemesis so don't you worry Mrs Roudnikova," she said calmly. As they all turned to stare at her in a mixture of awe and mystification, she made her resolved will clear. "I already have a plan. I shall turn him into a Daffodil; mark my words!"
Her eyes widened in defiance as she gathered Mrs Roudnikova's Persian cat under one arm, took up the ceremonial sword in her free hand and disappeared in a flash

of invisible lightning, leaving only the memory of that dark-lashed limpid gaze.

***

Bon Soir, Ana, how are you?

She was unable to answer Serge's question so he tried another. "Is there anything in particular which you'd like me to elucidate?"
There was only one thing she cared about in that moment. "Soul mates," she replied. "The alchemical union."
He smiled a little sadly. "There is only so much I can tell you. Some things must be seen and understood in ways beyond the power of words; but I will try to explain. Every soul unit comprises two co-equal androgynous parts, always in an imbalance of tension: the eternal masculine and the eternal feminine. The dissociation of these Androgynous parts constitutes the beginning of the Fall and between the two poles is a determined attraction of the series of centripetal forces - of union - and centrifugal forces or repulsion. In other words, sympathy and antipathy.
"The history of the formation of our world begins with the memory of the mysterious, mystical wedding, in the bosom of Eternity, of the two halves of the Androgynous. This memory is full of the passion of love that attracts, like hatred that divides. That is why many religions carry to the origin of the idea of the struggle of two divine principles. It is why the Initiates know the eternal active and the eternal passive search for each other and fight against each other. The attraction of the poles of the fallen Androgyne constitutes the Logos, that is to say, the Love that generates in time and the space of the element similar to that which is lost in Eternity.
"The Logos possesses the qualities of the Androgynous, but represents, in the world of the Fall, only the reflection of the pre-Eternal Androgynous. The origin of the deviation of the poles of the Androgynous, who made born the dual forces of the relative world, finds itself in the conditions of mystical marriage, in the beginnings that remain inaccessible to us.

The Logos that reflects in him the pre-Eternal Androgynous and the mystical marriage, also carries the roots of the fall potential that will be realised more materially tomorrow on lower planes.

"What we call involutive monads (Angels) help the evolutionary in their activity for the redemption of the world of the Fall. Knowing the law of the egregore, we can also say with precision that the struggle will continue until the moment where the axis of the enemy collective is destroyed (loss of the point central to the distribution of energy - quaternary law).

If this point is lost by the egregore, its constituent parts turn into a demoralised mass, confused with lateral currents and it naturally crumbles or is absorbed by the winning egregore.

We have learned that if the higher idea guides the monad or the collective of monads, this idea, in the measure of its moral depth, makes the axis of the Quaternary flexible and able to withstand all the blows during the battle.

On the other hand, doctrines based on the lower qualities of the soul are identified with evil in its quaternaries. They may have an offensive force, but no resistance. Evil can create any threatening force, but, encountering resistance inspired by the moral power of the idea, is infallibly a victim of the shock in return, his very offensive force falls back on him. The monad or the collective that acts for the occult evolution, will never suffer this shock in return, because its resistance remains without limit.

Let us also recall the help of the divine collaborators
to the enlightened monads. But heaven only helps men who help themselves: alone, they can count on spiritual protection, because the heavenly protectors respond only to a
great human effort. If the man does not give this effort the protection loses its meaning. In this struggle against the manifestations of imbalance, the emanations of evil on earth, he is sick, exhausted by life, unable to give the necessary support during incarnation".

There is a verse in Corinthians which encapsulates the soulmate principle, which his: "Nevertheless, neither is the woman without the man, nor man without the woman in the

Lord".

"It is a tragedy in equal proportion to joy that human beings are responsible for re-encountering, at least once in every incarnation, the Soulmate who is sure to cross our path. Even if it is only for a matter of moments, because those moments bring with them a Love so intense that it justifies the rest of our days[lxxxvi].

Love is the Alpha and the Omega of life. All else has only secondary significance. Man is born with the Alpha. It is the intention of the work to show the path which leads towards the Omega[lxxxvii].

I will also invoke the words of a great teacher and wonderful man, who wrote that: "The vision of such a romance has haunted the highest minds for thousands of years. We find it in platonic love, the basis of the singular romance in the myths of the Androgyne man; of Orpheus and Euridice; of Pygmalion and Galatea... This is the aspiration of the human heart, which cries in secrecy because of its great loneliness.

This romance forms the essential aim of esoteric work. Here is that love which will unite man to that being who is unique for him, the Sister-wife, the glory of man, as he will be the glory of God. Having entered into the light of Tabor, no longer two, but one drinking at the fount of true Love, the transfigurer: the conqueror of Death.

Spells of Attraction

For Isis raised up a loud cry, and the world was thrown into confusion. She tosses and turns on her holy bed, and its bonds and those of the daimon world are smashed to pieces

Three-formed Hecate, Stéphane Mallarmé

You, Artemis, have been bound by the fibres of the sacred palm tree, so that you may love Orion forever. And may no barking dog release you, no braying ass, no cock, no priest who removes magic spells, no clash of cymbals, no whining of flute; indeed, no protective charm from heaven that works for anything; I rather, let her be possessed by the spirit.

***

Hecate, you, Hecate, triple-formed, since every seal of every" [love spell of 190 attraction] has been completed, I adjure you I by the great name of A****
and by the power of A******,''' because I adjure you, you who possess the fire.... and those in it, that she, Ana, be set afire," that she come in pursuit of Orion, because I am holding in my right hand the two serpents and the victory of I** S****** and the great name B****** M*******, who brandishes fire . . . ,'* that she love Orion

Mr O'Ryan's acolyte had spent the best part of two days inscribing spells, intoning rites and otherwise trying to ensure that his Master's interests were taken care of. It had been an unusually frustrating process, resulting in not just less than ideal but truly inauspicious indicators of the spells' success or lack thereof.

Despite following instructions to the letter, it seemed as if every time he turned his back some hostile force or other sabotaged his best efforts. To make matters worse, the poltergeist – or whatever it was – had not only taken to ringing a cowbell loudly in his ear but insisted on blowing tobacco smoke in his face whenever he was trying to read something complicated. He was oblivious to the hostile Eidolon of Madame Blavatsky, who had been monitoring his actions very closely and was doing a first rate job of not just thwarting his aims but messing with his mind enough to rend the spells ineffective.

The much more daunting case of O'Ryan was still unresolved, but she had total faith that the Circles of Hermes and Avalon would prevail over him.

Her French pals were also on standby, but loathe to act on British soil without a definite invitation to do so from the King. The newly proclaimed King Charles III would be more than willing to issue such an invitation – especially to René, whom he had long admired – but it had not yet entered his brain to do so. As things stood, the three Parisian Mages waited in the Borderlands for the proper diplomatic procedure to be enacted.

"They've no idea I'm here, you know," Madame Blavatsky would confide in Ana whilst she readied herself for dinner, referring to the owner of the Castle and his clan. "In their triumph at your successful capture they became somewhat careless and forgot all about Mr Marconi and the possible outcome of his quest. Perhaps they thought he was too hapless a character to succeed at such a task as removing the abyss from before my eyes."

Ana had laughed at this. It was true that Marc did not make a wholly convincing-looking Magus but stranger things had happened, she supposed.

"But never mind him; 'you know who' is really going to try it on with you tonight". She glared at Ana. "You know this, I assume?"

Ana felt a thrill in the pit of her stomach, which was advertised by the blushing roses which burst to life on her pale cheeks. *I do hope so*, she couldn't help thinking.

Mrs Blavatsky glared at her even more fiercely. "Be careful what you ask for, my girl, because there'll be no relief if you get it!" She sighed and rolled another cigarette. "Anyway, what I wanted to tell you is to stay vigilant and don't be alarmed if anything spooky happens. That nasty little fellow – the one that brought you here - has been trying to write spells into the walls, you know – even up the chimney and in all the music cases – I keep having to mess them up. I've neutralised much of it completely but there's been so much put about by now that more likely than not some lost entity or other might stumble through by mistake."

Ana stopped fastening her earrings and stared at Madame Blavatsky in the mirror. "Whatever do you mean?" she said fearfully, "I hope it's nothing unchristian?"

Her guardian looked away a little shiftily. "Just keep saying your prayer mantra and it'll keep them at bay." *Anything to keep the girl in touch with the upward hierarchy,* she thought fervently.

Ana recited the prayer back to her obediently.

"Good", Madame Blavatsky muttered. "Keep that up throughout dinner – in your mind, of course, or he'll get suspicious - especially if he starts playing those Pan Pipes and suggests that you go and lie down. Remember this, Ana, it's very important!"

Ana tried not to giggle. "What if he sings, should I cross myself?!"

Madame Blavatsky inhaled sharply and took some more tobacco from the pouch as her current cigarette began to expire. At another time in her life she would have exploded in rage but those times were gone and by some Act of God she had discovered a certain degree of detachment, a Zen-like state of calm that was somehow accessible for the first time in her existence. She took a puff of the strong tobacco, then another and a third, until the second cigarette was reduced to a stub.

"I've a good mind to leave you to it," She said finally. "There are plenty of other things I could be doing. I've not seen my sister in over a century!"

I wish you would! Thought Ana ungraciously. She knew Madame Blavatsky was trying to save her from a fate worse than death and that to submit to the courtship of Mr O'Ryan would lead to a catastrophe of Cosmic significance, but she could not bring herself to care. She knew this was strange; that something within her had strayed from the straight and narrow path and was making its first tentative steps into the unknown. With each step she took, her recklessness increased exponentially.

That does it, thought Mrs Blavatsky. *It's time she came down a peg or two before a greater fall is risked.* "I'll be off then," she said casually.

Ana gaped at her. "What?"

"I'm sure you'll be fine; you look like you know what you're doing" HPB called disdainfully, over her shoulder as she

began her exit from the Castle. "I shall go henceforth to Tiflis, via the Sardar Palace, where I shall reunite with my husband and family. Good luck. You're going to need it."
And with that, she was gone.
Madame Blavatsky's exit left a great hole in the atmosphere and Ana felt suddenly small, vulnerable and alone. She regretted being so rude to the remarkable lady and – to make matters worse - she had already had to wave goodbye to Serge, who declared after the second lecture that he had urgent business in his homeland and had to take leave of her. She instinctively felt she was on thin ice and began to repeat her prayers with a renewed sense of urgency.

***

Don't you remember how we first met, he asked her as she closed her eyes and leaned back into the lush velvet chair.
"No", she murmured, "tell me".
It was a long time ago, more than two and a half thousand Years. You were younger then but you looked almost the same, your golden hair was famed around the Hellenistic world. They said you were most beloved of all the Priestesses of Apollo. It was I who chose you to be Pythia, but I was also the one who took you from the sanctuary...
"Did I want to go with you?"
*Yes...*she heard his smile, even in the silent word. *You wanted it more than anything.*
"How did it happen?"
Try to remember...
"How?"
Listen to me play.

Stella Maris, ora pro nobis.

***

I am standing in the centre of a great rectangular hall with my head held high and my long, bright hair wound into an elaborate arrangement that is held in place by a gleaming diadem. My white linen robe is bound with gold and I am still as a statue, with one eye fixed upon the future as the other observes what is past.

The air is cool beneath the temple roof. The only sounds that can be heard are an occasional bleating of goats and the distant murmuring of servants as they make ready for the Spring Council, which is to be held here in three and a half days. I have already swept clean the marble floor and it shines like the full moon of Amalios. Early-morning sunrays flood the hallowed space, infusing every atom. Narrow gaps between the thick, rounded pillars reveal sections of a motionless scene, silent as if time had ceased.

Happy are the men who enter this house and ask of me, "What do you see?" The wisest make the best of the answer they are given but others seek more, seldom to any avail, for there is a way that we do things at this place – here at the navel of the world - where the future is inscribed on lead.

It is on the seventh day of each month that the future lives of men are unveiled and they come from all parts of the Earth to know what the fates have in store for them. This is except for during the winter months, when twice-born Dionysus returns and natural chaos reigns in place of Apollo's reason.

When frost is on the ground and the sheaves of wheat have frozen back into the Earth – when the great white star of Maia appears on the horizon – then it is that nine wild maenads will herald the arrival of Dionysus. His body is buried close to where I am standing and during his season our dedications are made for the following year's harvest, while we pray that the sun God will return, his golden youth resurrected anew.

When I am satisfied that the purification rituals have been performed correctly and the Temple is perfectly clean, I walk towards the entrance of the great hall. It is lavishly decorated with all manner of votives – burnished golden shields, statues, cauldrons, tripods and bows - from all four corners of the

Earth. Counted amongst them are the ensigns and symbols of every noble family that is known to this world.

I instinctively look up before leaving Apollo's house, to above the entrance where a thousand garlands of laurel create fragrant canopies beneath the ceiling and pay host to the songbirds that sing his praises. The sweetest voice I ever heard belongs to the nightingale, who reveals to those with ears to hear the innermost longing of the psyche. A pure, shrill note breaks the silence and escapes into Echo's lonely realm. When daybreak comes I shall return.

The moment I step from the building and out into the dry, dazzling world, I behold a sea of olives undulating before me. It is a breath-taking panorama which stretches far as the eye can see. I could never grow weary of such a vista and I remain still for a few moments, breathing in the warm, sweet aura of tranquility, giving thanks for the grace of the gods which brought me here to live my days.

Anyone who has been here understands that Holy Mount Parnassus is the closest place to Elysium on Earth. From it springs the fountain of all arts and poets, artists and musicians – devoted lovers of the Muses – all pay testament to the prophetic mouth of God that wields power and influence here.

The Sphinx which guards both the entrance to our temple and mysteries of the world is made of a warm-coloured stone. It blazes in the sun like fire and I incline my head as I walk past it down the gleaming marble steps, still surrounded by the monumental dedications of various cities.

It is not long before I have entered the walled kitchen yard, where I immediately see one of the Tetrarch's slaves giving water to a package mule that is tethered to a small fig tree, already unburdened of the offerings he bore. My heart leaps for joy and his image appears at the front of my mind. Like rays of sun flooding into the Temple's cool interior, it casts deep shadows into hidden places.

The Tetrarch is the eldest son of the Tagos of Thessaly, a great aristocrat of Greece. His tribe, the Aleudae of Larissa, was founder of the Amphictyonic League, one of the most powerful military forces in the world. Now that Thessaly is the chief protector of Delphi, its surest and strongest ally, the

Tetrarch – as leader of the cavalry - commands more respect than almost any other man who comes here.

I take a few moments to pet the placid animal, which is dozing in the dappled shade. His velvety-soft muzzle tickles my palm and he bows his head for me to scratch his dusty forelock at its peak. The warmth of the sun penetrates to my bones and for a moment I feel relaxed and carefree, as any other 19-year-old girl on a halcyon summer's day.

As the slave returns to wash the mule's dust-caked flanks I make my way into the kitchen and examine a bundle of ingredients that were gathered on the seventh day of the moon. They are laid on top of a solid Myrtle-tree table, a gift to the sanctuary from Corinthian priests of Aphrodite. It is from these ingredients that I shall concoct the special elixir for my Earthly guardian - the Saint Timocrates - and the Pythia herself, a woman almost twice my age.

The production of draughts and medicines is a duty I perform often, but someone was once foolish enough to ask me what I was 'cooking', as if I were a common slave. As it was such an inappropriate question I simply declined to answer, as is my habit whenever a foolish or inappropriate question is asked of me. Then there are the questions to which there are no easy answers.

Once I was asked when he - Dionysus - first came here. At first I could only smile, for what is time to the kingdom of eternity? There are only hours of the day, seasons of the sun and cycles that are Marked by the passage of the moon. Most vehemently have I been warned by the Saints to never fall beneath the sway of time because that would bring death to all prophecy. Daily am I reminded that ordinary time is of no consequence and fate unfolds precisely as the gods command it. When this occurs is immaterial, the potential for all action being ever-present. We are chiefly concerned here with what is infinite, although men so often desire to make fixed points for the dead books of their history.

"For this reason", Timocrates informed me – quite gravely, in fact – when I questioned him on the matter, "the League has taken it upon itself to regulate all calendars of the civilised world that we might subjugate for perpetuity the menace of time at the centre of the Earth."

For the sake of the inquiry, it was sufficient to say that Dionysus comes at first sighting of the Pleiades, accompanied always by Euterpe, whose hypnotic sounds will soar over Parnassus from flutes poised like spears of moonlight on the muse's lips. What happens then, who can say? It is one of the mysteries we cannot share easily, for like dreams in the stillness of the night, memories of those days are as mist in the fire of morning.

Though my mind may roam free, my life here is wholly proscribed in many ways. Indeed, it is set in stone. I sometimes dwell on the fact that nothing ever changes and perhaps I wish it might, but I am more aware of my great good fortune and that I enjoy privileges that the majority of people, especially women, dare only dream of.

At the same time, I know all too well that I have seen nothing of the world beyond this temple and its outlying areas, although I frequently hear rousing stories of other lands from the men who come here. Stories I have over-heard, for the most part, or which come to me via my teachers, for it is not permitted for ordinary men to speak freely with a woman who is married to the God.

I most often hear about the great foreign kingdoms of Egypt and Persia – seats of wisdom and warfare, respectively - and of the various colonies founded abroad by generals and merchants of Greece, often upon the advice of my divinatory office. These tales can cause a sense of longing that I find difficult to overcome and there are times when I wonder if it is to the sea that I shall one day return.

I also wonder about the Tetrarch, who occupies my mind so fully that he is by my side in all but body throughout each day. We are bound, he and I, by ties both seen and unseen. There are ties for all to see because the Tetrarch is an overlord of Delphi and it was he that decreed I would be made Pythia when the former priestess was murdered during the war.

Then there are the unseen ties, because I alone have understanding of how much he means to me. Even my sisters do not realise the depth of this ocean. To my mind he is the

Earthly representation of Apollo himself and loving one enables me to increase my understanding of the other. My love for Apollo knows no bounds, for his light reaches even into places of darkness. He is my lord and my protector in times of danger, my guide through moments of chaos. He is the husband I cannot have, the mind which inhabits my own and requires me to master his world.

Recollections May Vary

We don't receive wisdom; we must discover it for ourselves after a journey that no one can take for us or spare us.

Marcel Proust, Remembrance of Things Past

Marcel Proust by Otto Wegener

It was towards the end

of the long Sacred War that I first set eyes upon the Tetrarch, who came with many horsemen under his command and at last razed Krisaioi to the ground, having already poisoned its waters with hellebore and put to death most of the town's irreverent people.
As the cursed polis burned, a desperate band of rebels somehow escaped and stormed the sanctuary, where they set about attacking the Saints as they prayed in the Temple. Some ran for their lives and Timocrates escaped their murderous intent whilst attending to God's holy flame in the Corycian Cave. He stealthily rescued me from my chamber and took me for hiding to the secret place of dedication, beneath the priceless earth. I saw the fear in his eyes as he spoke and girded myself for more terror.
"I must retrieve the temple scrolls, the words that were given to us by the Gods that none can replace. You will remain here - still and silent as a statue, my child - and pray with all the force of Psyche that Phoebus Apollo will save us."
Then he was gone, leaving me to cower like a new-born goat in the bowels of the Earth as I listened to the sounds of death and destruction crashing like cymbals on the ground above. While I devoted myself to fervent prayer in this hidden chamber, by their screams and the quickening of my heart I knew that a band of furies was raging above me. I pulled my veils closer to ward off the chill of that cold, dark grotto, my only comfort God's eternal flame. From this place I occupied myself with continual prayers to my beloved Lord of the Sun, until I was deep in his hypnotic embrace.
Over the course of the dark and hateful night the sounds of death progressively ceased, and after many hours I could see from the inexorable receding of darkness that the sun was beginning to rise. It was then that a ray of hope fell upon me like gold dust, for in that moment - with a clanging of metal, blood splattered but gleaming - a great warrior revealed himself at the entrance of the cave.
His sword was drawn but I recognised his Thessalian dress and saw the insignia of God upon his breast, so was unafraid.

More than this, I felt sure as halcyon day had followed the unholy night that Apollo himself had come to claim me, just as I had hoped and prayed he would. I got to my feet and approached him on my trembling legs, holding out my palms by way of supplication as I intoned a hymn of thanks for deliverance against evil. But rather than lower his sword he interrupted my chanting and addressed me in a cold voice.
"Stop and answer me now - are you a Cretan by birth?"
Even this did not startle me, so entranced was I by the certainty of deliverance from evil. I answered that I was not and a look of relief crossed his face, soon making way for a reflection of the wonder in my own. His eyes were like silver stars in the half-light and I was a small step away from him when he stretched out both hands to lift my veils. I held my breath as he twined heavy sections of my thick, golden hair around his fingers.
His tone became infinitely softer: "Who are you?"
"I am in service to the Temple" I whispered shyly, and revealed my true name to him beneath my breath.
I heard the dreamlike quality to my own voice as if it came from beyond me. So clearly did he resemble the god of my mind that I was dazzled by his longed-for manifestation. My world had been transformed in the twinkling of an eye, and with it the whole world above.
He repeated my name three times and I could not help but smile, flattered by his attention.
The Saints who tutored me were not like this man, who had come to me clothed with the sun. He was handsome as only the God could be, that much was clear, and never before had I experienced so clear an answer to my prayers. He did not say another word, just lifted me in his arms and carried me up to greet the new Dawn, clasping my golden head to his unyielding, burnished breast.
When he set me down again it was well away from the scenes of bloodshed, in an area where the servants slept. He got to one knee again and studied my face with an air of fascination, turning my chin towards the light and taking once again the weight of my hair in his hands, spreading his arms to measure its length. As he slowly opened his fingers it fell like skeins

of golden silk around my shoulders. My eyes drifted closed and in the split second before I fainted, I felt him lean towards me and kiss me on the cheek.

When I next awoke it was to find grandmother Hekate and her maid Corinthia bending over me anxiously.

"Thank God she is safe!" cried Hekate, who had nursed me for as long as memory served me to recall and my blessed mother before me. I sat up to put my arms around her.

I became aware that the Tetrarch was watching us with great attention. Silence descended, bringing with it a gentle breeze of warm, sweet air. It came suddenly upon us, as if it were the breath of Aphrodite.

"The Aura," he said quietly, putting a finger to my cheek again. His voice fell almost to a whisper. "I can scarcely believe she is mortal - in her face I see the divine…"

Hekate gave him a sharp glance at this but Corinthia overflowed with pride. "Oh, she is fair as the sun, my Lord. Such hair as there is on her head we have never seen the like of before or since!"

Without so much as a glance at her, removing neither hand nor eyes from my face, he asked: "You know, do you not, that the High Priestess is dead?"

I was shocked at his words for this had not occurred to me at all until that moment but the Tetrarch addressed me once again with an air of calm expectancy. "Now she is gone, what will you say to me, daughter of Apollo?"

I was afraid, then, for I had never before been questioned by such a man in this way. As I searched Memory for an appropriate line of hexameter the dry voice of Timocrates suddenly flew to my aid and the Saint's cool shadow veiled my bewildered face.

"May the God be with you now and always," he responded, "and assist you in fulfilling a glorious destiny, as befits the one who brought the light to Delphi in her darkest hour."

He got to his knees before the Tetrarch with arms outspread. "I give you my heartfelt thanks that she has been spared the fate which befell the others. You have saved her," he added simply. My noble guardian hung his head with such an aspect of total supplication that I was quite taken aback.

The Tetrarch did not appear surprised, but instead smiled broadly, dazzling us all with his countenance and appearing so handsome that I stared at him in amazement. He laughed merrily. "My dear friend Timocrates, there is no need at all for this attitude, please arise! I believe we have found the natural replacement for she who departed in the black of night." He paused and scrutinised my worried-looking guardian with a hard expression. "They cannot possibly object now we are free of the Cretans", he snapped."

Timocrates replied in a tormented whisper. "It has been a bloody night and we must make sacrifices for the dead. He turned to look at me, "we should wait....."

I saw at once how this resistance irritated the Tetrarch, who raised his voice before Timocrates could finish. "It is essential that the office be occupied by one who is loyal to the friends of Delphi and I believe this girl will remember well the way I saved her life. "Besides," he added thoughtfully, once more fixing his eyes upon me, "it is only fitting for the counsel of Apollo to be given by a golden-haired maiden in his days of greatest glory".

He pulled a shining blade from his boot and before I had time to think cut a lock of the hair that had fallen onto my arm. He carefully wound the long, golden threads around the hilt of his dagger. Timocrates stepped forward and bowed his head, but I was rooted to the spot without real comprehension of the scene I was somehow playing a part in.

The Tetrarch departed soon after and I was unaccountably rend in two by a sharp and hitherto unknown sorrow that would bind me to the moon by a silver thread, destined only to wax and wane as he came and went throughout the years.

From that day on, though he did not reside at Delphi but far away in the horsemen's hills of Thessaly, I would seek his face in every crowd, as the head of a flower will bend towards the sun. At night before sleeping I would touch in my mind his untarnished image, longing for the moment when he might really touch me, though I feared it would never come. It was shortly after this first encounter that I became the high-priestess of Apollo, and so it was that two great loves became intertwined in my Psyche for the whole of time.

Percy

"I hardly move, yet far I seem to have come."

Parsifal, Richard Wagner

Parsifal, Richard Wagner: "Then suddenly the heavenly splendor fell And flamed and glowed within the sacred cup." - Etching by Rogelio de Egusquiza, 1917

"You see, my son, time turns here into space."

Mr Morgan laid his hands out on the table and addressed the little gathering in his kitchen. "So, it's decided. We shall meet with EMESH at White Leaved Oak and advance as one Circle to the Keep. We shall fervently hope the King awakens and admits the French in time to meet us there. One of Nina's circle will send him a dream to hurry things along. From what Marc says, we should not expect to see Elena but we are authorised to utilise the Stone of Cintamani in our quest to free the Priestess."

The word hung in the air like the pendulum of a great clock which had come to a standstill, as if uncertain of which way to swing. It was the first time he'd said it out loud and Ana's father took a deep breath as anxiety twisted in his stomach. It was like Delphi all over again. "Regarding the Stone, we are yet to decide which one of us should wield it? Did your experience in the White Room give you any indication?"

Marc, who was still wearing his Tuaoi ring and radiated so much confidence that the others around the table felt strangely reassured by his presence, scratched his chin thoughtfully. "I can only repeat what Elena told me, which is that the purer the soul, the stronger the action of the Stone."

Both men scanned the faces of those present, including each other. There was Tristan, beside himself with anguish; Colin, busy working on an elixir that would help strengthen their auric shields against the Bacchic hounds; John, quiet and brooding, his mind fixed on trying to solve the unhappy sequence of events at Glastonbury. Mrs Pixley, of course, who was there to facilitate integration with the EMESH and to strengthen their astral sheaths with her special Armour of Light formulas.

Percy.

Both pairs of eyes settled on the pale young man simultaneously. Both lit up at the equally synchronous realisation that here was the man for the job.

Absorbed in a glorious technicolour magazine which commemorated the life of Queen Elizabeth II, it took Percy several minutes to realise that the room had fallen silent and *all* eyes were now on him. He sat up in his chair, surprised. As the youngest member of the party he had not expected to be given such an awesome task as wielding the Stone of Cintimani for the first time in over a century. "Why me?" he stammered, wondering what on Earth he was in for.

"We need someone who is able to wear the mantle of the Fool and react with the stone in pure innocence, free of all personal intention." Mrs Pixley was looking at him intently. "You shall bear the stone to White Leaved Oak, where we shall proceed with the Mysteries and advance upon the Keep".

The Pleiades

*"Lo he has come as Orion, lo Osiris has come as Orion....
Thereupon shall come Thoth, who is equipped with words
of power in great abundance, and shall untie the fetters".*

Pyramid Text, Utterance 442

Johann Bayer's Uranometria showing the constellation Orion

When she awoke,

It was to feel the sun on her face, as if it were the sun that shone on Mount Parnassus.
The sound of Mr O'Ryan's dog barking outside on the drive served to rouse her. As she opened her eyes she noticed – somehow for the first time – that there was a glittering star constellation engraved upon the ceiling. Sun-seeker Orion, beloved of Moon-Queen Artemis, whose love holds him there in perpetuity. Strange that she hadn't noticed it before.
She swung her legs over the bed but whilst the feel of the cold floor beneath her feet was jarring, it did not fully wake her. She felt as if she was still in a dream as she walked over to the dressing table, sat before it and gazed at her reflection I the mirror. She didn't know how long she'd been sitting there when a gentle knock on the door caught her attention. "Yes?" she called uncertainly, "who is it?"
"We've just come to say hello!"
The young-sounding female voice caught Ana by surprise and she stood up at once. Who could it be? Upon opening the door she was amazed to see not one but six young women dressed in white. They beamed at her with radiant smiles which enhanced their beautiful faces to quite an extraordinary degree.
One of the girls stretched out her hand. "I'm Maia. We've come to help you get ready."
"Ready for what?"
"It's Sunday!" Maia replied as if that explained it all. "Come, sit back down and I'll dress your hair. The others can entertain us!" Another girl, whose dark hair tumbled over her shoulders in thick, glossy girls, spoke up as they crossed the threshold. "We've brought you this drink. We made it ourselves and it's rather delicious, at least we think it is! I hope you like it!"
She held out an inviting looking brew in a tall glass cup of what appeared to be a sort of tea, topped with fresh mint leaves. The aroma alone was tempting and Ana took it gladly, savouring the warmth of the cup against her cool hands.
As Maia began to comb out her hair with long, slow strokes,

the other girls, who had retreated to the window seats, began to sing a curious verse. The words were somehow familiar, Ana thought, half-remembering and half completely lost in the abyss of time.

> *Call Thesmophorus, spermatic God [Dionysos],*
> *of various names, who bears the leafy rod:*
> *Mises [Misa], ineffable, pure, sacred queen, two-fold*
> *Iacchus, male and female seen:*
> *Illustr'ous, whether to rejoice is thine in incense offer'd,*
> *in the fane divine;*
> *Or if in Phrygia most thy soul delights, performing with*
> *thy mother sacred rites;*
> *Or if the land of Cyprus is thy care, well pleas'd to dwell*
> *with Cytherea [Kythereia] fair;*
> *Or if exulting in the fertile plains with thy dark mother*
> *Isis, where she reigns,*
> *With nurses pure attended, near the flood of sacred Egypt,*
> *thy divine abode:*
> *Wherever resident, blest pow'r attend, and with*
> *benignant mind these labours end*[lxxxviii].

***

Despite his prolonged absences which marred my happiness, when he returned the Tetrarch paid large measures of gold to have me sit alone before him in the Temple, high up on the tripod in my lightest veil. On such occasions my sisters would peer out at us from their secret place between the walls and columns that surround me on three sides.
"It seems to me, he loves her" whispered Erato to Calliope, knowing full well that I could hear every word of her musical voice. "I have seen how his eyes follow her form – as if she were a doe and he the stag – and now he sets another king's ransom before us!"
Calliope laughed in delight: "Love, sweet love - the story of a lifetime!" I could tell she was thrilled by the very idea and felt a flower of hope take sudden, reckless bloom within my

heart.

"Oh yes! And he shall write songs for her by the dying embers of day as he prepares to seek her presence in the sacred realm of hypnosis!" Whispered Euterpe to our dainty sister Terpsichore, who airily remarked that she would "dance for joy" to mark such a happy occurrence.

"It will all end in tears" checked the fateful Melpomene. "What mortal man has the right to desire one so beloved of Phoebus Apollo?"

I bow my head as I contemplate how such a thing might come about. Tears had not passed often from my eyes, for I had my sorrows but still more pride.

"If it is written in the stars that they are meant for each other then nothing can change things, nor unfix that which is set with fire upon the face of heaven," my clever sister Urania announced in portentous tones, causing me to lift my gaze that I might capture this spark of truth.

"It is true, dear sisters - no man can put asunder those who have been joined by God," murmured serious Polyhymnia with a meaningful glance towards the heavens, at which the curly-haired Thalia laughed and said it was "all rather amusing if you think about it!"

"We must end this speculation, which will – as you shall see! – disturb our peace. The fact is that every man on Earth seeks God's attention and many come bearing gifts for our sister."

Thus were the sanguine ruminations of my solemn sister, Clio.

I was thankful my hot cheeks were shielded by the veil as I struggled to breathe more easily. My almost irresistible urge to run towards him was kept in check by the unmoving force of the god which held me in place. The result was that I could not deviate an inch from the position in which I found myself, suspended between Heaven and the Abyss in a state of profound tension. I yearn above all else to feel the tender fire of our first meeting, the touch of his hand on my face, his lips against my cheek.

I have vivid memories of the last winter Tristeria, which left me with a sense of dissatisfaction that I cannot place. I wonder if my love for Dionysus has grown too strong. In my

unfulfilled longing for the Tetrarch the allure of the twice-born youth has power to move me beyond my present confines. I am drawn to follow him further in a way that would be impossible to resist were it not for my oaths to Apollo. Whether I might share more fully in Dionysus' gift of Renewed life without sacrificing my first allegiance to the Sun-King is a matter that occupies my mind greatly, most often when darkness falls.
I cannot safely confide these thoughts to anyone on earth, for if I do not remain true to Apollo and above the temptations of passion then none will have faith, his rule shall end and Delphi will crumble to dust, taking me and all the Saints to the same earthly grave. Time and again I wonder how I might reconcile the forces of reason and passion, duty and desire, which have somehow become opposed within me.
"The successful resolution of antinomies is a hallmark of mastery," Timocrates reminded me one sultry afternoon, when I complained – still without revealing my secret - that a growing fire in my heart might one day consume the clear, detached mind that was the gift of Apollo.
"If Apollo and Dionysus are perpetual rivals and both make Delphi the centre of the world - with me at its heart - then how am I to unite them within me when it seems they would rather break me in two?"
That night I spread my heavy hair about the fleecy headrest and gaze at the glittering constellation engraved upon the ceiling. It is the sun-seeker Orion, beloved of our Moon-Queen Artemis, whose love holds him there in perpetuity. I contemplate the virgin huntress of heaven who raised her bow at Apollo's behest and claimed the life of her lover unawares. With this as my example I must learn how to subjugate the crackling flames of desire, by which I shall make the love of my own life immortal.
The next morning, my sister brushes my hair out into sections and begins to finely weave it into braids, while I sit still with a cold, damp hand pressed over my eyes. The boundaries of my mind are starting to disintegrate and wonder if I will have the strength to bear it when God speaks through me.
She sets down the comb and places her soft hands upon my

shoulders, gazing down at me with lowered lashes and appearing as an Oread nymph in the priceless Egyptian glass.. She senses my anxiety and bids me in her heavily accented Greek, to 'look into the glass again, Priestess', as she sets alight a tightly wrapped bundle of leaves from a flaming lantern which hangs beside the doorway. The acrid scent of the smoke is pungent and soon I am becoming hypnotised by my reflection in the shimmering glass. I realise she has been singing to me for some time in her low, harmonious voice. The words she utters are in her native tongue – a language I know but a little of – and the stream of mysterious audition mingles irresistibly with the smoke until I feel the very air about me has become a vivifying incantation.

The nightingale bursts into song with a voice full of longing and I feel my eyelids flickering like the wings of a butterfly as it gathers pollen from swollen summer blooms. Before I have the chance to drift off into sleep the sensation of cold metal being pressed upon my crown sends a shock down my spine. I open my eyes onto the mirror and focus on the golden diadem that Maia has placed around my temple, fixed to the gleaming coils of tightly braided hair. I am captivated by the glittering of gold in the warm glass and when she hands me the sprig of Daphne I chew it unthinkingly, unable to tear my gaze from my own reflection.

I have lost my sense of time and see that I am changing. The golden band is shifting shape and blurs before my unblinking eye. I feel as if a wholly irresistible force is holding me still upon the seat, commanding my mind to empty as the shimmering golden snake slides around the left side of my face and cups my chin. In the next split moment there is no face at all that I can see, simply the image of a lyre, clear as the glass itself, defined and unmistakable. A single note – a perfectly tuned string from the top of the octave – sounds in the centre of my mind. It radiates outwards so it inhabits every space around me, clear as light and purer than untainted gold, herald of God's presence. The snake bites its tail. The form of another inhabits my own entirely.

Then comes music.

Orphic Sacrifice

It was the Moon-goddess, not the Sun-god, who originally inspired Orpheus

Robert Graves, The White Goddess

Diana and Endymion, Francis Job Short, 1891

A coven had gathered

At White Leaved Oak, the like of which had never been imagined in all the great ages of what remained of the King Tree and it's offspring.
Prominent amongst the gathering was Nina Roudnikova, away from Lost Continents for the first time in more than a generation. With her in the astral was the cream of Russia's intelligentsia, persecuted by the Bolsheviks and only just emerging from their self-imposed century of silence.
Also with them in the circle were representatives of the Company of Avalon, consisting of three Druids and two Anglican priests. Mrs Pixley had attracted a vast entourage of Spirts that stretched back as far as the cottages beyond the field. They were kneeling in reverence around a Holy Well that was blessed with the essence of the Grail.
At the centre of the circle stood Marcus Marconi, with his father's scrying glass in one hand and ceremonial dagger in the other, which was held aloft to show the Stone of Tuaoi to as many of those assembled as possible. Percy was standing beside him with his eyes turned reverently downward, continuing to pray without ceasing as he held aloft the Stone of Cintamani. As in answer to the music of the ancient crystal and meteor skimmed across the sky, trailed by a glittering retinue of fire and ice.
Missing from the company were some of their friends. Valentin and his wife, Maria, had elected to stand vigil in Westminster Hall, where HRH Queen Elizabeth II was lying in state ahead of her funeral. Joined with them through a covenant of the heart – and holding the fort in their Motherland - were, of course, the Spirits of poor Father Pavel Florensky (1882-1937), Daniil Andreev and Vladimir Solovyov, who lamented in Kaluzhskaya square, where the church of the Mother of God of Kazan had once stood.
Serge had not been heard of since rushing to Ukraine, where he had positioned himself in Luhanshchyna, close to the Russian border. There whereabouts of Marilyn, no one knew, but Mikhael had reassured them all that she would rally at a time of her own choosing. John had remained in Glastonbury

where, as agreed by the Druids, he would oversee purification rituals to undo any damage inflicted by rogue occult orders at this pivotal time in history.

As they prepared to advance upon the Keep and engaged in their opening rites, unbreakable bonds were formed between the masters of East and West who had gathered on England's sacred soil at the place of the King Tree. Mrs Pixley had led the group in a potent reinforcement of the Armour of Light via a series of exercises she'd devised herself, with a focus on the Golden Cone of Confidence.

The prayers of Valentin and Maria were also clearly discernible, as they mingled with prayers of the nation for the safe deliverance of Queen Elizabeth's soul to Heaven, a vast and solemn ritual which usefully paralleled the course of their own. As the sun began to set at precisely 19:07, they were all fully unified in a hymn of praise to the Lord.

And so it is said that after death, the tutelary genius (daimon) of each person, to whom he had been allotted in life, leads him to a place where the dead are gathered together[lxxxix].

I want to seek out the Tetrarch but my pride is too strong. Besides – and bitter medicine though it is for me to swallow - I know it is better this way. Better that I do not even think of him, for I cannot be married to him or any other man when I am Pythia, wedded to a God. I would be cast from the Kalki Scala in an instant, left to make the endless fall alone, abandoned by men and gods alike.

Notwithstanding the promise of such terror, my restless heart cannot stop yearning for the sign that relief is near. I scan the star-studded night for the sight of Orion. When the hunter reaches his apex in the sky, then shall wandering Dionysus return and no longer must I think of riddles to settle men's minds while my own is harbouring a storm. "Oh, Mother," I whisper into the star-studded night, "will you not set me free?"

It is seven days into the moon of Boedromiōn when I am awakened late at night with a start of instant arousal, as if some loud noise had penetrated my dreams but died before echo could greet it. My pulse is racing and my body is damp with sweat, oblivious to the chill of the night air.

I fling aside the covers and throw my feet over the side of the bed. At the first touch of cold stone I hear the familiar rhythm of the timbrels, the melodies of the aulos, and my heart rises up into my mouth in a single beat. Its rhythm matches the hypnotic pounding of drums, traveling to me across the earth from the deepest mystery of night.

IOI evoeI

***

Silently watching the start of the dance from the cover of the forest, the 12 were tense, but resolute.

It is time, thought Mr Morgan, prompting the 12 to disperse along rays of starlight to equidistant points in a wide circle around the moat of the Keep. For his vantage point in the North Colin started to beat the ancient ceremonial drum, slowly and softly at first. As one man/woman they began to raise the Cone of Power.

Also observing – in his case from the top of the Tower - O'Ryan had clenched his jaw so tightly that he was starting to grind his teeth. His hypnotic regression of Ana to the first life she'd spent with him had been so successful that it had taken him aback. Her latent power, formerly so veiled and passive that it was difficult to discern, had emerged with such force that it now far exceeded his. If she were to avert her gaze and thereby break their connection before the ritual was done, it would break him completely.

He struggled to stay in control of his mind. He could not risk losing sight of the mission of so many lifetimes. Hard lives, some of them. A two and a half millennium-long Nigredo was the price he had paid for his desecration of the Temple through violation of its Priestess. He had learned a lot in those long years, overcoming all tests and challenges. Now he had reached the point where their alchemical union in the darkest hour before dawn, was within his reach. There she was outside his home, losing herself in the dance and the firelight mead, oblivious to the appeals of her clan in the midst of the potent feminine constellation.

The enemy covens had joined by now and he sensed the strong cone of power extremely close to his home. It was very strong and contained some strange elements that he did not recognise. He would like to have sent Monsieur into the woods but he couldn't risk the hound running straight to the fire behind the castle, where it might frighten Ana out of her trance.

He would gather his men for the Orphic sacrifice. The 18-year-old girl who'd been in the basement for the past 3 moons would be given in honour of his Gods. His power would increase so much that neither Ana nor her clan would be able to thwart him. He took the iron knife from an ornamental case that was fixed to the East wall of the tower. Two dark stones glittered on the hilt, one of them deep blood red, the other charcoal grey. He would take the girl's head with it, in honour of the eternally dismembered Orpheus.

First he wanted Ana to plunge it into the maiden's heart. She had naturally befriended the eidolons of six earlier sacrifices, who were out there enjoying the firelight dance with her at that very moment. He paused so he might better hear the sound of their music and laughter drifting up to his Tower from the rear of the building. Catching Ana's distinctive joyous laugh he allowed himself a smile. His faith in her had been justified. The long years of waiting were almost over. The Priestess would be his again. From Orion would manifest Osiris and the cycle could begin anew.

***

The exquisite sound of the lyre was distant but Ana perceived it from the first note, which reached her from the top of the tower despite the louder noises in her near vicinity. She stopped dancing around in a circle with the other girls and stood still to listen. Her heart skipped a beat. It was Him!

Maia, Electra and the other girls sighed and began to melt away from the light of the fire, towards the edge of the castle moat, where they hid behind the shadow of a large willow tree and took up a poignant lament in the softest of tones.

They must be sad because he's calling me and not one of them, Ana thought, pitying them, her pupils already widening in anticipation.

The circle of 12, which had been slowly but steadily advancing over the course of an hour was now just metres away from the far edge of the moat, the cone of power towering above them in a vortex of inverse light. It was almost invisible to the naked eye of anyone but the most perceptive or gifted of onlookers. Ana was aware of it but, much to their consternation, she did not attempt to join with the energy of her clan. She was deep in hypnosis and entirely under O'Ryan's spell.

Mrs Roudnikova, though her concentration had not broken, could feel herself become more anxious. She had never known her great granddaughter to be unresponsive to even the slightest spiritual or psychic vibration, even if she failed to understand its origin. It was clear by now that Percy and Marc would have to cross the narrow bridge across the moat very soon and defeat the black coven with more direct forms of magic. Maybe even something more basic, she thought in Old Russian, a hint of desperation dripping into her mind.

The others stopped in their tracks at the sudden alteration in their circuit of force. *Gareth!* Her thought vibrations grew even stronger, forming a plaintive command. *You must give Percy the garter and then I shall give him my blessing.*

As Gareth Morgan was almost opposite Mrs Roudnikova at the other side of the circle, it took some time for Percy to get back to where she was standing, close to the bridge. Arriving at her side, he dropped to her knees in ardent prayer, an action which was immediately mirrored by the others present. Only Nina Pavlovna stood upright, blessing the young knight from the tip of a small silver sword.

Arise, Percy...

Just as Percy got back to his feet, Tristan stepped forward. *I'll go with them.*

Take my dagger, said Mr Morgan, handing him a dangerous-looking blade. *And don't be afraid to use it if you have to. You'll know if the time comes.* Tristan took the weapon, which had never been used in his or Gareth Morgan's lifetime, and the three men advanced as one towards the footbridge.

Ana, meanwhile, was answering the call of the lyre and was walking back towards the rear entrance of the Keep. The mystifying music now filled her entire being, leading her towards it like an orphan to the pied piper, though its origin appeared to have shifted. Whereas once it clearly came from above her, high in the Tower of the Keep, it now seemed to be emanating from the cellars, somewhere she had not yet been.

As Percy, Marc and Tristan set foot on the slippery wooden slats of the bridge, Ana's slippered feet alighted on the top step of the cellar stairs and paused on the cold, unyielding threshold. A strange orange glow was emanating from the space below, which carried with such a dark aura that something deep within her hypnotised soul gave pause for warning. *There's danger, don't go there*, her Guardian Angel whispered, urgently. *Go and see your father and great grandmother!*

Come to me Ana.

The words of the Tetrarch drowned out the angelic voice and cut through the atom of fear, splitting it into a forward compulsion of reckless desire.

The Crossroads

I began the presentation of the esoteric doctrine of the triad of categories of consciousness by identifying their ontological prototypes: Apollo, Dionysus and Prometheus. Having completed this task, we can now proceed to the study of the refractions of cosmic principles in the concrete evolving consciousness of man.

Vladimir Shmakov, Pneumatology

Belvedere Apollo

A loud and eerie cry

Rends the night in two. I cannot tell if it is made by bird, man or beast and am chilled to the bone, as if the strange call had seized my own breath. Then I see him standing beneath a Laurel tree, a dark silhouette in the waning light.

It seems as if invisible wings of air are lifting me over the stones towards the edge of the dark forest, where all other knowledge is obliterated by the realisation of his presence, standing in the shades. I tremble like a leaf in the wind as he leads me to the place where his horse is tethered. The danger we face is great and long we travelled that night, for the roads to and from Delphi are winding.

Whilst I feel a kind of desperate joy at the nearness of his heart against my cheek, with every fleeting step my fear increases. The further I slip from the Temple, down the steep and unforgiving road, the further it seems I am falling - either from or into an illusion - where once was my certain self. The further I flee from Apollo, the keener I feel the loss of his priceless gifts.

With mounting dread, I contemplate what it would mean if He - the one who has protected and nurtured me since birth, heaping upon me the most abundant blessings - were to turn against me. Much as I have turned away from him with my unholy actions. Will my erstwhile protector become my mortal adversary?

As we flee over the crossroads kept sacred by my grandmother Hecate, I experience the new sensation that my destiny is no longer laid out straight before me. It has entered into the unknown regions I cannot even speak of. Yet even as the dreadful fear tightens its grip on my psyche, I perceive the seed of something else. I know that ships are waiting to carry us away across the inky-black ocean of Poseidon. So often have I dreamed of the crossing, but only ever glimpsed the waters from afar, a glittering haze in the heat of the sun on the horizon.

I must have fallen into a trance-like sleep, for when I next hear his voice we have slowed to a halting pace. The hooves of his steed are soft upon the forest grass. At last, we come to

a standstill and I look around with shy, wary eyes.
As he jumps from the horse to help me down, I see faceless others materialise from the shadows of the trees, keeping a respectful distance. I bow my head in confusion and shame but catch my breath as something new assails my slumbering senses. An unknown fragrance is alive on the cool night air and the *sound*....it is like nothing I have ever heard before.
I see him smiling through the darkness. "Come, at last I can show you...." There are subtle notes of pride and joy in his voice as he guides me away from the dark forest path towards the moon-drenched horizon.
My heart is fluttering like a bird within a cage as the low, relentless roar grows louder. Slowly he draws me to the edge of the world and grips my hand as I gaze in wonder at the churning mass which stretches far beyond us. I gasp in delight, unable to contain my joy. The sea, at last!
He laughs with me. "This is the sea, Priestess, and soon we shall be upon it." He pointed to a deep cove, almost hidden from sight. "See my ship? When it has borne us to our destination and you are safe, then we shall perform the rites. You can dance in the firelight and bear witness to the glory of Dionysus once again."
He leads me down a narrow path to a small boat which transports us to the Pandia – named in honour of all that is Divine. The thrill of the irrepressible waves surging beneath us lifts my heart. Is this not, after all, what I always wanted?
The cabin below is sparsely decorated but warm enough, for it has been hung all about with lamb's wool. The flame from a small lantern crackles and sparks, casting strange shadows as the wooden boards tilt with the waves. I sit awkwardly upon the fleecy bed, trying to disguise the tumultuous emotions surging through me as he fills two cups of honey mead and puts one into my hands. He raises a toast to my freedom and there is a pregnant silence as we drink together.
Alone like this with a man in strange a bedchamber, I start to grow afraid again, as if I am not where I belong. I think of the comfort of my rooms at Delphi, the serenity of the moonlit temple, the laughter and companionship of my sisters. They are alien to me now, further away in spirit than Persia or

Egypt. The Tetrarch looks somehow unfamiliar and I feel a stab of terror. It is too late for me to run. Where has all my power gone? It is worthless as sand and I only have myself to blame.

He has been watching me carefully throughout this inner turmoil and now he finally speaks. "You need not fear me; you are a very great prize – the greatest of them all - and I shall honour you accordingly. We shall be married when we arrive at our destination, but would you grant me something ahead of that time?"

How could I refuse? The ship has already sailed and we both know full well that I am at his mercy. Moments ago we stood together watching as the shores of Hellas faded from view and the rash confidence of my inner child was blown into nothing by the restless wind. I nod mutely in answer to his question, struggling to calm my terror.

He knelt before me and put a warm hand to my cheek. "Do not fear, love, I would only unbraid your hair." As he began to unwind the intricately woven braids, slowly and gently, combing the strands with his fingers, my eyes closed and fear gave way to pleasure. I recalled how I would think of him with such longing when my hair was being dressed and felt as if my sisters' efforts throughout my life had been preparing me for this moment.

My heart was racing like the horse which had borne me, as his touch provoked a feeling like no other I had ever experienced. Was this the work of Eros, I wondered, or even Phanes himself?

I had wondered he might ravish me with force, as Gods do their nymphs, but his hand did not stray to the curve of my smooth throat. Nor did they touch my bare arms, spread on each side like slender branches of laurel as the golden ropes of my hair unfurled around them.

My eye flickered beneath their lids as I remembered how we had met, when he had knelt before me as he did now and measured the length of my hair with the same gesture of awe. Silence ran deep into the atmosphere and - just as it did on that first day - the aura came over us like dawn, gilding the shadows with divine promise. Sensing the Goddess draw near to us, I at last looked into his eyes and confessed.

"I dreamed of you…"

My voice faltered and he put a finger to my lips, halting the words before more could fall. He caressed my throat and longing suddenly surged in me like the churning waves. As if he could read my emotion as easily as an inscription above the Temple door, he removed the golden pin that held my peplos in place. It was a gift he had given me himself and as it was removed the fine white material fell down across my breasts, like blossom falling from a tree.

The breath of the Goddess touched my brow like a ray of light and it seemed as if every drop of blood in my body was transformed into a measure of liquid gold. He whispered my true name and my limbs wove around him like ivy, their knowledge exceeding my conscious understanding, even as one star died and another was born between us.

Kalki Scala

Beauty is mysterious as well as terrible. God and devil are fighting there, and the battlefield is the heart of man.

The Brothers Karamazov, Fyodor Dostoevsky

Fyodor Dostoevsky, 1876 {{PD-US}}

Ana began her descent,

Taking care not to tumble down the narrow and hazardous staircase, disappearing into the livid orange light emanating from the bowels of the Keep.
Moving just as cautiously across the old and rickety footbridge, Percy found himself gaining courage with every careful step. They crossed the wide moat without incident, having scrupulously avoided looking down at the cold dark water, resplendent with water lilies and moonlit bullrushes.
"Let's go round the back", Marc urged, "it'll still be open".
They ducked close to the castle wall and quickly reached the rear of the building, which was bathed in the glow of the collapsing fire. The cone rose above them like the shadow of the Queen's pyramid, rippling with a protective force so strong it made Marc's hair stand on end.
Tristan, who was bringing up the rear, hesitated on the threshold of the back door as a barely audible sigh reached his ears. He looked around in surprise. It had definitely been a feminine-sounding voice, he thought. Or multiple voices.
"There's no time!" Percy whispered urgently, sensing his companion faltering.
"I heard it too," Marc murmured, "we could look for them later."
Tristan looked round and gestured for them to move on. No sooner did they step over the threshold of the Keep than strains of the lyre abruptly ceased. It was a relief to be free of the hypnotizing effects of the music, but the new-found silence brought a more sinister kind of menace. They stopped again, attempting to reorient themselves in the unsettling gloom. The Cone of Power was effectively shielding their presence from those within the Castle walls, but it could not shield them from the evil atmosphere within.
Marc shivered on the spot, as if someone had walked over his grave. "Poor Ana, she must have been terrified. I don't understand why she didn't leave at once, the moment we arrived to help her escape!"
"She's drugged and under hypnosis," Tristan muttered, his voice grim. "These guys are very dangerous."

Marc nodded but didn't reply. He felt sorry for Tristan that the woman he loved was quantumly entangled with another man, let alone a necromancer. His heart began to pound as he considered what O'Ryan as capable of. "Let's say a prayer to strengthen our astral centre."

The three of them crossed themselves together and began to intone the prayer.

Ana was still as a statue of Kore, with the Archaic smile of a Delphian priestess, staring into the Tetrarch's eyes with look of intense concentration. He had met her at the foot of the stairs and placed a veil over her face before leading her to the altar. An oil lamp was burning above the head of the Seventh Sacrifice, who was bound unconscious to the stone slab.

O'Ryan was half speaking, half singing, a curious verse, half-remembered by Ana, half lost in the ocean of time. He placed the knife into her right hand. *What is this for?* She queried, as if in dream, still staring at him with moonstruck eyes.

It can represent the East, he reminded her, the element of Air or the Initiation of Swords.

Yes. Thank you. I don't know how I could have forgotten something so simple.

"Ana. Repeat after me…"

Before he could begin to intone the sacrificial rite he was struck dumb by the sudden manifestation of a dazzling female figure who shone with the fierce blue light of Venus. *What magic is this*….he wondered in confusion, as his power drained out of him with alarming speed, flowing towards her with a tremendous magnetic force. Before he could gather his wits and lower his gaze, she batted her lashes and captured O'Ryan with a beam which shot from her left eye.

Surely this is the Goddess, he thought in dumbfounded awe, hastily revising his plans of the past 2,542 years. Could he really be bothered to keep an innocent priestess under hypnosis for the rest of time. Why bother when Venus was already here and he could be Mars!

The Goddess was standing close to Ana's right shoulder – thoroughly outshining the submissive maid – with her wrist on one hip in the manner of a Dionysian priestess. The fingers of her other hand, glittering with priceless gems, were twined in her stylised hair, which was brighter than white gold.

A timid voice from the past piped up, reminding him about the lost rite: "What should I say, I didn't hear you?"

"Hush, child..." he answered dreamily, his eyes still riveted on the glorious apparition which rendered Ana all but invisible.

Ana's face took on a wounded expression,stung beyond measure as the realisation dawned that she was no longer the centre of his universe. Following his gaze she looked over her shoulder at what or whomsoever had usurped her so successfully, lifting the edge of her veil to see this vision more clearly.

Helen of Troy!

She gasped out loud, prompting the vision to remove the hand from her hair and put a finger to her lips, without breaking eye-contact with O'Ryan.

Trust me, Ana, I'm a friend. With a uniquely undulating gait the vision moved forward and perched on the edge of the altar, widening her eyes so they sparkled like sapphire stars in the flickering light of the lamp. Mirroring her movement, O'Ryan also stepped forward. He had a haunted look on his face, his own eyes burning like black coals as they drank in the sight of the unequalled female form.

She gave a winning smile and made a suggestion.

Kiss me love, with heavenly affection; hold me close to you... With all your heart's protection.

As millennia of emotion finally burst out of O'Ryan's chest with the force of Niagara, Ana squeezed her eyes shut against the hot and bitter tears that sprang up. She did not dare watch as O'Ryan was pulled irresistibly closer, like a man possessed.

Thrill me with your charms; take me, in your arms...

Oblivious to anything but the Divine Feminine force whose victory was almost complete, O'Ryan sank to his knees before the vision and begged her to use him in any way she pleased. She put a satisfied finger to his mouth, completing the Eleventh Arcanum with such supreme mastery of her art that she couldn't help laughing in delight.

As Ana let out a sob of misery there came a great cracking of the ether, which tore across the room like a dark thunderbolt of Zeus, to shocking effect. The girl who was tied to the altar awoke from her own drugged stupor and let out an echoing cry. This was too much for Percy, who rushed out of the shadows, flung his heavy cloak over her naked body and quickly began to untie her.

At the exact same moment Monsieur – who thanks to the Cone of Power had been sleeping in the Tower dreaming of hares – charged down the stairs howling in rage, skidded on the slippery stone and landed at Tristan's feet. The latter, upon receiving the fright of his life at the sudden arrival of what appeared to be a hellhound, whipped out the iron dagger and plunged it into the belly of the beast.

Finally coming to her senses, Ana whipped around and immediately began to scream as she witnessed the horrifying scene. Tristan rushed over to her side as O'Ryan prostrated himself to kiss the feet of the apparition, whose heavenly aura was on the verge of transporting him to Corinth.

Make my life perfection... he pleaded quietly, his forehead touching the stone. The air itself began to sigh. A fall of bright yellow petals drifted down upon his head - sadly but sweetly - transporting him to the Temple of Apollo at Delphi with the velvet kiss of time past.

Outside, beyond the moat, those who remained in the circle had fallen to their knees in ecstatic relief at the sudden release from their struggle. "It is done!" said Nina Roudnikova from the centre of their circle. "Ana has been released from the spell and the Goddess has conquered O'Ryan. Percy has found the missing Grail Princess. Hades has agreed to discharge its prisoners in time. The Mysteries are complete and the Rose is on the Cross."

With that she expired, disappearing entirely from the outer world and leaving the others holding hands around the space where she had once been. In her place was a wondrous flower, a perfect red nelumbo nucifera, also known as the

Indian Lotus, native to Russia and the Caspian Sea, which resembled in colour the secret Hrit Chakra.

"My Initiate has made the crossing," said Butator with pride. "The way is now open."

"Oh!" The small note of surprise from his wife made all of them turn to the West, whereupon they saw a second flower, golden as the Grail, of an unearthly variety.

"And Mrs Pixley has achieved the perfect citrinitas!" the moustachioed mage announced with palpable satisfaction. All we need do now is wait for Dawn.

With the Tuaoi stone glowing on his finger with such amazing brilliance that it conferred a hitherto untold energy upon him, Marc dropped the sword and leapt up the stairs with Vril-like speed as a massive surge of adrenaline struck him.

Barrelling out of the cellar stairs he made an instinctive dash for the nearest source of light, which was coming from the still-open back door and flooding into the hallway of the castle from a brilliant source beyond. Once he made it outside he was momentarily dazzled and pulled up in his tracks with a hand before his face.

Squinting against the blinding glare, Marc noticed an arresting sight. There in front of the fire – strange that he hadn't noticed it on the way in – was a circular sculpture atop a plinth which altogether stood five metres high. Glittering fiercely in the ultra-violet light, the figure in the centre of the circle, which had four arms and was standing on one leg, appeared to be made of pure gold. As the appearance of the strangely dynamic object came more into focus, he felt a shock of recognition. *My God!* It was the Nataraj Shiva.

Marc clutched his hair in panic and tried to stop himself from hyperventilating. *Get a grip, you Fool!* he thought fervently, as the limbs of the statue began to move in mechanical splendour like the arms of Swiss watch. The analogy made him think of checking the time, as if it might concretise some form of reality.

Fumbling in his breast pocket for the old-fashioned fob watch he'd bought in a curiosity shop close to his hotel in London, Marc read the dial with supreme astonishment.

4:32

Wow. OK.

He looked back up at the statue, suddenly serene. The module had worked. He had reached the Final Infinity.

It was the start of singularity; he was One.

***

When Marc reopened his eyes he astonished himself further by hardly skipping a beat and carefully slipping off the ring, which he left in his trouser pocket. He smiled broadly and gestured at the statue that was shining in the bright sunlight, perfectly offset by the deep blue sky.
"I must confess I've always wanted to see this," he admitted to the small huddle of scientists who surrounded him. "It's a wonderful piece, really evokes the forces of nature," he added, to nods and smiles of agreement.
Ignoring Nick's sullen face – the guy was a shitty wingman, Marc decided – he accepted a spontaneously made invitation to visit the legendary room whose walls were adorned on every available surface with ancient spells and incantations. "I wouldn't miss it for the world", he enthused, smiling at his host.
He was rewarded with a meaningful grip of the Director's hand. "It would be our pleasure Mr Marconi, I'm sure you'll find it as fascinating as we have done. Especially since we the breakthrough in September when we finally began to decipher the texts," he added confidentially." The man glanced down at the Split-Second Chronograph Patek Philippe watch on his left wrist.
"It's just gone half past twelve. After we've been to the spell room I suggest we break for lunch, go through a few more parameters for the module and then start getting ready for the Equinox party". He smiled pleasantly at Marc. "Of the two rites I can't help favouring Spring. He gestured at the carpet

of yellow flowers which were covering the grassy areas between buildings like a magic carpet. "Just *look* at the daffodils, they really are remarkable this year!"

If anyone had been looking at Marc's face in that moment, they would have seen he had gone pale and a haunted expression was in his eyes. Clearly he had lost six months.

"Where does all the time go…" he murmured softly, to cover his discomfiture. It doesn't seem like a week since Queen Elizabeth died." Irrationally, his next thought was that he'd been in England on the cusp of the biggest parade in half a century but had somehow missed it.

Then there was the matter of the daffodils. He almost let out a low whistle. It was *a riddle, wrapped in a mystery, inside an enigma*[xc]

A bespectacled man piped up from the edge of the scientific huddle. I'm suddenly reminded of what Edith Sitwell said about Marilyn Monroe: "She has a daffodil beauty, but in repose her face is strangely tragic…"

Marc's jaw dropped open and the Director smiled his appreciation. "What a wonderful description, very apt. The ancient Greeks believed daffodils were a symbol of death and grew in Hades".

The young man wearing the glasses nodded keenly. "And did you know that bulbs of the Narcissus are so poisonous they can paralyse you. Roman soldiers took them into battle in case of capture or terrible injury, as the modern-day equivalent of a morphine pill".

"How fascinating!" said the Director, thoroughly entertained. "And I quite agree, Mr Marconi," he added, turning back to Marc, apparently oblivious to his stunned demeanour. "Time really does fly! It's only six weeks until Beltane and that really IS a spectacle, we have a huge fire, light shows, dancers, musicians and all that, lots of big names turn up for that one. Here we are." He gestured to the doorway in front of them and began to turn the handle. "Inside here we shall find a spell for summoning the Vimana. Then it won't just be time that flies, we'll be on our way to Mars before you know it!"

To the sound of urbane laughter he pushed open the heavy wooden door and stood aside to let Professor Marconi pass through first. "If you look carefully you might even see one of the prototypes your illustrious namesake bequeathed to us! Just be careful when you approach the portal entrance, though, Professor; the photon crystals are incredibly powerful and the plasma field can be overwhelming if you're not fully prepared. The electro-acoustic mechanism will start up automatically as soon as you scan your chip in the starting device."

Marc paused on the threshold as he took this in, his brain working overtime again. *They must have accessed the secret Tesla papers*, he realised, wondering what he would find behind that door.

"Who knows, we might even reach the Omega Point!" joked someone at the back of the group; *Pierre*, Marc thought at once, without knowing how he knew the man's name.

"You know, someday", Pierre continued, "after mastering the winds, the waves, the tides and gravity, we shall harness for God the energies of love, and then, for a second time in the history of the world, man will have discovered fire."[xci]

"And remember, Marc," said a serious-looking bespectacled man with a moustache, "Science cannot solve the ultimate mystery of nature. And that is because, in the last analysis, we ourselves are a part of the mystery that we are trying to solve."[xcii]

Pushing his spectacles back up his nose, Marc took a deep breath and said a quick prayer to himself, crossed himself, and finally stepped over the threshold.

Epilogue

The victory achieved in solitude....what glory and what danger it comprises at one and the same time! ...it is the most real and the most serious spiritual danger which exists.

Meditations on the Tarot, Letter VII, The Chariot

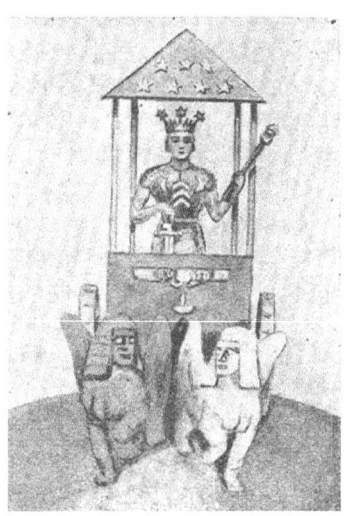

Marc knew Atlantis

Was central to the Russian and British occult schools, as well as the Edgar Cayce group that was head-quartered at Virginia Beach. Recklessly perhaps – and in light of his recent excursions - he was willing to attempt an astral visit to the underwater realm,, as Dark Journalist had suggested when he interviewed Marc for the show. Broaching the subject later with Olivia, she had suggested he ask for angelic protection before attempting the journey.

Later that night – Lammas, as it happened - Marc lay down on the spare-room bed with a curious sense of inner nonchalance, rather like a false sense of security. He had decided not to make too big a deal of it, failing to realise that he was feigning bravado so as not to die of fright before even starting.

He thought back to the phone call with Olivia and decided a prayer to the archangels, Michael in particular, was probably in order. It went something along the lines of:

DJ and Olivia think I should go to Atlantis, would you please protect me if you, like them, also think I should go?

In a matter of seconds, much to his surprise, a large fish-headed being began to approach him from seemingly out of nowhere, appearing above the bed where Marc was lying and inclining somewhat to the left.

Hey, that's weird. Gazing at it fixedly with his inner eye (his real eyes still wide open), Marc reflected that he had never seen anything remotely like it. The fish-headed being was rather fat and whiskery and appeared irritable, as if it had been roused against its will from a great long sleep. It reminded him both of a medical doctor he'd once encountered and a former tutor at Yale who had not been very impressed with him.

The idea that it was some kind of catfish drifted in and out of his mind. By some force of will or form of telepathy Marc was led to understand it was the first threshold guardian of the gateway to Atlantis. Bypassing his conscious self, ego and outer ears entirely, it communicated directly with his spirit, etheric or astral self to gauge his true intention. Thankfully for Marc, his intentions were innocent – at any rate, satisfactory enough – for in the twinkling of an eye, everything changed.

One moment he had been lying immobile in bed with all eyes glued to the inquisitorial fish, but following a split second where he lost consciousness – and *with no warning whatsoever* – he found himself at the bottom of a shadowy green-grey ocean, half hidden by seaweed, staring in astonishment at a half man, half fish.

Or maybe it was a half-man, half-serpent, for its winding corkscrew tail was hideously large. Longer than a double-decker bus. Maybe two buses. Whereas the sight of it had a striking resemblance – as he would later realise - to an ancient sigil of Ioannes, the situation he found himself in was uniquely terrifying. Deep water was one of his primal fears and there he was, sitting at the bottom of some ocean, observing an appalling scene. How was he even breathing?

The huge entity was approximately 33 feet away from where he was hiding behind a large clump of seaweed, visible only in profile. It was dark as the shadow of the deep, with short curly hair and arms held at right angles from the elbow in an oddly stylised gesture, as if he was holding something in his hands. Whilst his torso was like that of a statuesque man, everything beneath the waist consisted of the great spiral tail. *If I can see him, what if he turns and sees me!?* Marc could only wonder in abject terror. And what would happen if the creature *did* see him!? This panic-worthy possibility vied with his life-long fear of deep water to a dangerous degree, one step away from loss of either breath, control or both.

"Fervently praying he would not be spotted, a sudden 'Eureka!' moment struck him like a thunderbolt as for some bizarre reason the word 'Capricorn' sprang up in him. The effect of this apparently random word emerging from his mind made him feel as if he'd fathomed some great secret without particularly trying.

His sense of euphoria was so great that it brought him to the surface in the next split second, back into his body in the bedroom. As if there were some part of his deep unconscious which knew more than the rest of him, Marc was somehow sure that he'd passed some sort of arcane test that he didn't even know he'd been taking.

After just enough time to take another breath and register his own safety, Marc was drawn back into the astral or spirit world, whatever it might have been. When his eyes next opened it was onto an utterly tranquil scene, finding himself walking on a path beneath an azure sky, a perfect unforgettable blue that always evoked the spiritual world. The path unfurled before him, leading him towards a low, white wall with an opening in the middle, marking the threshold of a building which had not yet come into view.

Sitting on the wall, just to the left of the opening, was a young woman with very long black hair, tied up at the sides but flowing free down her back, wearing a knee-length white robe. She was angled to her right so she was in profile and was shielding her face from view with her left hand.

No sooner had Marc registered her presence when he arrived at the next scene, still walking forwards but this time inside the building with the girl walking beside him, to his left but just out of view. He vigilantly tried to observe his surroundings for outstanding detail, but it was quite dark inside, maybe even under ground. Everything within the windowless structure was smooth and solid stone.

The room they were in was not normally shaped, comprising of weird angles, apparently some form of a corridor, or an inner continuation of the path outside the threshold. There were columns at the back and he wordlessly expressed some disappointment at the lack of decoration or other defining features that he could use as reference points.

Also without speaking, the guide indicated that he should look down at the floor, whereupon he saw that they were following a path of square tiles, some 12" across, that were uniformly patterned with simple black swastika-style crosses. He was reassured that they were not the subverted Nazi swastikas, but a much more ancient form of the universal symbol.

They turned an acute corner to the right, arriving at once in a pitch black chamber, devoid of any form of light whatsoever. The guide placed a book in his hands which glowed white like the moon, as if illumined from within, opened onto a blank double page. Peering at the pearlescent surface, he was intrigued to see writing manifest swiftly and seemingly of its own accord, with letters appear from right to left.

The words which materialised on the surface of the page were composed of mostly – but not entirely - triangular letters and short diagonal lines in parallel. Marvelling at this strange script, which rapidly filled the page, Marc couldn't help wishing he'd learned a few dead languages. What could it possible mean?

Later research on his computer would indicate that the alphabet resembled a form of ancient Phoenician or Athenian. Recognising some of the triangular letters, he decided that the first word to have appeared on the page was either 'EDEN' or 'DEAD'. The angelic script of Eden now lost to mankind, perhaps, or the language of Atlantis, just as dead to the world as the long-lost civilization?

He wasn't able to study the page for long before the scene changed once again. In a baffling development, his entire field of vision was filled by a host of smooth, grey, pleasantly rounded objects. He did not realise at first that he was lying face down on a wide pebbled beach but, as he lifted his face, he saw before him the shore of a clear, calm, green-grey sea. Perhaps it was early in the morning, for rather than being that glorious blue, the sky was now a colourless grey, very much like the ocean itself.

As he gazed out to sea, Marc was struck with the most profound sense of wonder and mystification he had ever experienced. He was certain that just a moment before he had been in a building – an entire land! – that was apparently now somewhere beneath the waves.

Getting to his feet, his eyes still locked on the calm, grey ocean, he wondered how he had been able to see the sky so clearly if the place was underwater. He was seized by an irresistible impulse to dive back into the water and tried to rush forwards, but a hand grabbed his shoulder from behind, making him jump out of his skin.

He leapt round to see a man with black skin, shining eyes, short dark hair and an angelic smile. Despite the friendly appearance of the fellow, his presence was so unexpected that – on top of the unprecedented earlier events – it was a shock too far for Marc.

He must have expressed his terror because the man looked wounded and the smile left his face. Immediately contrite, but without any more bandwidth left in his blown mind, Marc apologised profusely, gave the man a quick hug and then reverted back to his body on the bed without further comment or ado.

When he discussed these strange events later in the week with DJ and Olivia he was met with a surprised response:

Oh man; we meant the Atlantis bookshop on Museum Street.

Marxists or Rosicrucians?

"I place this work as the goal of my life, for the benefit of all humanity, its freedom, its progress. The organisation or order of EMESH is supposed to present itself as a group of select individuals based on their superior morality and the cultural development of an individual, and who are ready to devote all, all of their personal life, for this goal."

Testimony of V.K. Chekhovski, 1928

Left V.K. Chekhovski & right E.K. Teger

𝒟uring his interrogation

Given on 28th June, 1928, whilst in prison, Vadim Karlovich made a strenuous attempt to engage his captors in a debate over who would have the more civilising force on humanity by wielding the more effective magic: Rosicrucians or Marxists? Thus began a very serious attempt on the part of the EMESH Redivivus to convince the Soviet authorities that cooperation with the global occult centre and heirs of Atlantis could only benefit their aims.
The matter of Atlantis was – and still is – fundamental to the occult doctrine of the Russian Rosicrucians. In his testimony Chekhoski said: "I believe in these more powerful, in these incomparably more complete cultures of humanity, such as Egypt or India or Atlantis, but especially the high culture of Atlantis".
Through a series of brilliant letters written from his prison cell, the Vadim Karlovich went to great lengths to explain their world view, in one series via a discourse between a Mystical Christian, an Occultist and two materialists.
Less hopeful but equally desperate, perhaps, was the so-called suicide letter he would write the following year -1929 - from the Solovki prison camp, after a failed attempt to organise a prison break with other inmates. Two weeks after writing it – at the age of 27 - he was shot dead along with his father. Evgeny Karlovich Teger, who had also been arrested and sent to Solovki, was transferred to Petropavlovsk and Tashkent on account of his ill health. In 1937 he was arrested again on charges of fascist activities.[xciii]
Most of our knowledge about this highly secretive order comes from the official testimony of its founder, Chekhovski, who was in turn profoundly influenced by the Martinist ideas of G.O. Mebes, Papus and Stanislas de Guaita. In accordance with long-established kabbalistic principles, the universe was perceived as consisting of five planes:
At the apex is the divine plane of Olam ha-Aziluth, the subtlest, finest and least materialistic, the realm of Ein Soph. Here is the plane of spiritual fire and the alchemical

salamander. Below this is the mental plane of Olam ha-Briah, world of Creation, signified by the Mother letter Aleph. This is the realm of transcendental reason and first causes, from which emanate the ten Sephiroth, the Spirit of Christian Hermits and elemental world of fairies and sylphs.

The third realm is that of Olam ha-Yetzirah, the World of Formation, the astral plane and the Mother letter Mem, the spiritual water. Here is the world of transcendent emotion, spiritual hierarchies and secondary causes, the seven planets and 12 zodiacal signs. It is the Soul of Christian hermits which resides in the Yetzirah plane, along with the Undines, elementals of water.

Fourth is the world of Olam ha-Asiah, the physical world that is governed by the Mother letter Shin. Here is also the zone of illusion or Maya and the Body of Christian hermeticists. With the element of Earth come the corresponding elementals, which are gnomes. The fifth and final level in this hierarchical structure is the lower abyss.

It was through this structure the EMESH hoped to both transform the individual human being and − by extension - restore the ancient magic and knowledge of Atlantis. This overriding mission would be taken up by a successive magical circle, the Rosicrucian "Order of Orion-Khermorion" led by Vsevolod Belustin, with the blessing of his friend and teacher, Vladimir Shmakov.

The task of contemporary man is reintegration, the restoration of unity, the mastery of lost perfection.

Members of the Order saw the history of the world and humanity through a Gnostic lens, as a perpetual struggle between good and evil, light and dark, 'White (Tsarist)' Russia and the Red Terror. This inescapable duality, as they saw it, necessitated the conferral of both 'light' and 'dark' initiations, so that members would not fall prey to the dark side, but instead learn how to overcome and control its forces. In this they followed G.O. Mebes, who also had a 'know they enemy as well as thyself policy'.

Whilst the figure of the 'Light Bearer', Lucifer, is more

veiled in the earlier works of Mebes, the Orionists openly attempted magical contact with the fallen angel and Lords of the Astral Element. Lucifer in this context is seen by them as perfectly balancing the poles, beyond the endless strife between forces of good and evil. They believed it was for the adept to decide whether to implement either or both of these forces in pursuit of their own goals.

The last word on this matter may to Vadim Karlovich, who told his interrogators:

"Not one government in the world can satisfy me politically. In the political milieu of the world I see a mixture of concepts, lies, political battles and forces in altercation with each other. I reject the political system and deny it. Whilst I evolved and was raised by several conservative persons, I came to an individual and very liberal conviction. For me – meaning for my I, mind and heart – there are no concepts such as nation, homeland class, rank, state or country. My homeland is where my ideological friends and brethren reside…all of humanity must exist freely in all respects…the greatest happiness and prosperity is freedom of thought and conviction; freedom of will and activity in agreement with their convictions. People of the entire world need to group together based on their convictions, whether they be one or millions. Let there not exist among you any kind of coercion. Freedom! Freedom! Freedom!"

Dramatis Personae

It will have been noted by all who read The Eidolons that there are cameo appearances from several figures from the occult world, for whom some background information may be useful and hopefully interesting. Pictured above is Valentin Tomberg, who I'm supposing most readers will be acquainted with in some way and who therefore needs no introduction. Sadly, we have been unable to find any kind of photograph, drawing or painting of Nina Roudnikova.

G.O. Mebes (Butator) (1868 – c1834)

The college professor Baron Grigory Ottonovich Mebes was born in Riga in 1868, devoting himself to the 'secret knowledge' in 1991, after graduating from the Physics and Mathematics Faculty of St. Petersburg University.

At the end of 1910, Mebes became the Inspector General (Secretary) of the St. Petersburg branch of the Martinist lodge, a branch of the French Kabbalistic Order of the Rose and the Cross, which was founded in Russia by Gerard Encausse (Papus).

The following year Mebes began his lecture course on the Encyclopedia of the Occult, which his students would eventually compile into a book, which became the text book for occultists throughout the Russian Empire and – ultimately – beyond. In August 1912 Mebes began to extricate himself from the tutelage of the Paris leaders and proclaimed the independence of the Russian Martinists. The Apollonia lodge, headed by Mebes, (with the initiatory name of Butator) was declared a great lodge and led by the "Invisible Master" (Mebes himself).

In 1913, St. Petersburg Martinists, led by Mebes, formed a special autonomous chain of O.M.O.R. with a pronounced Templar colour, which in 1916 was transformed into the "Order of Martinist Eastern Obedience". It was ruled by the Order of the "Invisible Master" or the Father (G.O.M.). His official representative was the student of Mebes, Inspector-General I.K. Antoshevsky (the initiatory name Hyacinthus). In the summer of 1917, when I.K. Antoshevsky was killed, he was replaced in this position by another student of Mebes – V.V. Bogdanov. The Chapter of the Order consisted of seven persons and the official print organ of the Russian Martinists was the occult magazine, Isis.

In 1918-1921 Mebes gave lectures on the Book of Zohar in Petrograd, and his second wife Maria Nesterova lectured on the history of religion. The declarative goal that the Russian Martinists had set for themselves was, on the one hand, to prepare the one going for the Highest Initiation (maximum programme), and on the other, to expand the esoteric secondary education of those who were not recognised as capable of the Highest Initiation. In addition to purely theoretical studies, practical work was carried out in the "school" to develop its capabilities for telepathy and psychometry among its members.

Aleksandr M Aseev, publisher of the book "Occultism and Yoga", contended that the three main branches of the Russian initiating movement – Freemasonry, Martinism and Rosicrucianism – were separate and independent organisations, but all led Mebes. The three orders worked in close contact and often included the same persons. Martinist and Rosicrucian lodges were located, according to A.M. Aseev, in the beautifully furnished apartment of Mebes and his wife in St Petersburg.

The secretive activity of the Mebes and Nesterova groups continued until 1925, when the OGPU began to show a serious interest in their work. In the middle of 1928, the Leningradskaya Pravda and Krasnaya Zvezda newspapers reported: *"...an investigation into the Great Lodge Astraea, led by 70-year-old Black Occultist Mebes, was opened by KGB agents"*.

According to AM Aseev, Mebes was arrested after being betrayed and died in the Ust-Sysolsk camp in 1934.

The vehement persecution of the 'intelligentsia' in general and occultists in particular was a hallmark of the Bolshevik Revolution from 1917 onwards, throughout the civil war years of the early 1920s and beyond, even to the present day.

In the febrile and paranoid atmosphere rumours abounded about conspiracies – real or imagined – which were attributed to certain members of society, fueled by the fact that Alexander Kerensky, de facto ruler of Russia from the summer of 1917 until the October Revolution, was openly a member of the Masonic Lodge since 1913.

All of this took place within a context of deeply engrained anti-semitism in earlier Russian regimes and society, which found appalling expression in the work of the Black Hundreds and gave birth to the idea of a Jewish-Masonic conspiracy. The fact that the radical Leon Trotsky – characterised by his vehement fight against God - was Jewish, added fuel to the dark fire. An excellent natural orator, Trotsky returned to Russia in spring 1917; according to the economic historian, Antony C Sutton, with a cheque for $10,000 which demonstrates his American backing. As rumour has it, Trotsky was a changed man, whose oratorial skills and powers of persuasion had reached incredible heights. In appearance and behaviour he was said to resemble an Egyptian priest and was able to control the minds and will of the crowds, skills which were also attributed to Lenin himself and Hitler after them. Some attributed Trotsky's newly acquired gifts to his association (whilst on US soil) with the freemason, Charles Crane, considered the 'gray cardinal' of American politics. He was alleged to have passed secret knowledge onto Trotsky, the application of which was readily apparent for all those who witnessed his triumphant return to Moscow at the start of the Revolution.

The writer Nina Berberova, who worked for years with Russian Masonic archives confirmed Trotsky's affiliation with the order, which she said he had joined at the age of 18.

With the fascinating paradox which is so characteristic of Russian history – especially occult history – many of the White Russian emigres who escaped their homeland saw the Soviet Union as the triumph of freemasonry.

In his book, "From Peter I to the Present Day" published in 1934, Vasily Fyodorovich Ivanov wrote that in 1918: "a five-pointed star rises above Russia - the emblem of world Freemasonry. Power passed to the most vicious and destructive Freemasonry, the Red Freemasonry, led by the Freemasons of high initiation, Trotsky and his henchmen, the Freemasons of lower initiation: Rosenfeld, Zinoviev, Parvus, Radek, Litvinov..."

Viewing international Freemasonry and socialism as aspects of the same dark egregore, Ivanov mused in his later book, Secret Diplomacy, that by the early 1930s Russia was becoming "the purest and most consistent Masonic state, which pursues Masonic principles in their entirety and consistency... The goal of Freemasonry and socialism is the same. They only temporarily diverged in their methods of action." This view is confirmed by the words of Soviet People's Commissar, Vyacheslav Molotov himself, who towards the end of his life admitted to being a communist who also "managed to be a freemason".

In contrast with many other members of various occult orders, masonic or otherwise, G.O. Mebes considered is main role to be apolitical, focused instead on the initiation of young people into esoteric teachings.

Nikolai Georgevich Rogalev Girs (Nabusar) (1898 – 1979)

In the 1920s, Russian esotericist, Catarina Sreznewska-Zelenzeff, was readying to leave Europe for Brazil when her friend, Nina Roudnikova – an inner circle initiate of G.O.M. and fellow 'White Russian' emigrant, gave Catarina the notes she had written on the Minor Arcana of the Tarot, as taught by G.O.M. to the Promethean Group. Nina asked Catarina to transfer the legacy to someone 'dignified' and capable of preserving the lessons for humanity.

Years later in Brazil, Catarina met Nadia Iellatchitch, widow of Gabriel, who had also been a friend and disciple of G.O.M. The ladies decided to live together and invited Nadia's brother, Alexandre Nikitin-Nevelskoy – another Mebes follower – to stay with them. With his profound knowledge of esotericism, Alexandre proved to be the 'someone dignified' who would translate the Minor Arcana into Portuguese.

Nicolas Georgevich Rogalev Girs was born in St Petersburg on June 15 1898 and came under the spiritual tutelage of G.O.M. at the age of 21, receiving the Martinist initiation within the Nordic Star Order on December 20 1919.

As was the case with fellow student, Nina Roudnikova, Girs escaped the Bolshevik Revolution, although it is unknown if they left Russia together. Whilst Nina gave her notes from the G.O.M. course to Catarina Sreznewska-Zelenzeff, Girs went with some other students to Germany where he continued the work, forming new Martinist lodges and conferring initiations.

Having survived the Bolsheviks, he would go on to experience the similarly egregious advancement of Hitler, who put a stop to the initiatory schools and persecuted occultists. Whilst Gris himself managed to survive both terrors, he decided to leave Germany for Chile on August 14, 1948, with a view to dedicating his life to painting and the restoration of art works in Santiago.

It was during this time in Santiago that Girs encountered a

group of Martinists who'd kept the flame of the tradition alive. A new Martinist movement was thus born in Chile and by 1957 there were several orders across the country, one of which had a direct connection with the Paris Order led by Philippe Encause, son of Papus, from whom were received new rituals and administrative rules. Girs was nominated as the great national delegate for Chile and tasked with forming a major council.

Girs was known to engage in very profound and intense spiritual work and by 1960 had done much to advance Martinism in Chile. In addition to his affiliation to Martinism, for half a century he was also a member of the sovereign sanctuary of The Ancient and Primitive Rite of Memphis and Misraim. Thus he represented, in his own Grand Lodge, the latest initiate in the uninterrupted chain of Russian Martinists and Freemasons founded in Moscow in 1788, directly linked to Louis Claude Saint-Martin himself through Prince Alexey Golizin.

The "Occult Encyclopedia" of G.O.M. – published in English as the Tarot Majors Course – was Girs' primary initiatory study material. Through his contact with other Russian initiates living in Central America he also obtained the notes of the Minor Arcana which were used to configure the South American Autonomous Martinist Grand Lodge.

Nicolay Rogalev Girs passed away on December 12 1979 and was buried in the Russian cemetery at Puente Alto.

Vladimir Alekseevich Shmakov (1887(?) - 1929(?))

Predictably, perhaps, given the well-documented purging of the Russian intelligentsia in general and occult schools in particular, there is little surviving information about Shmakov's life. We know that he was born in Moscow in the 1880's (1887 according to one testament) and died whilst still a young man in Argentina, 1929. He was highly educated in the outer world as well as the inner, being a railway engineer by profession. He displayed a lifelong passion for esoteric philosophy and spirituality, which in the pneumatic world of fin de siècle Russian high society attracted a group of like-minded souls to his salon.

He was still living in Russia as late as 1923 – a year after Stalin came to power – where he stood at the centre of an esoteric circle of approximately twelve regular members and a few secondary figures. The pressures of the Stalinist regime proved too great, however, and in 1924 he left the Soviet Union with his surviving family, moving first to Germany, then Prague (in some accounts, Switzerland), before settling in Argentina and remaining there until his death. It seems he had small children with him when he arrived in South America, presumably also his wife, but it has not been possible for anyone that I know of to trace his movements there or anywhere else. If ever there was a 'hidden superior' or 'unknown philosopher', it is him.

He published two major works in his relatively short lifetime: the present volume, The Holy Book of Thoth, Great Arcana of the Tarot (1916) and Fundamentals of Pneumatology (1922). After a 70-year hiatus his works were republished in Ukraine and later again in Russia. Another title - The Law of Synarchy and the Doctrine of the Dual Hierarchy of Monads and Multitudes – materialised in Kiev in 1994. The outline ideas of synarchy were presented by Shmakov in early articles which appeared in German philosophical journals prior to 1916. He is also thought to have outlined a work entitled The Basic Laws of the Architectonics of the World Unity - a Biner, Turner and Quarterion, but the text of this latter (if it exists at all) has not yet surfaced.

The interchangeable qualities of the concept of Synarchy and the archetype of Sophia are discernible in Shmakov's thinking, with its strong orientation towards the divine feminine principle. In Foundations of Pneumatology he considers Sophia in relation to that most occult Sephira, Daath, whilst Isis and Astarte are presented as binary Goddess forms, analogous to the Holy Spirit and avidya (ignorance) respectively.

One of Shmakov's fellow esoterists and students, Vsevolod Belustin, wrote that: "different Moscow mystics gathered around Shmakov, sometimes they appeared, and then disappeared again from Shmakov's horizon. Among them, there was a famous mystic-priest Pavel Alexandrovich Florensky." According to Belustin, Shmakov was assisted in his escape from Russia by the President of Czechoslovakia, Tomáš Masaryk.

Konstantin Burmistrov supplies some interesting insights into these interrelationships in his essay, Esotericism in Soviet Russia in the 1920s–1930s, where he examines The Order of Orion-Khermorion (Order of the Moscow Rosicrucians and Manichaeists). Founded by Shmakov in 1916, the Order was restructured around the leadership of Belustin in 1926, two year's after Shmakov's departure from Moscow. The order operated until 1933, when it was destroyed by the NKVD.

Vsevolod Belustin (1899 – 1943)

The investigative file about the aristocratic Vsevolod Vyacheslavovich Belustin is preserved in Russian archives. Here it is recorded that he was born into the family of a military general who later became a senator. He spent the civil war years in Crimea but did not serve in the White Army and did not go into exile. In 1922 he returned to Moscow and would spend the period from 1924 to 1932 working as an interpreter in the People's Commissariat for Foreign Affairs.

A graduate of the Alexandria Lyceum with a degree in philology and linguistics, Belustin developed an early interest in astrology and occultism. These interests could only expand when he came into contact with Vladimir Shmakov, into whose occult society he enthusiastically entered and was welcomed. Shmakov invited him to read a course in the philosophy of mysticism and hold practical classes in kabbalistic arcanology, which propelled Belustin to an immediate leading position in the occult circle.

Belustin was held in such high regard in the occult underground that he soon became known as the 'Moscow St Germain'. He was arrested in 1933 in the case of the

Rosicrucian Manichaeist Order, released, then arrested once again in 1941.
He was sentenced by military tribunal to 10 years in labour camps by a military tribunal and it is not known exactly when he died. 1943 is the usually given date of his death and it is knownt hat he was 'rehabilitated' in 1957 at the request of his widow Natalia Borisovna Salko (1909 - after 1996). They had a daughter, Olga.
Belustin was already a cult figure by the time Vladimir Shmakov appointed him as successor to his Moscow society of occultists. Along with Mebes, Tomberg and – of course – Shmakov, Belustin is considered one of four key figures who form a Quarternary of inner plane guides for Russian and Eastern European occultists today. His mission was to effect a Rosicrucian revival on Russian soil, via a closed magical circle of 16 individuals. (This is in contrast with Shmakov's open society where many people came and went with regularity). Other members included the engineer Fyodor Petrovich Verevin (1899 - 1967), biologist and chemist Mikhail Ivanovich Sizov (1883 - 1956) and the physician Maria Vadimovna Dorogova (1889 - 1980), who successfully practiced and taught the occult work until her death in 1980.
In his book, Andrei Nikitin wrote of Belustin: "Was he really another incarnation of that magician of antiquity, who we know under the names of Christian Rosicrucian, and later - the Count of Saint-Germain? In any case, this was the idea suggested by the seemingly limitless knowledge in the field of occult sciences that this man possessed. "
In 1926 he founded the Moscow Order of the Rosicrucian Orion Rite, which he registered with the Soviet government. The group never exceeded more than 16 persons and its ranks included but weren't limited to the knight of the outside tower and the knight of the inside tower. The higher order included the anthroposophist, Mikhail Ivanovich Sizov, who had assisted in the building of the Goetheaneum in Dornach.
In the 'Dinner' chapter you can find an extract from his Arcanology of Hermes, Arcanum VIII (Justice), where he looks at the 'Orientation of the Mystery to the Constellation of Cancer'. He is also quoted in Marilyn's musing on the

Sphere of Eros in the Chapter, The Golden Chain. You can read the report of his testimony given during interrogation on 22 April 1940 in the End Notes[xciv].

Serge Marcotoune (1890–1971)

Born in St Petersburg to a royal doctor and the daughter of a Ukrainian orthodox priest, Serge Marcotoune) had a lifelong interest in politics and spirituality. His masterful quest to reconcile these opposites made him influential within Martinism and European diplomacy.

His occult initiations and political commitments took place in several countries, always within the Martinist Order then headed by Papus.

In 1917, partly in response to the Russian Revolution and the ramifications for Ukraine, Marcotoune founded the Martinist Lodge St Andrew the Apostle No. 1 in Kiev in 1917. He also established the Young Ukraine political group, in sympathy with Symon Petlyura and Pavlo Skoropadski. The latter came to power and Marcotoune was appointed his secretary, becoming renowned for his diplomatic skill. His initiatory connections enabled him to assist his fraternity through the conflict. In 1920 he was forced to leave Soviet Ukraine for France, where he received a patent to found his own lodge from French Martinist leader and author, Jean Bricaud, also known as Tau Jean II. Thereby was the Renaissance Lodge (later St Andrew the Apostle No. 2) inaugurated. He headed up this lodge in person until 1945 and later in Spirit from the Canary Islands until 1953, exerting a strong influence upon the Golden Chain of Russian Martinism through Robert Ambelain, Armand Toussaint, Daniel Fontaine and others.

Whilst in France Marcotoune also served as secretary of the Association of Slavonic Masons, facilitating the emigration of refugees fleeing the Bolsheviks. In The Eidolons are two long extracts from Serge Marcotoune's seminal works, The Secret Science of the Initiates and the Practice of Life.

S.A. Malsagoff (1893-1976)

An exert from S.A. Malsagoff's (or Malsagov) account, Solovky Prison Camp: An Island Hell, Life in a Soviet Prison in the Far North, is featured in the Persephone chapter as part of a speech given by G.O. Mebes' character ('Butator'). It should probably be said that it is unlikely Mebes himself would have been so effusive, as his interrogation records indicate a rather formal but incredibly well-reasoned and lucid character, rather than someone who is easily overcome with emotion. One reason why I 'synchronised' him with Malsagoff here is because Mebes was also sent to the White Sea Islands following his arrest in the infamous case of the Leningrad Freemasons. (More details of which can be found in the English language translation of the Tarot Majors course (Shin Publications).

Whilst the details of Mebes' personal experience in the gulag are still lost in the KGB archives, Malsagoff's harrowing account caused a sensation when published in the West in 1926 (also the year of Mebes' imprisonment). Malsagoff wrote and published his work after an incredible escape from the notorious Solovetsky Island prison camp in the Soviet Arctic in the 1920s. I feel his account is so important a work that anything I could have imagined writing myself by way of description myself would pale in comparison. You can read the full work here:
https://archive.org/details/1926AnIslandHellMalsagoff

Leonid Nikolaievich Andreyev

A portion of L.N. Andreev's S.O.S! (Save Our Souls) is shared in the Virgin Atlantic Chapter. The author's collection of essays detail the seismic upheaval occurring in his motherland of Russia, written in the last two years of his life from his vantage point across the Arctic Ocean in Finland. As reviewer Sophie Benech, says of this work: "Whether he analyses the effects of censorship on writers, the ascendancy taken by Lenin over the Russian people, the way in which savage revolt takes precedence over revolution, or the unleashing of barbarism under the guise of great and noble ideas, he gives free rein here to the lyricism and passion that characterise him: He considers things more as a poet than as a political analyst". I agree with Sophie's excellent analysis and believe Andreyev is a clear link in the 'Golden Chain'.

Nikolai Belotsvetov (1892-1950)

Nikolai Belotsvetov was a Russian officer, poet and mystic, who had participated in an underground occult groups and activities. Forced to flee Russia in 1920, he channelled his experiences into a vast autobiographical novel called 'Michael', which explored what Konstantin Burmistrov describes as "the complex relations between occultists and the Cheka after the revolution, the flirtation of the "magi" with the regime, and the Bolsheviks' attempts to use occult forces to strengthen their power".
Michael caused a sensation amongst his peer group of fellow occultists, who successfully petitioned for him to destroy the work, which one assumes had the potential to cause grave difficulties for those who were left behind in Russia. Burmistrov raises the possibility that the book exposed "a link between the Bolsheviks' occult interests and a Jewish group within the party and the Cheka".
Sadly for the historian, only fragments of what could have been an invaluable record survived, within a rare 1921 book called "The Proletarian Missionaries' Commune".
Belotsvetov was an intimate friend of Valentin Tomberg, who married Belotsvetov's first wife, the Polish aristocrat, Maria Demski. Beotsvetov married his second wife, Anna, around the same time in the 1930s and the four of them remained firm friends through good and bad times, until Nikolai's death in 1950, which was a great blow to Valentin Tomberg.

Marilyn Monroe

Marilyn Monroe's presence may appear incongruous at first but there are good reasons for it. As arguably the most successful pupil of drama teacher, Mikhail Chekhov – himself an initiate of G.O. Mebes' Order of Light in St Petersburg - and a respected student of anthroposophy, she is a direct link in the Chain. Secondly, the story required a character who was the epitome of femininity in body, mind, soul and human memory. She sits at a table with those of her Chain who appreciate both magnetism and beauty as powerful signifiers of the astral light in human 'pentagrams'.

I also wanted to recognise that the great work is not only carried out by those who wear their habits out in the open! How many artists, of whatever disciplines, have proved just as great, if not better, at the work in question, touched, as they are, by the Muse?

* For more on G.O. Mebes see the Tarot Majors and Tarot Minors courses and for details about Vladimir Shmakov please refer to The Holy Book of Thoth: Great Arcana of the Tarot, all by Shin Publications. You can also find out more via the Youtube Channel: @alchemicalweddings7489

The Higher and Lower Minds

From Pneumatology, Vladimir Shmakov

The higher mind is revealed in empirical consciousness only in its approximation to the individual Self, in the assertion of its identity. Brushing aside the touch of the phenomenal, he tears off the chains and veils from the self-sufficient dignity of a single being. A person becomes capable of cognition in the higher mind only because he will be able to realise himself as a special unity, designed to become an original axis of the Universal and recreate it in himself. To be capable of this higher knowledge means, first of all, to be aware of one's own spirit, to rise above the changeable cycle of forms and phenomena and thereby join immortality.
Only immortality has the gift of higher knowledge and, conversely, the element of the higher mind is the element of immortality. Wisdom (Chokmah) is the first revelation of God. There is His essence, there is His basic predicate, there is a living connection of the Unconditional and Eternal with this vale of sorrow.

"She is the breath of the power of God and the pure outpouring of the glory of the Almighty: therefore nothing defiled will enter into her. She is a reflection of eternal light and a pure mirror of God's action and an image of His goodness." Wisdom of Solomon 7:25.

As love is the nature and element of the hypostasis of the Spirit, so Wisdom is the nature and element of the Logos. Wisdom is the living tablet of the Almighty, and this doctrine has been equally proclaimed to us by the Upanishads and the Zend-Avesta, Hellas and Plotinus, the Bible and Hegel, and revealed in the initiatory mysteries in all ages and among all peoples. Knowledge in the higher mind is the only way to

God, to eternal life; revelations of Wisdom descend from heaven, and only they elevate the earth, sanctify it and raise it to heaven.

The lower mind reveals itself in the removal of actual consciousness from the individual Self, in the dispersion of its identity. Subject to the synthetic category of periphery, a person learns here the diversity of reality as a total set of individual elements. Each of them is studied separately by him according to his external qualities and relationships with others.

***

The degree of divergence of the lower mind with reality is directly proportional to the complexity of its concepts claiming to be universal. The element of cognition in the lower mind should be imagined as a kind of cavity, only in contact with reality at the base, and then continuously going away from it into the space of imaginary extension. The lower mind, as such, in its isolation from the life-giving trends of the higher mind, is an imaginary reality, and all its activities are fruitless. Moreover, in complete solitude, it ceases to exist at all, goes out without a trace into nothing. It is only in conjunction with the initial intuitions of the Logos that it comes to life, but it is here that the specificity inherent in it actually manifests itself.

Paralysing the tension and the law of true knowledge, it outlives the descended transcendental gifts in useless speculations and constructions of the imaginary world of abstract schemes. Every formula of the lower mind is either a conditional designation or an enumeration of the qualities of an object. Unable to reach the differentially small components of qualities, the lower mind accepts its initial, so to speak, "atomic" qualities of some finite magnitude and intensity. It distinguishes them from empirical activity, objectifies and asserts them as some initial constant quantities. Their number can increase to an arbitrarily large value, but always remains finite.

It is obvious that in this process there is a significant

distortion of reality. Firstly, everything accepted as an elementary quality is in reality an infinitely complex synthetic whole, and the representation of reason in no way conveys its true versatility. Secondly, this whole is essentially concrete and valid only when applied to a given object and under given phenomenal circumstances. Therefore, when abstracting it and recognising its applicability to all other objects, two opposite mistakes are made. On the one hand, some of the overtones essential for this object are lost in the representation, and on the other hand, some other part of them is unnaturally transferred to other objects. Thirdly, as a consequence of what has just been said, the representation itself remains completely indeterminate and changing according to elusive laws, since in the application to each new object it includes some part of its overtones. Fourthly, each person invests in such a representation subjectively inherent overtones, but, unable to grasp this due to the lack of proper, regardless objectivity in the representation, he simultaneously loses the freedom to express his identity, and cuts off the desired community of expression,

So, every representation of the lower mind necessarily suffers from two polar-conjugate disadvantages: on the one hand, it loses all connection with concrete reality in its abstraction, and on the other hand, it has no internal stability and is inevitably subject to random subjective overtonal colours, both from each cognising subject and from the object being cognised in each given case.

If all this is true in relation to the simplest, "atomic" representations, then in complex representations these profound shortcomings are amplified to an extreme degree. The single predicates of a complex object here begin to play the same role as the overtones of the simplest representation. Here, too, only some of them are captured, and the partial is mistaken for the general, and some aspects of the general are ignored or discarded as partial. The more synthetic the cognisable object is and the more complex the representation about it, the more steps in the hierarchy of representations apparently connecting it with the initial elementary ones. With each transition from the lowest stage to the next, a number of new distortions appear, and therefore the hierarchically higher the inductive construction, the more it is far from reality.

The peripheral nature of cognition in the lower mind turns its striving for objective generality into the exsanguination and desiccation of reality, into separation from concreteness and immersion in the chilling waves of abstraction. Instead of delving into the nature of being and discovering living figures in its depths, weaving a pattern of external forms with the relentless luxury of diversity, instead of creative and joyful merging with the streams of the stream of life, the empirical consciousness of a person freezes in the indifferent calm of an outsider spectator and replaces the splendour of life with the squalor of a primitive scheme.

Just as a child or a resident of primitive caves draws people and animals with the help of a few circles and dashes, so the lower mind, proud of its shameless poverty, worships its schemes and formulas, considers them more perfect than life itself. Immensely impoverishing the surrounding world, the lower mind also immensely humiliates the dignity and vocation of man. He sees in it only a thinking machine, only an apparatus that constructs and manipulates circuits, devoid of any special value inherent to him personally, because all thinking human machines are only successful impressions of the same stamp to varying degrees.

The schemes of the lower mind that claim to be universal are devoid of any extension of depth; internal hierarchical perspective. They try to recreate this universality from the outside by an exhaustive enumeration of the main objective characteristics, and therefore the introduction of at least the slightest signs of subjectivity into them is a violation of the basic principle of construction, there is a failure to achieve the goal.

In the higher mind, the approach to the unconditioned is carried out only through the development of individuality, because only in its extreme tension does the part reflecting the whole in itself get the opportunity for the first time to realise this reflection of the whole and to join its universality. The pathos of the lower mind is polar opposite: it seeks to destroy all individual identity and through this achieve universality.

The lower mind reveals itself in its pure nature only in the removal of the actual consciousness from the individual Self, in the extinction of its identity. By detaching a person from organic communication with the surrounding phenomenal environment, he reduces his consciousness to the cold emptiness of the abstract. A person becomes capable of one-sided cognition in the lower mind only because he breaks away from his personality under its influence, plunges into the element of ossification, merges with the cold of its sharp crystals and will live only its dying life.

The lower mind is, therefore, an attack from the world of triumphant beauty. There is a revival of outlived shadows and frozen moments with its own blood, there is a challenge to the joyful luxury of life, there is a desire to be outside of being, to give victory to its underside, to make life a reflection of the shadow. Falling out of existence is a failure into non-existence. There is an ecstasy of wasting strength and dying, there is a plunge into absolute nothingness, into non-existence.

Only absolute nothingness coincides with the element of the lower mind; only this is the absolute limit that includes Absolute Being in order to create, and vice versa. The lower mind is the element of absolute dying. The lower mind is the first revelation of the immanent environment, its primordial multiplicity of atomic crystal forms frozen in immobility, is its essence, is its basic predicate, there is a deep connection of non-existence, absolute illusion with the world of becoming forms and intermittent phenomena.

The lower mind is the natural tablet of Death, the immeasurable anguish of life forever flying away and fading into the depths of emptiness. His gloomy cult arose only in our time. This is the law of the majority and the tyranny of collectives, this is the worship of the fetishes of the scheme and the audacious trampling of freedom and the impulses of the diversity of real life, this is the triumph of vulgarity and bringing everything under the stamp, this is the depersonalisation of peoples, their cultures and everyday life, this is the relentless triumph of the "average" person, deprived of connections with both the Upper and the lower, and therefore and with its own beginning of identity.

This cult carries the deepest distortion and degeneration of consciousness, where it begins to look for patterns of life and be content with them, loses the ability to penetrate into its creative flow and covers its own inactivity with a flicker of peripheral feelings, thoughts and sensations. The lower mind is an artificial means of separation from life, detachment from its storms and collisions, to an illusory victory over its elemental expanse in dissociation from its waves; the lower mind unfolds in the desert of the spirit, and only it is able to remove a person from life, to give peace of solitude, to extinguish dangerous impulses in the thin air of abstraction.

Just as each lower level of the hierarchy receives meaning and justification for its existence only in submission to the higher, so the lower mind becomes powerful and beautiful when it is the challenge, realisation and completion of the higher mind. Here it becomes the executor of the supreme law, a visible symbol and prototype of human nature, his phenomenal tool, method and support, his ultimate concrete realisation. In any binary of the first kind, the thesis ontologically precedes the antithesis, but it is revealed and reaches actual concreteness only in the evolutionary activity of the latter. This doctrine, in particular, is perfectly expressed by V. S. Solovyov:

"Higher, more positive and complete images and states of being exist (metaphysically) above the lower ones, although they appear or open after them. This does not negate evolution; it cannot be denied - it is a fact. But to assert that evolution creates higher forms entirely from lower ones, that is, finally from nothing, means substituting logical absurdity for the fact. The evolution of the lower types of being cannot by itself create the higher ones, but it produces material conditions or provides an appropriate environment for the manifestation or revelation of the higher type."

It is precisely in this creation of material conditions, that is, in the initial preparatory organisation of the multiplicity of the knowable, that the true vocation of the lower mind lies. Here, too, he remains only an instrument for the formation of schemes, he also translates the inexhaustible richness of life into the language of abstract relations, replaces its ever-quivering and iridescent flow with motionless forms of abstract principles and their mechanically dominating phenomenology. Finally, he also eliminates here the amateur activity and diversity of individual figures and reveals the yawning emptiness but the powerful influences of the higher mind, the life-giving gifts of the spirit carried by the Logos, bring abstract creations back to Life, include them in the element of creative self-consciousness.

The periphery, coupled with the Centre, ceases to be isolated and lifeless. In unity with him, she penetrates the reality of his being, includes him in all her divisions, responds to him and organically reflects him. Here the periphery becomes the otherness of the centre, its mode; its multiplicity is permeated by unity and subordinated to it, and the unity of the centre begins to actually include its diversity. Here, the entire periphery is only a differentiated, but also a single centre, and the centre is a periphery that has realised its unity.

Thus, the lower mind on the harmonic path becomes only the threshold to the higher mind; the ecstasy of the abstract scheme, which leads to extinction in Emptiness, under the all-resuscitating grace of the Logos, catastrophically degenerates into the ecstasy of the organic mind of self-aware life, and the process of cognition is transformed into a "Great Work", into the sacrament of a cult, into the theurgic self-creation of an individual being.

A completely different lower mind is closed in itself; here there is only detachment from reality and withdrawal into the world of bizarre bends of the abstract. Living in nature and drawing all the powers and possibilities of his being from the Universal, a person builds a completely special world in his consciousness, belonging to him alone. Usually he is even very little aware of this, because, gradually losing the gift of direct communication with the living essence of the surrounding, he also loses the ability of independent self-esteem.

Man is the final link of the cosmic process; being the highest stage of organic evolution, it is at the same time the last stage of the descent of the spirit in its higher nature. His vocation consists in the realisation of the actual unity of the upper with the lower, in the concrete actualisation of the first and in the victorious enlightenment of the second.

Man is the true centre of the manifested world and the axis of its life and evolution; it is in him that the synarchic law is recreated, for he penetrates with his unity all the stages of all hierarchies and reunites them again in his synthetic unity.,

The entelechy of the human path can be adequately defined as the achievement of complete immanence with the cosmos, a complete creative fusion with it in its entirety and divisions, and in the highest development of individuality - awareness of oneself as an original axis of the universal, freely in harmony with the comprehensiveness of the Absolute.

Here the individual does not dissolve into the vastness of the Universal, but it does not close in itself; asserting its identity, it organically interacts with everything, and reflects everything in itself, and recreates everything in itself. The lower mind is an absolute caricature of its entelechy - the higher mind – and, therefore, is characterised by polar opposite properties. Evolution in the category of reason, which at its highest stage should lead to an immanent fusion with the cosmos, begins with the ever-increasing development of man's complete alienation from it.

If the entelechy of the path consists in the highest affirmation of individual identity, then its first links lead not only to the loss of the original memory of individuality, but also to the dispersion of subjective qualities of the phenomenal personality. The periphery of all forms and constructions of the lower mind deeply regenerates primitive consciousness. At first, the category of mysticism awakens in a person, and his whole life, knowledge, activity and aspirations are determined by instincts. Here man is a true "child of nature", for the mystique of his being determines his initial unconscious immanentism with nature.

***

The entelechy of the development of the lower mind, as such, can be adequately defined as the achievement of complete isolation from cosmic Reality, both as a whole and in all divisions, and the assertion of a self-enclosed abstract world, impersonally and independently embracing the diversity of concreteness of the real in general formulas by the method of integral substitution.

Here the individual does not develop a creative interface with the Universal and does not reflect it in itself, but closes itself in the pathos of constructing abstract schemes, extinguishes its identity and seeks to reveal the universal through the highest tension of abstraction.

V. Ern penetratingly defines rationalism as a great meonic myth. Indeed, the concept of nature as a mechanical product of abstract impersonal laws and the initial passive atomic environment expels all life from it, immensely degrades its own dignity and makes it only an appendage to the system of abstract principles.

Already one of the founders of humanistic culture, Galileo, said: "La natura non si diletta di poesie" ("Nature is not amused by poetry") and this defined the basic nascent worldview. All nature is mechanical and does not include freely developing concrete principles, and therefore it is dead. Its apparent vitality is only a haze of naive observation, there is only an illusion cherished by the arbitrariness of fantasy, because in reality all the processes of nature, both inorganic and organic, are only concatenations of causes and effects, and therefore are always mechanical in everything.

Such a worldview considers lifelessness, that is, Death, Nothingness, non-being, to be the main principle of nature. Man is a part of nature, and therefore he himself is also only a machine. The periphery of his nature and constructions are elevated into the basic ontological principle, and the whole universe is proclaimed the kingdom of sovereign Death.

Like any idol, the lower mind has its own special cult. To ascend into it, you need to break all ties with life, you need to drown out the ever-lurking longing for the Eternal, you need to vulgarise and debunk a fairy tale, you need to uproot poetry from your heart, you need to become deaf to the Verb of Beauty spread in the world. This is the conversion of a person alive into a mummy, into a soulless automaton, the awareness of oneself only as an "epistemological subject".

The further a person moves in this direction, the more he even resembles death in his appearance; such, for example, are Voltaire and Kant. But also whole complex cultures of human societies are degenerating under the chilling influences of the lower mind. The organicity and spontaneity of life are replaced by the artificiality of norms and forms of social structure, the ugly perversion of guiding aspirations and imaginary ideals, the soullessness and superficiality of all human relationships. The social organism turns into a machine that immensely oppresses everyone, no matter how perfect its abstractly conceived idea may seem.

The laws of the majority and the mechanically formed public opinion, levelling all original manifestations, paralyse not only creativity as a free advance, but even the ability to properly assess what is happening, oppress any free perception. The need to consider and conform to formal norms in all aspects of the life path gradually corrupts every person, extinguishes the sacred flame of the dream of the ideal. Innate boldness and thirst for heroism in the vast majority is stifled even in their youth, senile infirmity of spirit comes early, cold indifference to everything that goes beyond the threshold of everyday life, and only cynical mockery of every impulse to rise begins to reign.

The supreme mind fills the whole being of man with sublime and mighty joy. Awakening a person from the painful sleep of a phenomenal life, the higher mind awakens the memory of the primordial dignity of the spirit and its radiant fatherland. He sees the vanity of his surroundings and the futility of his sucking drives, he not only cherishes the dream of the ideal, not only conceals in the depths of his soul a smoky reflection of the kingdom of Truth and Beauty, but also concretely realises the immutable reality of the heavenly insights, and the hidden immeasurable power of his own spirit, and the timeless promise of the Heavenly.

He is not a lost traveller in the fata morgana of a changing world, obediently drawn by the raids of its chaotic waves, but an inquisitive researcher of the depths and originality of his spirit who realised his mission, who came to this vale to accomplish concrete experience and behaviour to his neighbours. Everyone to whom the gracious gifts of the Logos have been bestowed is not only enlightened with his whole being, but also tirelessly strives to attach all other people to his insights and cheerful happiness. Wisdom is a true unquenchable light, and its all-illuminating rays make the consciousness tremble, inhale the thirst for a feat, call to sacrifice and make all the accepted sufferings all the sweeter, the greater the pain they cause.

Thus arose the feat of selfless service to the truth, voluntary acceptance of the cross of overcoming the suffering of the errors of others. In complete self-denial and oblivion of personal immediate interests, man included in himself the transcription of splits, shifts and tears of consciousness, restless in the host of disorganised duality of the world, and in the very throes of tearing admired the ecstasy of victoriously born truth.

For some, the ardent desire of the spirit to share the feat of Bringing Light, enlightening everyone, prompted them to go to certain death in the cruellest torments with the gospel of the highest Truth and the Highest Knowledge, others were satisfied. the revelations of the whole sorrowful path of the terrible ascent to the luminous height of Truth with its slips, bruises and failures were being made in themselves, the third, having taken a vow of poverty, went into the wilderness for persistent and terrible work of consistent comprehension, the fourth burned in the ecstasy of a fiery, but still premature take off to the Sun.

The lower mind is always filled with endless longing. He tends to withdraw into himself, separate himself from the flow of life and move only in his own thoughts. He carefully pursues all the last remnants of the real and tries to replace everything with abstract schemes and constructions. Accordingly, the process of mechanisation of human consciousness and self-perception takes place.

Being carried away by the construction of schemes, a person himself imperceptibly adapts to the artificially created kind of life. He not only ceases to see anything different from the schemes, but also organically loses the very opportunity to do so. A number of potencies are finally atrophied: the categories of mysticism and will lose their independent meaning and freedom of original manifestations, becoming only contributing tools to achieve the goals of the intellect. The whole surrounding world and all internal processes begin to be perceived only through the prism of the lower mind, and vice versa - it becomes the only imperative of all efforts and desires. Everything that does not quite correspond, and even more so - does not correspond at all to the tendencies of the intellect - is declared either absolutely insignificant, or at the lowest stages of development.

Hence, naturally, there is a tragic collision of such consciousness with the surrounding. No matter how the significance of the other two pneumatological categories is suppressed, this can only be achieved in part, and on the other hand, direct experience invariably has an awakening effect on them. Therefore, a person can no longer limit himself to the abstract assertion of his worldview, but finds himself forced to defend it and fight for it, And the further he has moved away from real life, the more inevitable the collision with it, the more stubborn the struggle with the world and within his own consciousness.

In parallel, another kind of disharmonic collision naturally arises. Underlying the periphery and schematism of thinking, a person dissociates himself from the higher regions of consciousness. The prophetic gifts of the intuition of the Highest are denied and ridiculed by them. He closes himself in his limited swamp, and every impulse that seeks to pull him out of the lowlands he loves meets him as a daring encroachment. Having bound himself with heavy chains of soulless mechanicality, he accordingly lowers the hierarchical dignity of consciousness and the possibilities that prevail over him. Revolving only in the lower sphere of the rational principle, he equally breaks away from its higher depths, and from the creative darkness of ancient chaos.

He is equally alien to the subtle fluid of the bright, all-pervading and all-encompassing Apollo, and the twilight glare of bizarre, incredible forms flashing and rushing to life in the standing waves of the unborn. By his isolation and the heaviness of his movements, he becomes deaf to the springs of being, and, closing his eyes to the immeasurable ocean of all-illuminating Light, he wanders, attracted only by the barely glimmering light of the life still remaining in him (Arcanum IX).

But he is not able to overcome the gift of listening to the worldly from very ancient times. No matter how sensitivity to the inclinations of Eros is suppressed, no matter how the higher centres of perception degenerate in inactivity, it is enough to weaken the armouring tension, so that immediately the soundless noise of the wings of Eros soaring in the world pierces consciousness and throws it into awe.

And the highest experience, both sweet and heavy, instantly returns to insignificance the exhausted temple of the scheme, powerlessly spreading at all seams. To listen to the revelation means to burn everything that he has worshipped before, and to worship everything that he has burned. And now a person begins to strive with his impotence to overpower the power of the Almighty... He is straining all over, ignited by a wild hatred for everything that is alien to the familiar world of the banal, and enters into a fierce struggle with it.

Every higher illumination is a daring encroachment on cute fetishes, every dream and call to the wondrous and sublime, the very longing for the freedom of unconditioned beauty is not only madness, doubly dangerous both in incurable and strange contagiousness, but also immensely criminal in its habitual challenge and in the desire to devalue and overthrow all this.

The lower mind is modest and only vulgar only in its impotence. But if he has enough power to actively intervene in life, to turn from a closed-in spectator into a concrete participant in it, striving to subordinate everything to his laws, then he becomes a tyrant, indescribable in his ferocity. His soulless mechanism is always cruel; the depth of life is alien to him, its bends and momentary impulses are incomprehensible, sometimes more concealing than a long chain of large and open events; interfering in life, he always breaks it, distorts its own course and, like a blind force, considers only himself. Bursting into a child's, not yet sophisticated soul, he mercilessly tramples the flowers of dreams and poetry and tries to throw their sadly fallen petals out as unnecessary and harmful rubbish.

The awakening of the lower mind is always the twilight of spiritual youth. The outgoing immediate simplicity takes with it an innate sensitivity, a person loses understanding of the language of nature, communication with beauty without words and knowledge without memory. The enchantment of the fairy tale still seems like a distant echo, and the dying song still trembles in the heart, but the person is no longer the same, the internal substitution that has happened in him is already putting its seal. Everything close and dear, to which the soul is about to reach out again, is rejected with pain and annoyance, because the hour has come for attempts to create a homeland in an inhospitable foreign land. He breaks with the old and rushes forward on the path of suffering, because the ancient law of passing through the void on the verge of two worlds must be fulfilled in order to return back, wise by experience and found himself in the search for the outside.

From the very beginning of its origin, the lower mind manifests itself as a ruthless destroyer of the initial simplicity of Eden. He is the "great killer of the real", about whom the ancient wisdom of India preserves the memory. His entire development is the incessant growth of the exsanguination of life, the imposition of iron chains on nature and on man himself in the process of cognition.

The vast majority of people are content here only with replacing the direct creativity of experiences with their schematic formulas, not fully including them in themselves and not fully identifying with them. Initially, the prevailing simplicity of life gives way to an equally passive - simple following of general formulas, only the type of drowsiness changes, but not the attitude to Maya's dreams.

However, the substitution of the dream object, the superficiality and inner emptiness of the schemes constructed by the intellect after the rich luxury of the kingdom of the primitive fairy tale can no longer quench the thirst for search, no matter how weak it may still be. Sometimes a person is deceived, and the same nurtured ghosts give satisfaction and fill life for a while, but this always lasts only a few moments of self-deception, after which dissatisfaction and aimlessness of life rises with even greater force.

The path of the lower mind is the path of painful, deaf and incurable longing. No matter how entangled a person is in the nets of abstract schematism, no matter how he shuns spontaneous impulses, no matter how he suppresses dreams of another world - beauty and freedom, the eternal memory of the freedom of the spirit continues to glow in his being, and on his life path he cannot help but constantly make sure that "nothing the transitory cannot satisfy a person" (Upanishads).

On the other hand, the path of earthly life is a path. Suffering. There is no side of a person's being that does not painfully remind him of his existence; it can be said that in this vale a person is conscious of himself only insofar as he suffers. This suffering and burdensomeness of a person's life path comes primarily from the fact that he does not know the true meaning, purpose and justification.

The heaviest suffering is borne by a person relatively easily when it is justified or attracts him to a higher Goal; on the contrary, even a minor obstacle, a transient and weak suffering can become truly unbearable when it seems meaningless to him. Ignorance of the goal, ignorance of the source, misunderstanding of the cause is the heaviest burden, and it always weighs on a person when he outlines the area of his searches with the narrow limits of his phenomenal personality and the conditions of the phenomenal environment.

The seal of hopeless despondency and boundless longing weighs on all who seek only earthly truth, only earthly justification. Lifeless pessimism reigns in all searches, both in the field of science and in the field of art, when they stop looking for the source, causes and purpose beyond the world of changeable forms and transient phenomena.

If the path of the lower mind is painful, and its gifts are cruel to the own consciousness of every person following it, then this is even more powerfully manifested in relation to its active leaders and guides. For most people, the influence of the nature of the lower mind is limited only to the surface of consciousness. Its deeper sides remain mostly undetected at all, and the little that has manifested itself actually or has only made the actual Self aware of the very fact of its existence lives completely apart and independently, acting and developing without any externally visible dependence on stylized peripheral processes.

These two sides of consciousness not only get along together, despite their opposition, but there have even been attempts to legitimise this unnatural discord once and for all. Over the past two or three centuries, not only almost the entire intelligent mass, along with the fanatical worship of materialistic civilization, at the same time retains the ability to dream, poetry and religion, but also among great people there are numerous examples of complete enslavement by schematics of the intellect, which goes next to deep religiosity and in general the ability to erotic admiration.

From the point of view of the lower mind, this blatant inconsistency is only a transitional state, when the atavistic attraction to absurd fantasies and obsolete religious grovelling before the terrible Unknown, destroyed in a direct struggle by the triumphant enlightenment of the intellect, still shamefully nests in the back of consciousness, still trying in vain to escape from the darkness inevitably approaching it, where the dregs of the historical process rot.

A strong and truly enlightened paladin of reason must uproot all these ridiculous remnants of the distant barbaric past. There is one supreme absolute substance - mind, and therefore it must take its proper position in consciousness, become the centre and the only imperative. Everything that is not with reason is against it, and therefore is insignificant and should be thrown out like a rotten worthless rag.

If in the superficial mastery of consciousness by the lower mind there is only a decrease in the intelligence of life, impoverishment of the worldview and mechanisation of the life and activity of consciousness, then with a deep penetration of its chilling stream, a complete rebirth of the entire psyche takes place. The consciousness schematised on the periphery is only pale and disappearing. To create a really deep crystallisation of consciousness, to reveal the abyss of the formalising element in oneself, to covet the introduction into its depths and boldly rush into them is the lot of very few.

Grasping the ecstasy of the Arctic beauties of a world forever frozen in immobility, which has finally embodied its ideal intellectual plan, a person vividly understands the vulgarity and insignificance of everyday life and complacently realises his special distinction and cold aristocracy. If passive adherence to the regulatory norms of activity and perceptions developed by a schematised civilization only dries up a person and suppresses his initiative, then a truly powerful challenge to the real will be born only in great boldness, carries bizarre, unimaginable delights, generates the laws of a special perverted Logos - the black sun.

There is no majestic goodness of the divine order, there is no radiance of the primordial light, gentle and caressing, there is no sonorous clarity and life of facets, as there are no eternal overflows from facet to facet, the sparkle of everything in everything and the sweet apotheosis of each part, penetrating everything and becoming everything and shining each with its own light.

They are replaced here by the sharpness of divisions and the screaming cold of mutual alienation of petrified schemes hanging over each other; here reigns the beauty of yawning abysses of contrasts, the irreconcilability of designs and the futility of attempts to merge, the chaos of bends and dips flowing out of the Black Darkness, piercing with its dead rays everything from the outside to the middle.

This is the frozen song of triumphant Death, this is the eternal moment of absorption by the formless Emptiness of what has been achieved. The kingdom of Life is a stormy stream of ascents and descents; but everything once achieved by one's soul ascends into the Light and as an "intelligent force" becomes a servant of the world Throne, and returns one's exhausted body to Nothing from where it came.

Death and non-being are the eternal springs of being, and they also constitute the dual triumphal gates of the microcosm reuniting with the Absolute. In order to ascend in spirit into the kingdom of Life and Light, one must give one's body to the kingdom of Death and Annihilation and through this triumph of exultant Life by death overcome Death and thereby make one's body immortal.

But in a lonely approach to the eternal mystery, the merging of Being with Death is a genuine touch with the all-consuming Abyss. Here a person is threatened with death from the black sun. As in the approach to the Highest, the human soul can burn up in the flaming ocean of Apollo, so in the high ecstasy of crystallising forms, the limit comes when penetrating black rays from everywhere from the outside extinguish the brightness of the facets, and the forms frozen in immobility disappear without a trace in the sinkhole of the gloomy ocean; the abused and rejected Dionysus hides the perverted Apollo; two abysses, absorbing each other, return to nothing.

This is the last limit of the spontaneous development of intelligence. Only absolutely isolation can people rise to this terrible stage, but even in the very approach to it, the winds of the abyss are heard for a long time. Every goal set by man is an entelechic idealisation of his present qualities; every phenomenal quality is a caricature prototype of noumenal reality; the evolutionary movement towards the goal set is at the same time a recollection of it, a recreation of it, and identification with it.

***

Every inductive worldview is always based on a system of myths: they form the fulcrum, based on which alone it becomes possible both to begin cognition and all its further processes. The deductive worldview also unfolds its essence in the system of myths on the periphery, but their nature is completely different.

The higher realities are provided with a mythological appearance only for the possibility of introducing to them those to whom direct intuitive contemplation is not yet available. The esoteric myth is a symbol that in its essence empirically coincides with reality; the positive myth is only an auxiliary and only relatively regular reduction from the concrete empirical. Hence, as a consequence, it follows that esoteric myths are catholic, and positive ones are only sectarian postulates.

Including all kinds of possible binary relationships, esotericism accepts every positive statement, indicating its hierarchically inherent place in the holistic worldview. Positivism, on the contrary, proceeding only from particular certainties, cannot but enter into a struggle with others based on other certainties, or only on other methods and methods of classification. The basis of esotericism is the living truth, and therefore it is identical with life; the basis of positivism is abstract principles, and therefore it is alien to the organicity of life.

Having risen in the XVIII century to a worldview claiming to be exhaustive universality, the lower mind could not immediately but declare a merciless war against the established system of life. This struggle took on a bright political colouring and caused a long chain of revolutions, wars and all kinds of economic upheavals that continue to this day.

But all these are only external consequences of an incomparably more important and interesting internal struggle between schematising and classifying reason and the organic nature of life. The natural way of life began to be denied not for its particular shortcomings, which could be very deplorable, but entirely, fundamentally. Until now, the life of peoples and all their historical processes have not been governed by the unconditional dictatorship of the intellect, only extra-rational forces have acted. But since there is only blind chance outside of reason and only pathetic scattered glimpses of the same reason, then the whole story as a whole is only a play of chance and ignorance.

This inner emptiness was only covered up by the fetish of tradition, and therefore, first of all, every tradition must be destroyed. Man is supposedly devoid of innate ideas, the

difference of individuals is only a mechanical consequence of heredity, upbringing and environmental conditions, and therefore it is enough to equalise all these conditions according to the ideal of reason, as all the problems of social life will be solved, all people will become. reasonable, and therefore virtuous, which will create an earthly paradise.
The struggle against traditions and individuality is the slogan of the militant lower mind. But since the lower mind assumes all truth, all goodness and all justice, then every opponent is an enemy of humanity and everything is allowed in relation to him.
The world must be turned into a paradise by violence, and therefore the sea of spilled blood is only a necessary payment, there is a redemptive sacrifice before the altar of the Intellect. From the blood and the lamentations of the victims, the monstrous idol of the new Moloch rallied, mocking unfortunate humanity to this day. We live in a terrible time when the soulless lower mind lays out humanity with unprecedented boldness on the procrustean bed of its schemes and tries to drown everything beyond its limits in blood.
But all his efforts are in vain! One day, this bloody nightmare of the dialectical elimination of the lower abyss of Apollo - Mephistopheles will also be a thing of the past, as the elimination of the lower abyss of Dionysus - Baal-Zebub - in the cruel cults of Astarte, Melita and Derketo has gone. The lower mind, having revealed itself to the end, will take its proper subordinate position in the life of every person and Entire peoples, and a new page of history will begin. Then everyone will realise the great truths that Dostoevsky's genius says in the words of Shatov in "Demons".:
"Not a single people," he began, as if reading from the lines and at the same time continuing to stare menacingly at Stavrogin, "not a single people has yet settled down on the principles of science and reason; there has never been such an example, Except for one minute, out of stupidity...Reason and science in the life of peoples have always, now and since the beginning of centuries, performed only a secondary and official position; they will continue to do so until the end of centuries. Nations are composed and moved by a different

force, commanding and dominating, but the origin of which is unknown and inexplicable.

This force is the force of an unquenchable desire to reach the end and at the same time denying the end. This is the power of continuous being and denial of death. The spirit of life, as the Scripture says, is "a living river," the exhaustion of which threatens the Apocalypse. The beginning is aesthetic, as philosophers say, the beginning is moral, as they identify. "Searching for God" - as I call it - is the easiest.

"The goal of the entire popular movement, in every nation and in every period of its existence, is solely the search for God, one's own, certainly one's own, and faith in Him as the One True One. God is the synthetic personality of the whole people, taken from its beginning to its end. There has never been a time when all or many nations have one common God, but everyone has always had a special one.

"A sign of the destruction of nationalities is when the gods begin to become common. When the gods become common, then the gods and the belief in them die together with the peoples themselves. The stronger the people, the more special their god is. There has never been a people without religion, that is, without a concept of evil and good. Every nation has its own concept of evil and good, and its own evil and good. When the concepts of evil and good begin to become common among many peoples, then nations die out, and then the very distinction between evil and good begins to fade. and disappear".

The instrument, result and vehicle of the lower mind is actually positive science. Of course, this does not apply to science in its true sense and as a whole, but only to those ugly bends of it that can only be called a parody of true science - "semi-science". The essence of semi-science is determined by its complete alienation from life, the denial of all the roots of being. V. Ern is deeply right when he says:

"I am convinced that for true culture there is no enemy more terrible than rationalism. Culture is the gathering and the highest creative organisation of the deepest elements of life, and rationalism, as we have seen, fundamentally and hopelessly consciously chaotizes life."

With even greater sharpness and vividness of thought, we read in the same creation of Dostoevsky about the bloody consequences of mankind's fascination with the pseudoscience of a one-sided lower mind:

"In particular, this was distinguished by semi-science, the most terrible scourge of mankind, worse than pestilence, famine and war, not known until this century. Semi-science is a despot, which has never come before. A despot who has his priests and slaves, a despot before whom everything has bowed with love and with superstition, hitherto unthinkable, before whom even science itself trembles and shamefully indulges him."

Complete soullessness, hopeless isolation from life, ferocious dogmatism, fanatical perseverance, satanic pride, fierce ruthlessness and cruelty of the fiery priests of semi-science - how infinitely far it all is from the quiet, but mighty and joyful light of the servants of the Logos! They know the commandment that "warmth does not always come from the bright rays of Truth, and blessed is he who has not paid for the gifts of knowledge with his heart," and therefore they have combined the revelations of reason with the revelation of love above in their soaring.

A true adept of Wisdom, attracted by erotic grace, is a genius, and "for those who have ears to hear, the very essence of genius is always joyful, like a trembling exciting news from the depths of their birth". The true Science of Light, enlightening everyone, enlightens the whole being of his disciple, and the power of knowledge he gains only strengthens and grows his inner peace, harmony of consciousness and erotic thirst for Truth, as the wonderful chords of Euripides proclaim to us:

"Blessed is he who is immersed in science with his soul:
He knows no malice against his neighbour;
Criminal acts, unrighteous thoughts
Temptations were despised by his royal mind.
He contemplates everything with an inquisitive soul
The Imperishable Nature of the divine system;
Where did it come from? And how? And when?
And low passion is forever alien to him!"

End Notes

[i] "On the occasion of our meeting," wrote British poet, Dame Edith Sitwell (1987-1964), of her 1953 meeting with Marilyn Monroe (1926-1962), "she wore a green dress and, with her yellow hair, looked like a daffodil. We talked mainly, as far as I remember, about Rudolf Steiner, whose works she had just been reading. In repose her face was at moments strangely, prophetically tragic, like the face of a beautiful ghost – a little spring-ghost, an innocent fertility daemon, the vegetation spirit that was Ophelia."
Marilyn was known to have been a student of Rudolf Steiner and borrowed many books from the Anthroposophical Library at 211 Madison Avenue, New York. She was introduced to Steiner's work via her esteemed drama teacher, Mikhail Chekhov (1890-1955), nephew of the famous playwright, Anton Checkhov. Mikhail Chekhov had been a student of G.O. Mebes and also Konstantin Stanislavski, who described him as his most brilliant student. By 1927, like others in his circle, Chekov found himself in conflict with the Communist regime and rather than risk arrest, torture and even death for his spiritual interests, instead left Russia, first for Germany, then Lithuania, England and later America. The Wikipedia entry for Chekhov states: He developed the use of the "Psychological Gesture", a concept derived from the Symbolist theories of [Andrei] Bely. In this technique, the actor physicalises a character's need or internal dynamic in the form of an external gesture. Subsequently, the outward gesture is suppressed and incorporated internally, allowing the physical memory to inform the performance on an unconscious level.

[ii] www.peacehost.net/peacechurch/

[iii] This note appears in The Truth about Madame Blavatsky by V. Jelihovsky and is reproduced in Madame Blavatsky's Baboon, Theosophy and the Emergence of the Western Guru, by Peter Washington.

[iv] Youtube profile: @alchemicalweddings7489
https://www.youtube.com/watch?v=AJZ0memWlUw

[v] Olena Petrovna Blavatska: Born 12 August [O.S. 31 July] 1831 in Yekaterinoslav (now Dnipro, Ukraine) – died 8 May 1891 at Annie Besant's house in London, England.

[vi] This is a most extraordinary statement. I will not vouch for its truth and cannot even hazard a guess as to the nature of the offence. Indeed it raises a suspicion that the American fraternity was a brotherhood of the 'Left', especially when taken in conjunction with what follows

[vii] About 1874

[viii] Isis Unveiled, a Master-Key to the Mysteries of Ancient and Modern Science and Technology, First Edition, Helena P. Blavatsky, 1877

[ix] 'chain' is a term used in certain occult schools to denote their lineage, both down through the ages and in the present time. In this respect, members of a particular tradition are considered as 'links in the chain'.

[x] Nicholas Roerich, The Key from the Gates

[xi] "The Letters of H. P. Blavatsky to A. P. Sinnett", TUP, Pasadena, California, 1973, 404 pages, Letter L (50), see p. 121.

[xii] The apartment building owned by the insurance company "Life" in Moscow.

[xiii] 1905

[xiv] The extract was published in an article by HPB in the 9th April 1881 edition of "The Pioneer", Allahabad, India. Boris de Zirkoff, who compiled HPB's Collected Writings, reports:
"This article is pasted in H.P.B.'s Scrapbook, Vol. XI, p. 67, now in the Adyar Archives. Though unsigned, it is most likely from her own pen." In the quotation provided she is describing her observations of the Moscow populace who'd just learned of the death of the Tsar.

[xv] Ibid

[xvi] No relation to the dramatist, Mikael Chekhov who is quoted at the head of the chapter.

[xvii] United State Political Administration, the heiress of the Cheka and the forerunner of the KGB of the USSR.

[xviii] The order EMESH Redivivus had its roots in the Martinist Order in St Petersburg, led firstly by the Pole Czesław Czyński and then G.O. Mebes. It is thought that the earliest incarnation of an EMESH group in this city existed from the turn of the 20th century and initiated the Moscow Order founded by the Russian-Polish physicist Vadim Karlovich Chekhovski (who had a Polish father) and the Russian-German diplomat Evgeny Karlovich Teger, both of whom were disciples of G.O.M. In 1919 Chekhovski became involved in a group of devoted Russian Orthodox called the Order of Worldwide Secrets, whose members were united in their mistrust of the Soviet government. As an employee of the Moscow Department of the Leningrad Bekhterev Brain Institute, Chekhov was responsible for the practical side of the work, whilst Teger, whose diplomatic work took him to missions in Afghanistan and Western China, was an expert in occult literature. Teger may have been the more radical of the two. According to Daniel Shubin in his book, New Rosicrucians in Soviet Russia, in 1905 Teger took part in the December battles in Moscow on the side of the anarchists, which resulted in his exile to Yakutiya in Eastern Siberia. An amnesty in 1913 meant he was able to return to Moscow and rapidly became interested in occultism. In 1914 – at the outbreak of World War I - he was detained once again on account of being a German citizen.

[xix] In an indication of the grey magical area the group's founders were working in, the proximity of the EMESH HQ to that of the Lubyanka prison – scene of much torture and bloodshed - was thought to enhance the astral potency of the vicinity, through the heightened energy released by suffering souls, described by them as martyrs. Chekhovski's associate, V.V Preobrazhenski, recorded a conversation between himself and Teger regarding the selection of their group HQ: "First, the building is in the centre of the city; and second, their cellar is located underground right alongside the cellars of the OGPU, where blood of the executed is spilled. As it is well known, they said, the blood of martyrs nourishes the ghosts who comprise the kingdom of gloom and darkness, and it is only the current of light from mystical rites conducted there that can destroy the prison."

[xx] This latter was the pseudonym of Leonid von Fölkersam, a member of the French "Société magnétique" and "Centre ésotérique de France". In the 1910s – at the same time as G.O.M - he gave a course in St Petersburg on "how to develop hidden mental forces", also teaching practical occultism by various means.

[xxi] Chekhovski worked in Leningrad in the mid-1920s, where he met his wife, Sophia Albertovna. Their son, Mikhail Vadimovich, was born on 8th July, 1926. During his twice-yearly trips to Moscow he taught students the mystical and occult concepts

he'd learned from G.O.M. and was even able to revive the Order of Secrets. However, there were too few initiates to create a stable group. See New Rosicrucians of Early Soviet Russian by Daniel Shubin.

[xxii] OGPU officials raided the home of G.O.M. on 16-17th April 1926 and the Master himself – along with his Martinist associates – was sentenced to three years' exile at Syktyvkar (earlier known as Ust-Sysolsk) on 20th May. Three more years were added once this initial sentence finished. You can read more about this – and the workings of the EMESH group - in Daniel Shubin's work.

[xxiii] These nine levels were further divided into three groups, each of which had three successive stages. The first of these was concerned with the periphery and the second with the centre (EMESH) as a mechanism for establishing the global occult headquarters. The third group was concerned with the world centre for occult magic that would implement the magical works in the service of culture and humanity. "Thus," says Burmistrov, "the Order's goals were hugely ambitious and extended to the attainment of world supremacy".

[xxiv] During his interrogation, Fyodor Petrovich Verevin testified against Teger and Chekhovski but did not give up Belustin.

[xxv] When the OGPU entered the secret laboratory they found and arrested Chekovski, Teger and about 20 other young people, several of whom were also members of the Orion order. Some were released but most were charged with violation of Section 58-4 of the Soviet Criminal Code on 31st May 1928: the distribution of anti-Soviet propaganda and counter-revolutionary activities. Another was charged with espionage and another with aiding and abetting the enemy. Several of them were held at the Lubyanka prison. There was no actual trial. Teger, despite his earlier expressed allegiance to the Soviet government, was sentenced to 7 years' imprisonment at Solovki concentration camp. Further arrests and trials occurred until the early 1940s, at which point no more information about him can be found.

[xxvi] Edgar Cayce's Atlantis, Gregory L. Little; Lora Little and John Van Auken

[xxvii] We realise the timeline is little off here as the pipeline was actually blown up on 26 September 2022 and Seymour Hersh wrote his bombshell report - How America Took Out The Nord Stream Pipeline on 8 February 2023. According to Hersh: "Last June, the Navy divers, operating under the cover of a widely publicised mid-summer NATO exercise known as BALTOPS 22, planted the remotely triggered explosives that, three months later, destroyed three of the four Nord Stream pipelines, according to a source with direct knowledge of the operational planning". Link to the article: is here: https://seymourhersh.substack.com/p/how-america-took-out-the-nord-stream

[xxviii] Vladimir Dal

[xxix] Nikola Gogol

[xxx] Nina Roudnikova, The Solar Way, Arcanum XIV.

[xxxi] Leo Tolstoy

[xxxii] S.O.S., Leonid Andreyev, 1919.

[xxxiii] As Jack Parsons' Scarlet Woman, Marjorie Cameron, described UFOs, saying they were as prophesised by Aleister Crowley.

[xxxiv] Serge Marcotoune, La Ciencia Secreta de los Iniciados

[xxxv] HPB, Philaletheians

[xxxvi] From the Caves and Jungles of Hindostan, Helena Petrovna Blavatsky.

[xxxvii] René Guénon, East and West (abridged).

[xxxviii] Ruler of Jupiter according to Peladan's book, How to Become a Mage.

[xxxix] Ruler of Mercury according to Peladan's book, How to Become a Mage.
[xl] With thanks to Charles Salvo for his insight into the thought of Rene Guenon comparative to Gurdjieff
[xli] Éliphas Lévi, Dogme et Rituel
[xlii] Josephin Peladan, How to Become a Mage
[xliii] Ibid.
[xliv] From René Guénon, The Crisis of the Modern World

[xlv] За здоровье ('to your health' in Russian)
[xlvi] Belyustin, Arcana of Hermes
[xlvii] This son is fictionalised, but 'Victor' is someone referenced in the English edition of the Holy Book of Thoth as an acolyte of the Shmakov school of occultism who tried to trace the steps of the Master by various means.
[xlviii] "The famous Wearyall Hill Holy Thorn tree, alleged descendant of an original planted by Joseph of Arimathea, was planted in 1952, the year of the Queen's Accession. When horribly vandalised in 2010, a cutting had been taken and cultivated in Kew Gardens. It was ready to be planted in Glastonbury, this time in the safe setting of the garden of St Dunstan's House, where Glastonbury Information Centre can be found, a location in the immediate proximity of the Abbey that our foundation myth affirmed Joseph had founded. The event presented continuity and the theme of regeneration to nicely mark the advent of the new King. On Saturday September 24th, the new Thorn was planted as the climax of a tree-blessing processional ceremony that took in our Rowan memorial (where photos of recently deceased Glastonbury residents are placed) and a recently planted oak that was part of a nationwide Jubilee tree-planting initiative". Paul Weston, Pax Cultura Avalon of the Heart Glastonbury Royal Jubilee.
[xlix] Paul Weston, Richard Whiting, Last Abbot of Glastonbury Abbey: http://www.paulwestonglastonbury.com/richard-whiting-last-abbot-of-glastonbury-abbey/
[l] With thanks to Brother Ramon for highlighting this quote!
[li] Letter of Philip Oyler, to Wellesley Tudor Pole
[lii] G.O.Mebes Tarot Majors, Arcanum VIII, Justice; Lex = system of Law
[liii] Head of a Monastery; Abbott.
[liv] Extracts taken from the autobiographical account, An Island Hell, by S.A. Malsagoff, who'd been committed to Soviet Gulag's, including Solovky, during the time frame in question. He managed to escape to the west by swimming across the Gulf of Finland. When his book was published in 1926 it resulted in a worldwide scandal.
[lv] Leaves of Moraya's Garden, Book I, The Call, Nicholas Roerich
[lvi] Nina Roudnikova, The Solar Way, Arcanum II
[lvii] Ibid
[lviii] Linked with these activities was the Russian officer, poet and mystic, Nikolai Belotsvetov (1892–1950), who had participated in an underground occult circle and lodge in the Motherland. Forced the flee Russia in 1920, he channeled his experiences into a vast autobiographical novel called 'Michael', which explored what Konstantin Burmistrov describes as "the complex relations between occultists and the Cheka after the revolution, the flirtation of the "magi" with the regime, and the Bolsheviks' attempts to use occult forces to strengthen their power".
Michael caused a sensation amongst his peer group of fellow occultists, who successfully petitioned for him to destroy the work, which one assumes had the potential to cause grave difficulties for those who were left behind in Russia.

Burmistrov raises the possibility that the book exposed "a link between the Bolsheviks' occult interests and a Jewish group within the party and the Cheka". Sadly for the historian, only fragments of what could have been an invaluable record survived, within a 1921 book called "The Proletarian Missionaries' Commune".

[lix] Chekhovski spent two years in Germany, where he studied anthroposophy under Rudolf Steiner.

[lx] Teger encountered revolutionaries whilst interred in 1914 and did come down on the side of the Soviets after the October Revolution of 1917. He even participated in the Civil War as a Red Army Commander, which leads us to wonder – given his pivotal position in the Moscow occult community – whether he was a spy for the White Guard during this time or later. At any rate, his outward allegiances enabled him to obtain good positions in the regime, eventually becoming a diplomat of the Russian consulate in Kashgar, China and Kabul in Afghanistan. Upon his return to Moscow in 1928 he somehow became acquainted with all of the important esoteric groups in that city and Petrograd.

[lxi] This extract from Belustin's testimony can be fond in Daniel Shubin's book, New Rosicrucians of Early Soviet Russia.

[lxii] Meditations on the Tarot, Letter XXI, The Fool

[lxiii] G K Chesterton, The Flying Inn

[lxiv] Ibid

[lxv] The Mabinogion, The Dream of Maxen Wledig

[lxvi] Posthumously published

[lxvii] Published on the DarkJournalist Youtube channel

[lxviii] Ibid: quoting CIA psychic spy and Scientologist, Pat Price

[lxix] Ibid: Russell Targ discussing the death of Pat Price.

[lxx] Alois Mailander is thought to have been 'a secret Rosicrucian guide to at least 54 members of the Theosophical Society,' according to Mailander researcher, Christine Eike. This has contributed to speculation that this relatively unknown Rosicrucian teacher may have been the legendary 'M' introduced into occult lore by Madame Blavatsky. Mailander's students called him by his spiritual name of 'John' and some believed him to be the reincarnation of St John the Evangelist.

Mailander is reported to have been highly disapproving of certain occult practices, in particular astral projection. He even accused members of the Theosophical Society in London of perpetuating a hoax by claiming they could leave their bodies, adding that such out of body travel was both unnecessary and potentially damaging to spiritual progress. Whilst we would agree with this latter statement – that astral travel is both unnecessary and potentially dangerous, we dispute his assertion that it is impossible and that, therefore, individual claims of astral projection must be a 'lie' or a 'hoax'. In a comment thought to be about Kempten resident, Mailander, Madame Blavatsky said: "there is only one initiate in Germany today, and he lives in Kempten, but he is not of our school." This comment is published in Rolf Speckner's Friedrich Eckstein als Okkultist.

Nevertheless, Mailander did become a member of the Indian Theosophical Society, saying that their teaching agreed with their own, "in the main". On the other hand, he claimed to have nothing to do with either Helena Blavatsky or Colonel Olcott themselves, preferring to communicate with TS members. According to Eikie, Willy Scrodter, in his Rosicrucian Notebook, claims that Blavtasky was herself a pupil of Mailander in Darmstadt. Eike herself (as with many in her tradition) is keen to downplay the idea that Blavatsky was an actual student of Mailander, preferring to admit that they 'perhaps met once or twice, but to make a student and teacher relation

out of it is drawing it much too far in my opinion'.
We have speculated that Valentin Tomberg, whose karmic mission involved reuniting the (exoteric) Church of Peter and the (esoteric) Church of John, may have come into contact with the Mailander occult 'chain' whilst he was living in Germany during World War II. Tomberg and his friend Nikolaj Belozwetow discussed a possible Sophianic cooperation with the Christian Community of Emil Bock, who was the first to reveal the full name and identity of Mailander, (1956). Tomberg would have spoken with Bock around a decade earlier, in the mid-to-late 1940's. Bock rebuffed these efforts at cooperation, possibly because of the Tomberg controversy within the Anthroposopical Society.
In occult circles, from Jane Leade onwards, there was an expectation of the 'return of John', as part of the universal Spiritual renewal of mankind. Modern day students of Mailander appear to identify their Master with this impulse from the 'Church of John'.
Christine Eike's essay and other researching about Mailander, including earlier essays by Richard Cloud, which Ms Eike draws upon, can be found at: https://pansophers.com/

[lxxi] Anna Rudolfovna Mintzlova (1866 – last seen in Moscow, September 1910) features in Daniel Shubin's book, New Rosicrucians of Early Soviet Russia. Of very distinctive appearance and with well-attested mesmeric faculties, she learned Theosophy from Annie Besant and later became a pupil of Rudolf Steiner, becoming a leading proponent of Anthroposophy in Russia. She had some influence over the poet Andrei Bely. The description of her was given by Maximillian Voloshin.

[lxxii] Vladimir Shmakov did indeed keep Thomas Edison's autograph pasted at the front of his magical diary, as detailed in The Holy Book of Thoth by Shin Publications (publisher's afterword).

[lxxiii] The Secret Science of initiates and the practice of life (paraphrased and abridged).

[lxxiv] La Ciencia Secreta de los Iniciados, Serge Marcotoune

[lxxv] Ibid

[lxxvi] Ibid

[lxxvii] La Voie Initiatique, Serge Marcotoune

[lxxviii] From the Rubaiyat of Omar Khayyam.

[lxxix] From the materials of V.V. Belustin Circles of The Mind of Hermes.

[lxxx] Vsevolod Belustin, Arcanology of Hermes

[lxxxi] Uranus-1, Neptune-2, Saturn-3, Jupiter-4, Mars-5, the Sun-6, Venus-7, Mercury-8, Moon-9

[lxxxii] Vsevolod Belustin, Arcanology of Hermes

[lxxxiii] The Solar Way, Nina Roudnikova, Letter XIV, Temperance.

[lxxxiv] Prayer to Our Lady of all Nations, Valentin Tomberg

[lxxxv] Manly P Hall, The Initiates of the Flame

[lxxxvi] Paul Coelho, Brida

[lxxxvii] Boris Mouravieff, Gnosis

[lxxxviii] Orphic Hymns 41-86, Translated by Thomas Taylor. Hymn to Mises (Misa). The Fumigation from Storax.

[lxxxix] Plato, Phaedo

[xc] Statement made by Winston Churchill about the Soviet Union in October 1939 after the signing of the Nazi-Soviet Pact and the beginning of World War II

[xci] Pierre Teilhard de Chardin

[xcii] Max Planck, Where Is Science Going?

[xciii] The scientific and pseudo-scientific activities of EMESH represent the first attempt at parapsychological research in Russian history, as the idea of mental telepathy emerged as a theme in society and the press. Chekhov presented the results of his research at the Institute of the Brain, and at the Society for the Study of Psychology, Reflexology and Hypnology, without making reference to the occult order. His work was favourably received by fellow specialists and the media alike. The Department of the Society of Psychology, Reflexology and Hypnology in Moscow was a useful cover for his underground work, which gave him the excuse to hire the basement room where the OGPU would catch up with him.
The various colourful experiments conducted there anticipated later researchers who set up shop in top secret KGB laboratories
Sources: https://www.insur-info.ru/history/exhibit/details/464/
https://foto-programmer.livejournal.com/75955.html
[xciv] Q: Tell the investigation your autobiography.
A: I was born in 1899 in Leningrad. My father, Vyacheslav Vyacheslavovich Belustin, was a nobleman, had a law degree, served as a senator in recent years before the revolution; after the revolution he worked at the station of the Forty Murmansk Railway, died in 1926. My father did not have real estate, but he had large funds (he had several tens of thousands of rubles). In 1918, I graduated from the Alexander Lyceum with a degree in philology and linguistics.
In the same 1918 after graduating from the lyceum, I moved with my mother to the Crimea, where I lived until 1922. Living in the Crimea and being in the territory occupied by white troops, I was conscripted into the white army several times, but I was released from military service as the sole breadwinner of the family. At that time, my mother was dependent on me.
From March 1923 to April 1924, I served in the chemical part of the Main Artillery Directorate as the chief clerk. From 1924 to 1932 I worked at the NKID as a translator in the press department. Before my arrest in 1933, I worked as a lecturer at the Medical Association.
In 1933 I was arrested by the NKVD as a member and leader of the counterrevolutionary organisation of mystics in Moscow, but two months later I was released from arrest with the credit of pre-trial detention. From 1933 to 1938 I worked in Moscow in various Soviet institutions as a teacher and translator of English. In 1938, due to my straitened financial situation, I left Moscow for Stalinabad and entered the Stalinabad Pedagogical Institute as an English teacher.
Q: Tell us who your relatives are and where they are currently?
A: I am married to Natalia Borisovna Salko, born in 1909. She is an art historian by profession, works and lives in Moscow. My uncle Konstantin Frantsevich Neslukhovsky, a geographer and cartographer, lives in Leningrad; his daughter Irina Konstantinovna Merts lives with him, with whom I have been on very good terms for a long time. My uncle's son, Sergey Konstantinovich Neslukhovsky, lives in Moscow, works as a designer of calculating machines, I do not keep in touch with him. I don't have any brothers and sisters. I also have no relatives abroad".
Source: http://www.studfiles.ru/preview/3318851/page:30/
Belustin plead guilty to certain charges but categorically denied being a spy for British intelligence.
In 1941 the authorities in Moscow had accused Belustin of being the son of a tsarist senator, non-partisan, a citizen of the USSR, [who] in 1933 was arrested by the OGPU as a member of a counter-revolutionary Masonic organisation; before his arrest in 1940, he worked as an English teacher at the Stalinabad Pedagogical Institute.

In 1919, in the Crimea, he collaborated with the Denikin information agency. From 1920 until his arrest in 1940, he was an agent of the British intelligence agencies, on whose instructions he carried out espionage work on the territory of the USSR; he handed over to the British intelligence a number of espionage information on aviation, transport and the chemical industry.

In 1926, on behalf of the underground mystical organisation "Rosicrucians" organised by him, he concluded a concordat on joint struggle against the Soviet government with the head of the Masonic "Grand Lodge of Astraea", Astromov-Kirichenko. In order to misinform the State security agencies, he penetrated the secret staff of the OGPU and concealed the counter-revolutionary work of mystics and Freemasons known to him.

Further reporting on the matter claimed that Belustin: Being opposed to the existing Soviet system, in 1923 organised an underground mystical organisation "Rosicrucians" and in 1926 concluded an agreement (concordat) with the head of the Masonic organisation "Grand Lodge of Astraea", Astromov-Kirichenko, setting the task to fight against the Soviet building, against the ideas of Marxism and historical materialism and recruiting new personnel in order to cover a wider field in their anti-Soviet and [counter-revolutionary] activities.

Belustin was sentenced to be imprisoned for a period of ten years and without voting rights for five years, without right of appeal.

Source: http://www.studfiles.ru/preview/3318851/page:40/

www.ingramcontent.com/pod-product-compliance
Lightning Source LLC
Chambersburg PA
CBHW072044110526
44590CB00018B/3032